We Dance Because We Cannot Fly

From heroin to hope:
Stories of redemption and
transformation

Guy Chevreau

Sovereign World

Sovereign World Ltd
PO Box 777
Tonbridge
Kent TN11 0ZS
England

ISBN 1 85240 320 9

Cover design by CCD, www.ccdgroup.co.uk
Typeset by CRB Associates, Reepham, Norfolk
Printed in the United States of America

The last chapter in Humberto Fernandez's comprehensive treatise *Heroin* is titled "Heroin Addicts: Beyond Redemption?" He states his conclusions:

"Our perception of addiction as an incurable disease has not changed much. In 1930 Sirovich stated: 'Medical science is almost powerless to redeem these unfortunates.' Today we say treatment can work, but the fact is it works for relatively few, and these few are viewed skeptically, not embraced as redeemed members of society."

(Minnesota: Hazelden, 1998, pp. 295, 298)

One wonders what Fernandez might have written if he'd been to Betel.

"The point of departure is humility;
the destination is love."

(Bernard of Clairvaux,
On Loving God, *c.* 1135 AD)

This book is dedicated to Betel's house leaders, the *chicos* and *chicas* who graciously serve twenty-four hours every day.

> *"You are a letter that has come from Christ, given to us to deliver; a letter not written with ink but with the Spirit of the living God, written not on stone tablets but on the pages of the human heart."* (2 Corinthians 3:3)

Contents

Preface

We Dance Because We Cannot Fly is the story of Betel – a caring Christian community that is healing thousands of broken lives. It is a special story that needs to be told in a special way. Many have stopped, stared and marveled at the wonder of God's grace upon the Betel rehab communities, businesses, and churches that are proliferating around the world. Fewer have had the courage or the giftings to step inside and discern the deep work of the Spirit in our midst. Betel is much more than residences, farms, shops, tools and a large fleet of white vans. Betel is the *Betelitos*, those addicts and outcasts of all shades, colors and cultural backgrounds who have found new life in Christ and their place in His "mystical" Body. Dr Guy Chevreau has had the courage to draw near enough to get to know us, and he brings the prophetic and literary capacity to document our story in an exciting and vivid way.

We first came to know of Guy through our dear friends Bill and Melinda Fish. A few years ago our curiosity and hunger for God had been whetted by the stirrings of the Spirit in Canada. The Fishes and many of our dearest friends had experienced personal renewal in that visitation of God. They suggested that Guy come and minister in Betel of Spain. He has visited us many times since that first visit in 1997. Consequently, he has had intimate contact with all of the Betel leaders, especially through his involvement in a number of our regular leadership summits, our *cumbres*. He has toured Betel of Spain, Portugal, North Africa, France, Germany, Britain, Italy, and America.

Many preachers and teachers have visited and blessed Betel, but not all of them have touched our hearts. We have a street

expression that describes the process of an individual's identi-
fication with and acceptance by the Betel community. We say
someone *ha pasado por el aro* – that he or she "has gone through
the hoop," when they have gotten down, humbled themselves,
and become like us. This is no small or petty ritual of passage,
but a noble gateway of love erected by a people who have
fought marginalization and rejection all their lives. Everyone
has to pass through the *aro* in Betel: new addicts off the street,
new missionaries who come to help, visitors, guest speakers –
everyone. We caution new workers not to try and "preach" to
the addicts until they have won their hearts and a right to a
hearing. There is no formula or set time frame for this acceptance, but everyone knows when a newcomer *ha pasado por el aro*
and has become a Betelito.

Guy is a Betelito even though he is a Doctor of Theology and
an articulate expert on historic revivals and the great Christian
mystics. We know he is a Betelito because he has eaten with the
men and women and drunk their sweet coffee! He has hugged
them and loved them. He has slept in their homes and ridden in
their vans; he has picked up furniture donations and helped
them with their chores. He has joined our outreach teams and
walked the streets, parks and garbage dumps of Madrid, Lisbon,
Marseilles, Hamburg, New York, Birmingham and Naples in
search of hurting lives. Guy did not seem to notice or care that
hundreds of them were HIV-positive and sickly. For all of these
reasons, we believe he is a Betelito.

We Dance Because We Cannot Fly is a great story that is
powerfully told with graphic, unembellished truth by a friend
whose authority comes from God, and whose heart is knit to
the men and women whose stories are told within its pages.
Guy has conducted in-depth interviews with the Betelitos, but
they are not the only source for this book. His intimate
knowledge of God, and the transforming work of the Holy
Spirit enable Guy to trace the work of the Great Protagonist in
Betel.

We Dance is much more than merely another perspective that
compliments and enriches Stewart and Marie Dinnen's two
earlier accounts of Betel's history and life: *Rescue Shop Within a
Yard of Hell* and *Sacking the Frontiers of Hell, Rescue Shop 2*
(Christian Focus Publications).

In Guy's book, one does not just catch a glimpse of the addict's heart: one is able to feel, taste and touch the woundings that brought life to ruin. All the horrific circumstances associated with addiction are so pointedly contrasted by the wonderful unveiling of the Father's love that has transformed each of their tortured lives.

The story also tells of how a handful of WEC and Amistad missionaries, along with an army of ex-addicts, have stumbled upon the wonder of simple people finding love, acceptance and healing in the Family of God. It is a modern journey along "ancient pathways" reminiscent of humble, first-century Christianity. You will see that these *marginados* have a redemptive message for the whole Church.

Reading what follows is an exhilarating and joyous adventure that will enlarge your heart and take you to unfrequented depths and heights. So if you ready for the trek, *"Come, and let us go up to the mountain of the Lord!"*

Elliott Tepper
International Director of Association Betel
April 2000
Madrid

Acknowledgements

To all the Betelitos – *gracias, danke, merci, muito obrigado, grazie*, thank you – for letting me into your hearts and lives. You have shared precious gifts with me.

Elliott and Mary Tepper, Lindsay and Myk McKenzie, Kent and Mary Alice Martin – thank you for your fast friendships, and the honor and privileges you have extended to me. Thank you for all the help with the details of Betel life. What would we have done without e-mail?

Thanks to my translators Perry Lim, Guillermo Galvan, Ann Kathrin Langbehn and Jonathan Tepper. As you worked so hard asking and re-asking my questions, and struggled for the nuances of meaning, you added so much to the telling of this story. Thanks also for the laughs along the way!

Darlene Worsham and Ann Kathrin – thank you for your work transcribing the tapes of some of the initial interviews.

Thanks to Dr Barry Morrison for your steady friendship and support through this decade of change. Thanks too for your critical reading of the draft; I look forward to paying my debt of gratitude – on the golf course.

Blessings on Trish Posavad for your careful proof-reading and your faithful covering on the home-front.

To the Schleife in Winterthur, Switzerland, and Church of the Living God in Manchester, Connecticut, thank you for your apostolic support. May you be abundantly blessed for all that you have enabled.

Thanks to our Friday night house group for your prayers and practical care, and to Alan Wiseman for your ongoing intercessions and prophetic encouragement and insight.

To my wife, Janis: for all that you give, in all the ways you serve, and all that you teach me as you lay down you life for the gospel – grace, grace, grace.

My children, Graham and Caitlin: I love you tons. A few more years, and you can come to Betel with me.

A particular verse of Scripture, Romans 11:36, has directed me through the writing of this book.

> *"From him and through him and for him all things exist – to him be glory for ever! Amen."*

We Dance Because We Cannot Fly is offered in that spirit of gratitude and worship.

Guy Chevreau
Oakville, Ontario
April 2000
S.D.G.

Foreword

The message was clear. Guy Chevreau had telephoned to ask if I would write a foreword to his new book, *We Dance Because We Cannot Fly*. The message went on to say something about a prophecy I had given him in Toronto in January 1997. My response was immediate. I was honored to be asked – Guy knows many people around the world, and I was flattered and grateful that he should think of me. I was intrigued by the fulfillment of the prophecy and excited by the title. I wondered what they had to do with each other.

Guy happened to be in London when he left the message, and we spoke a few days later. I remembered the prophecy very well. Several thousand people had gathered for an anniversary conference at Toronto Airport Christian Fellowship. Guy and his charming wife Janis were sitting towards the front center section. The prophecy had to do with a new sort of fire in the church, new models of church, things that he'd never seen before.

I seemed to recall that I said the seeds for this would be sown within the next seven weeks. Well, the seven weeks came and went, and months later Guy told me that the word had not yet been fulfilled – and we joked about whether I had missed it or he had been disobedient! What we didn't know was that within that seven-week period a seed *had* been sown. Guy had received an invitation to speak at a church in Spain, one which was to open his eyes to different models of church, evangelism, prayer and community. This book is the result of that and subsequent visits.

I asked Guy why he had chosen the title, *We Dance Because We Cannot Fly*. It's a phrase I've used repeatedly – one of my best friends, singer-songwriter Noel Richards, coined it. We were at a leadership conference and someone asked, "Why, at Gerald's age and sagging shape, does he dance during worship?" Where Noel got the phrase from, I don't know, but quick as a flash he replied, "He dances because he cannot fly!" Later in the conference he spoke about how one day, in the age to come, we would fly instead of dance. The atheist turned born-again Christian Malcolm Muggeridge once said that when people love each other they don't just laugh *with* each other, but, because of the security their love gives them, they can afford to laugh *at* each other. It was Noel's turn to be laughed at. I walked across the stage and explained that this was a biblical nonsense. With mock repentance he bowed at my feet, to shouts of appreciation from one thousand leaders of our Pioneer network of churches.

However, the next year it was my turn. I had just read Psalm 90, verse 10: *"As for the days of your life, they contain 70 years, or if due to strength, 80 years, yet their pride is but labor and sorrow; for too soon it is gone and we fly away."* When I relayed that to Guy, there was a short silence on the other end of the phone and then laughter. He went on to explain his source, far more meaningful, profound and wonderful than any of the fun Noel and I had engaged in.

Guy told me it came from a comment made by Raul Casto, the first person in the Spanish church to give their life to Christ. He was to become the first indigenous pastor, and the first of their pastors to die an AIDS-related death. Here was a man who was once trapped in behavior patterns that had caused him to become sick, depressed and eventually to lose his life prematurely. Yet now he'd been born again, baptized in the Holy Spirit, and he had a new song in his spirit that overflowed with gratitude and praise for all that Jesus Christ had done for him. *We dance because we cannot fly* indeed!

I find this book very satisfying, perhaps the most exciting that Guy has ever written. It is likely to move you to tears, to challenge you about how much time you spend with the unconverted, the needy and those pushed to the margins of society. It has done that for me. This is a church that is helping people belong before they know what it is they have to believe. In a post-modern world, this is the only way forward for the majority who have yet to meet the Lord of the Dance.

I pray, therefore, that these words, stories and insights will help us understand that our future does not have to be a repeat of our history. There is a brand-new door opening to make life attractive and intelligible to those around us. It may not be with people like those Guy writes about in this particular book, but all people need Christ, all people need to receive love and to have value placed upon them. This book will help you do all of that.

Gerald Coates
Speaker, author and broadcaster
June 2000

Chapter 1

La Victoria Esta en Jesus

"Thanks be to God! He gives us victory through our Lord Jesus Christ."　　　　　　　　　(1 Corinthians 15:57)

Before me stood a thousand exuberant Spaniards. They were all on their feet, arms outstretched, their faces radiant with the glory of God. With thunderous enthusiasm, we were singing the church's signature song, *La Victoria Esta en Jesus*, "The Victory Is in Jesus." As an itinerant preacher, I'm regularly in front of large crowds. Lively, engaging worship is typically the norm. But this was no ordinary, "great" church conference.

It was my fourth opportunity to be with this congregation, the largest Protestant church in Spain. These brothers and sisters had captured my heart. I have been privileged to preach in over a hundred churches, in nearly as many cities, in over twenty nations. But the church in Madrid has no equals. It is the most redemptive and transformative community of faith I know of. To be with them is like stepping into the Book of Acts, only in color.

The majority of the arms raised towards heaven are heavily tattooed. Many of the wrists bear the scars of attempted suicides. There are few noses that have not been broken, few smiles that are not missing teeth.

Three-quarters of the congregation have been addicted to heroin. Nearly every church member has spent at least one night in jail; one in four has been behind bars for a year; one in ten, a decade. Because they are typically not strong enough to

19

steal, eight of every ten of the younger women in this church have been prostitutes.

Most of the gathered never knew their father. Many of the others wish they never did, and bear the scars to prove it.

Five years ago, half the church was HIV-positive. Presently, one-fourth of the church tests positive. Spanish health officials have joined many governments worldwide, and now make available a free and limitless supply of disposable needles. Clean needles have brought the incidence of infection down dramatically. In addition, the fear of AIDS has changed the habits of newer addicts – heroin is sniffed and smoked more than it was in the past.

The majority of the congregation is male, and unmarried. There are disproportionately few children. Most of these live with only one parent, either because of relational break-up, or death. The younger children rarely carry their parent's AIDS virus, largely due to more effective medicines, and those who are born infected are often experiencing remissions.

There are several hundred seniors in the congregation. These are typically family members of the recovering addicts. Mothers and fathers have come because the church cared for their children when no one else did.

The church in Madrid has grown to its present size in fourteen years, and has planted fifty new communities in as many cities in nine nations throughout Europe – Lisbon, Malaga, Almeria, Sevilla, Valencia, Barcelona, Marseilles, Hamburg, Naples, and Birmingham, England – and one in Melilla, a Spanish enclave in Morocco. There are two centers in North America, one in New York, and the other in Puebla, Mexico. The newest of the works has been established in northern India. A team of three missionaries and seven church members were sent out from Madrid to pioneer that work. All of them had to wait on visas; one had to finish his prison sentence, and receive the court's permission to leave the country.

Forty thousand drug addicts have come through the church's open doors. While the majority have left within the first two weeks, fifteen per cent are completely rehabilitated. Over 5000 men and women have lived in one of the ninety residences for at least a year, and senior staff estimate that seventy-five per cent of them have remained drug-free.

There is one statistic that is the most arresting. The twelve most senior pastors and their wives, all of them ex-heroin addicts, are living with a death-sentence hanging over their heads. Ten of the men and ten of the women are HIV-positive; four others have had sclerosis of the liver. Three of these four have experienced miraculous healings or remissions. Of the present forty-five ordained pastors (twenty-one couples and one single), twenty-six individuals (60 per cent) are HIV-positive. A few years ago, the percentage was much higher.

A double dynamic is at work here, because fewer of the younger pastors are infected, and, in the last six years, the church have buried four of their ordained pastors. As to funerals of senior leaders and close friends, there have simply been "too many."

The title *We Dance Because We Cannot Fly* was a prophetic comment made by Raul Casto, the church's first convert, and their first indigenous pastor, months before his AIDS-related death. After an extended time of worship, he addressed the congregation. The church is affiliated with World-wide Evangelization for Christ. With an eye to some of the more conservative WEC missionaries and other guests visiting, he addressed those who may have been unsettled by the boisterous praise. Raul simply explained their behavior: "We dance, because we cannot fly!"

As I worshipped with my friends, I thought of the Apostle Paul's words,

> *"No wonder we do not lose heart! Though our outward human-ity is in decay, yet day by day we are inwardly renewed. Our troubles are slight and short-lived, and their outcome is an eternal glory which far outweighs them, provided our eyes are fixed, not on the things that are seen, but on the things that are unseen."* (2 Corinthians 4:16–18)

Before me stood the most dynamic Bible commentary I had ever read.

The church's name is *Betel*, Spanish for "Bethel," "the house of God." The men and women that have formed this community of grace are affectionately known as Betelitos. This is their story of redemption and transformation in Christ.

Chapter 2

Descent into Hell

"The chords of death bound me,
  Sheol held me in its grip.
  Anguish and torment held me fast;
then I invoked the Lord by name,
  'Lord, deliver me, I pray'...
I shall walk in the presence of the Lord
  in the land of the living."   (Psalm 116:3, 9)

In the south-east of Madrid is an area known as *Vertedero*, "the Dump." Two kilometers off the highway, along a gravel road, trucks turn off to the auto wreckers, and further along, the garbage dump. Further still is the gypsy camp. When we were there in February 2000, it had only been established two months earlier but it was already the focus of the region's drug dealings. The Celsa gypsy encampment, a few kilometers to the east, was the previous center, until the government began tearing it down. Demolition, however, is no solution to the problem; the trade and traffic merely shifted location. Government officials estimate that the drug dealers in *Vertedero* serve 5000 heroin addicts daily, and turn $460,000 in trade every twenty-four hours.

When we arrived in *Vertedero*, thirty-seven cars were parked on the mud flatlands outside the gypsy camp. Most cars had more than one occupant. They openly smoked or injected their newly acquired heroin. Those who arrived on foot stood and indifferently bared their arms; several others dropped their

23

pants, squatted, and injected into their groin. One man held up a small cosmetic mirror. He was using it to see how to steer a needle into his jugular vein. Another, mirror-less, was injecting into the corner of his eyelid.

Twelve young boys were playing football (soccer)[1] on the edge of the flat. Thirty feet from the goal line, a man was standing with a needle in his arm. On the sidelines at center field, two men were huddled on the ground, their coats over their heads. In their heroin stupor, they were not only oblivious to the match before them, but to everything.

We opened the back door of the Betel van, and immediately guys started shuffling in our direction. They had come for the free packages of cookies and Nutella we were handing out. Few said, *"Gracias."* Nearly all of them took the flyer that read, *"Hemos escapado de la adiccion! Y tambien podrias tu!"* "We have escaped from addiction! You can do it too!" The invitation is surrounded by twelve photos of smiling Betelitos. No one threw the flyer away. Many takers carefully folded the paper, and slipped it into a pocket.

We arrived at 11:30 a.m. It was relatively quiet. Thirty cars drove in every minute; about the same number of people arrived on foot. Within an hour, over lunchtime, the traffic picked up markedly. The number of cars more than doubled, and parking was at a premium. There was a striking contrast in the vehicles – the BMWs and Audis had single occupants; the beaters, the twenty-year-old road wrecks, often had five or six sickly addicts inside. They were un-unionized taxis driven by addicts. As we moved further into the lunch break, the number of regular taxis arriving increased exponentially.

Two police officers cruised the area in a four by four Sport Utility Vehicle. They showed no interest in those shooting up. They intervene only in violent situations.

Thirty meters from the Betel van was a rehab services van. In front of it was a large bucket half-full of used syringes. There was a continuous stream of guys exchanging needles. Two men walked up and exchanged their needles, all the while talking on their mobile phones. A well-dressed businessman got out of his BMW coup, and walked over to the bucket. We overheard the exchange – seventy-five needles, old for new. He picked up a handful of free condoms, sterile swabs, and bandages.

It didn't seem to register that he was at the top of the heroin slide. Life at the bottom was standing immediately to his right. Another addict, stooped over, was searching through his tattered jacket for his used syringes. His toes were sticking through the holes in his shoes. His ears were black with caked-on dirt. The businessman returned to his car, and his neighbor hobbled over to the Betel van for cookies. Life at the bottom was prioritized as efficiently as the entrepreneur's: needles first, food second.

The Director of the rehab approached us as we stood beside his van. I was with Perry Lim, a WEC missionary originally from Singapore. It was more than obvious that we didn't belong in the *Vertedero*.

"What are you guys doing here?" His tone was cold and aggressive. Perry answered, "We're from Betel." The Director's posture changed immediately; he smiled. "Oh." We chatted for ten minutes together. Social Services holds Betel in very high regard.

The Director broke conversation to give a wreck of an addict a mini-lecture. Perry translated for me. The man had come, asking for needles. He had none to exchange. The Director gave him two new syringes, some swabs and bandages, and made him promise that he'd clean himself before injecting. He also had to promise that he'd return the used needles for new ones – that he'd only use them once.

Driving out from *Vertedero*, I noticed a newly erected retaining wall on the north side of the road. Barbed wire is strung along its length. The wall hadn't registered on the way in. Now, I didn't need to ask why it was there. It keeps stumbling drug addicts from wandering onto the railway line that runs parallel to the road.

Few readers will have been anywhere near a place like the *Vertedero*. Those unfamiliar with the nuances of the drug scene are referred to Appendix I, "Drugs and Drug Taking," for a brief introduction.

What follows is a candid account of one addict's drug experience. His name is Sean Davies, from the Betel in Birmingham, England.[2]

"I rolled my first joint of cannabis at age eleven. It was all bent and twisted, a pathetic looking thing. The first few drags, I felt nothing. Then my eyelids went so heavy, like lead. I couldn't move, and instead of just my heart beating, it was like my whole body was thumping.

"I got very sick to my stomach, but I was whacked, and it felt so good. I suddenly wasn't in a depressive space any more. I was so relaxed, physically and emotionally. In fact, I felt so relaxed, I felt I was stuck to my bed.

"With increased use, I learned to function. I smoked a lot of cannabis, and my head was cloudy all the time. All my reactions were so slow. It's no surprise it's called 'dope.' Cannabis just dulls everything. I would smoke a joint first thing on waking up, and then throughout the day. I was stoned all day long.

"It wasn't long before I graduated. I was out drinking, and a dealer I knew gave me some speed – amphetamines. It felt there was so much energy in my body when it came on. It was like a rush that started in my toes, and gradually worked its way up, till it hit my head, and I thought it was going to explode with WOW!

"Speed gave me confidence I didn't have before. I was afraid of girls – scared of being rejected. But on speed, I'd talk to anybody. I didn't care. I had the feeling that nothing could touch me.

"The bad side was coming down. The comedown off speed is really, really bad. You want so much to sleep, you're so tired, but you can't. Your mind won't let you sleep. It's still racing, even though your body has crashed. It is *so* frustrating; I used to cry out, 'No more, please. Let me sleep.'

"I've taken speed for fourteen, fifteen days straight. Why so long? I was afraid of the comedown. I tried to postpone it as long as possible. I never liked them days. I'd smoke so much dope trying to come down off speed – to feel relaxed, and heavy.

"One day, I found my mom's tranquilizers, temazepam, in 20 milligram tablets. One of them would knock you out for twenty-four hours. I'd been awake for seven or eight days. My body was in a bad way. My stomach was in spasm, because I hadn't eaten. (Speed suppresses the appetite.) I took ten of mom's tablets with a cup of tea, and ten minutes later, I felt it slowly come up, taking over from the center, working its way out. It felt like my body was humming. Then the drowsiness came on all at once. I felt like I just raised off the bed, and floated away. All of the anxiety and frustration of the comedown melted away.

"I started doing speed, and then taking diazepam, temazepam, Valium – any downers I could get. They eased the comedown. Till I discovered them, it was murder.

"I dropped a lot of acid – LSD. The first time I took it, I remember when I peaked: I was looking out of the window, and there were suddenly bright lights everywhere. The brightest I'd ever seen. It was wild.

"But I didn't really like LSD; it was horrible. Things just used to change, right in front of my eyes. Things would disappear, then reappear. You'd watch your hand melt . . . and sometimes, it would never come back.

"I took it many times, but it was not a favorite drug. I always felt I was being chased by shadows. It was really, really strange. I felt like I wasn't me; acid changed everything. It's a constant rush, for hours, and the comedown off it was horrible. I felt hollow inside, like there was nothing inside me.

"And when I would start to get drowsy, I couldn't sleep, because the shadows would still be chasing me. LSD is one of the worst drugs I've ever taken. I've done a lot of drugs, a lot of different drugs, but I quickly got bored with them. Cocaine was something else! On coke, it felt like no one could touch me. I'd get so high. I would do anything. *Without coke*, I'd do anything, but on coke, I was absolutely fearless. The first time I smoked crack, I felt like I was stuck to the ceiling. It was a good feeling. The high just killed every single problem I ever had. I smoked a lot of crack.

"This is embarrassing – it's said that 'smoking crack is better than sex;' and, yeah, it was. Being high on cocaine was as intense, but more prolonged than orgasm, like a million bombs going off in your mind all at once. I loved the feeling.

"The comedown was grim. I remember one time, I'd been awake, smoking crack, and taking ecstasy for a couple of days, then smoking a lot of cannabis, washing temazepam down with bottles of cider, but it wasn't really working. I couldn't sleep; I was out of my mind for sleep. A friend had some heroin to sell. He said it would help. I'd never taken heroin before, but I had seen people do it; how they cooked it up, melting it on a spoon, drawing it up in a syringe. The first time I did it, it seemed to come so natural. I put my belt around my arm, and pulled it tight with my teeth. I got a vein up, and put in the needle, but pulled on the syringe, and got some blood in it. I remember looking at it and thinking, 'Sean, I don't believe you're doing this.'

"But as soon as I started pushing in the syringe, the rush hit me right away. I couldn't believe it. It was like I was on another planet. I just leaned back, and went into a complete fantasy. My body felt *so* nice. It was like waves were washing over me, inside my body. I had pins and needles, nice pins and needles, in my head. I was violently sick, but as I was being sick, the buzz got more intense. So I actually enjoyed being sick, the buzz was so strong.

"Heroin would suppress all the badness I was feeling. It give me a nice cosy covering. I no longer felt guilty. I no longer felt ashamed. I no longer felt anything but good. When I was on a heroin buzz, inside my little heroin house, no one could touch me. Once I had injected, no one could get to me."

That last bit may sound almost appealing. Any sense of innocence will be duly shattered when you read the balance of Sean's testimony in the chapter 'Accelerated Grace.'

Before proceeding, however, the grim details of the heroin story need telling. The following is from an interview conducted with another long-term addict, also from the Betel-Birmingham.

Josh and his young friends experimented with what they could find around home: they sniffed Butane, solvents, and glue.

"The solvents introduced me to the world of hallucinations. I started chasing the high, from solvents, to cannabis, to amphetamines, cocaine, ecstasy, and LSD. With the amphetamines especially, I took so much that I got really paranoid, and in order to come down, I started to take heroin. When I had the money, I'd use cocaine.

"I was always chasing the high. Even though I didn't get that involved in crack cocaine, I used it. Crack killed some of my mates. I did drugs from the time I was twelve to twenty-eight – sixteen years of addiction.

"I took so much heroin, for so long, my tolerance levels kept increasing. I got to the point where I couldn't take enough to get as wrecked as I wanted to be. So I'd top it up with different things. I was taking diazepam and mogadon, on top of the heroin, ten a day, chewing them like they were Smarties.

"I had a very violent past. The reason I was violent was because I was afraid of people. Because I was scared of them, I made them scared of me so they'd keep away. I had my walls up, and nobody would come near me and I'd have my space. Anybody that tried to get inside, I'd bite, you know. But really, I was just scared. That's why I did so much heroin.

"Heroin was everything about me. Heroin was my strength, it was my temper and my violence; it was my character, it was my confidence. Heroin was all of me; it *was* me. Heroin was everything what made Josh, Josh. You know, it controlled my every thought, everything that came out of my mouth, the people I slept with; it was everything.

"When you're an addict, you develop tunnel vision, and it doesn't matter what's in your way, you're gonna get your money. For instance, I knew that my brother's fiancée had some money. One day I went around to the house, and I kicked the front door off. I walked straight in, and knocked her out cold. When she woke up, I asked her where her money was. She wouldn't tell me, so I hit her again. She came to again, and I asked her where her money was. She wouldn't tell me, so I hit her again. She came to; I asked her where her money was. She told me; I took it, and left her scared to death.

"I didn't feel anything because I was on heroin. You just feel the pain when you come down. And that's just one incident of tunnel vision. It doesn't matter what's in your way or what you have to go through. I've never hit my mother, for instance, but I've threatened her in many different ways. I've held a knife to her throat, demanding money.

"That's what it's all about, money, money, money. And that's when you get tunnel vision. It doesn't matter what's in your way, if it's a child of twelve years or whatever, if they've got something you want, you'll take it, by force, or by any means. That's addiction."

"My family wouldn't have me around because I'd done violent things to them. My father didn't want to know me, my cousins, my aunties, all my relations, anybody, my friends didn't want to know me, the girls I used to live with, they didn't want to know me. I don't blame them.

"I've stabbed people, I've sliced people, I've hit people with hammers, I've glassed people in the face. Just smashed a beer glass on the table, and stuck it into someone's face.

"I did a lot of dealing up in Glasgow, but that came to a quick end because I was involved in a violent assault. One night I was with one of my friends and a couple of girls. Next thing we know, someone is breaking down our front door. Two guys wanted to rip us off – our money, and drugs. It was our fault – we'd been showing off our money a bit. We brawled, and they took off. We found out where one of them was staying, and we chased him down. We kicked *his* door in, and shot him in the legs.

"This is typical life in Glasgow, this is what happens, this is gun life in Glasgow. You have to protect yourself. It's a life of fear and intimidation.

"I was growing enemies pretty fast. Stepping on people's toes, 'cause I was bringing heroin down in quantity and selling it cheaper than others were, just to get the business. I was getting threats; doors were closing all the time. So it was no more Glasgow. I couldn't go back up there.

"My business connections were gone. No more big scores, and no more money. All of a sudden, I was alone.

"As my life was caving in, I was also getting weaker and weaker. My heroin habit was getting worse and worse, and as an addict, I never ate. You just eat sweet things and you go to McDonald's and get a milk shake. I was losing weight and lookin' terrible; my eyes were sinking deeper into me 'ead, but I couldn't see it myself. I thought I was lookin' all right, fit and muscular and all that. To anyone else, I was looking like death warmed up.

"From that time on, it was just a down-hill thing. More and more drugs, and to support my habit, I was thievin' all the time. It just got crazy; there was no way I could get as much heroin as I needed. I was breaking into people's houses and tying people up. I'd get their bank card, and then threaten them physically, till they told me their PIN number. Then I'd go to the bank just before 12 midnight, and take the maximum draw, wait a few minutes till after midnight, and as it was a new banking day, I could take another draw. Sounds tough, but I was scared. No, not scared, paranoid.

"This is about a year before coming to Betel. Things had got so bad I couldn't go anywhere, I was so paranoid. I thought everybody was after me. Even though people weren't, I thought they were. I couldn't knock on my friends' doors because I thought they were after me. I couldn't go to a bed and breakfast 'cause I didn't have the money. I couldn't go home 'cause my family didn't want me.

"I kept sinking lower and lower. I was losing the will to live, basically. Life meant nothing to me. No meaning, no purpose, and everything was drifting away. All I wanted to do was just die."

Josh and Sean have a lot in common. The drugs, the violence, multiple prison terms, deteriorating health, and a growing desperation brought them both to the place where they had nowhere to go but Betel.

Sean was staring at the floor as he finished telling his story. It hadn't been easy to recount the details of his past. He slowly shook his head back and forth: "Heroin, cocaine, speed, ecstasy, LSD, cannabis; all a lot of highs; a *lot* of lows. So much pain . . . "

Then he straightened up, lifted his head, his face beaming: "Glory to God *that's* over. Love brought me out of all of that. Thank you, Lord. Glory to God, I don't ever have to go through all of that again. I don't have to live that lie any more. Thinking that everything can be made right by putting some brown powder on a spoon, cooking it in water, and sticking it in my arm. I no longer have to cover my problems with a quilt of chemicals. There's a new way to live."

Notes

1. All subsequent references to "football" refer to what North Americans know as soccer.
2. His name has been changed.

Chapter 3

When You're Too Sick to Steal

"If you give of your own food to the hungry
and satisfy the needs of the wretched,
then light will rise for you out of the darkness...
you will be called the rebuilder of broken walls,
the restorer of houses in ruins."　　　(Isaiah 58:10, 12)

In the midst of the Arab market in Marseilles, France, is a man, talking on a mobile phone – his "Betelephone." He is standing in front of a stall that sells used clothing, and has just called London, England. He is speaking to Malcolm Hayday, one of the Directors of the Charities Aid Foundation. They are talking about a start-up loan for an export-import business to help finance a new work in northern India.

This is the globalized world of Elliott Tepper, the International Director and co-founder of Association Betel. Elliott oversees 110 residences, more than 80 thrift shops (known as *Rastros*), a dozen church properties, and over 250 vehicles, in fifty metropolitan areas and nine countries around the world. His monthly phone bill is considerable.

The telephones are not just used administratively, for Association Betel cannot be reduced to numbers and statistics. It is in its essence relationships. The mobile telephone enables Elliott and about a hundred senior Betel leaders to stay in continuous and intimate contact with one another. The phones, perhaps more than any other dynamic, are what keep the Betel organism from degenerating into an organization. As needs arise, and as the leaders feel God quickening their spirits, the calls go out. *"Hola, buenas tardes..."* – "Hello, good afternoon...' The right call, to the right person, at the right moment, is the secret to many of the miracles they have witnessed. With their antennas up, the men and women at the forefront of Betel are continuously nurturing their spiritual vision and faith. Seemingly oblivious to their phone bills, they are quick to call and encourage one another.

In these ways, the mobiles sustain the relational links that keep Betel vital and personal. After the conference in September 1999, Elliott took the team and me on a Betel tour. We mentioned to him how impressed we were with Jorge, the Madrid house leader, and Pepe, a junior leader. Elliott quite surprised us, for he not only knew about them in their leadership capacities, roles and functions, but knew details of their drug backgrounds, their conversion, and deepening maturity in Christ.

Sixteen years earlier, Elliott didn't know a single drug addict.

In July 1983, Elliott, his wife Mary, and their four boys arrived in Madrid from Mexico, to join the Spanish WEC team. On their arrival the mission's field leader, Billy Glover, picked them up at the airport. While waiting for them to clear customs, his portfolio was stolen – in it were his car keys, his wallet, and the keys to the Teppers' apartment. Their time in Spain began with a theft. It was to be a sign of the difficult times ahead.

Like a *burro*, a donkey, the Teppers tried to do what they had done in Mexico. While in Puebla, studying Spanish, Elliott's MBA from Harvard had afforded him the opportunity to teach economics and banking at the Universidad de las Americas, and that had opened all manner of significant relational doors with the university elite.

"If it worked in Mexico, it will work in Spain." The little missionary band went to the Universities of Madrid and Alcala, but after a year of frustration, they had met with little success.

The Teppers' apartment was in San Blas, one of the rougher suburbs of Madrid. They began to spend more time in their immediate neighborhood, handing out tracts on the streets. Most of those passing by showed no interest in their attempts to share the gospel. The only ones who would listen were the drug addicts, the homeless, and the prostitutes. The Teppers also seemed to attract people with mental problems, especially the clinically depressed and the psychotic.

Mary and Elliott, and Billy and Hazel Glover were joined by another WEC missionary. Lindsay McKenzie was raised in Melbourne, Australia, and while at WEC Missionary Training College in Tasmania, was inspired and challenged by a visiting missionary to consider Spain as his field of service. Lindsay arrived in August 1993, and combined his language training with street evangelism in San Blas.

The WEC team began befriending those on the street who showed some interest in the gospel. Reflecting on those early days, Lindsay says, "We really weren't thinking about what we were doing. It just sort of happened. We look back, and it makes sense now. We were trying to search for God's strategy – not some program. We walked around San Blas, praying, wandering around in a 'holy ignorance.' WEC had a vague, undefined missionary strategy – 'Go to where you feel God is calling you, and then, be led by the Spirit' – which we were trying to follow.

"We learned that even the most insignificant encounter can be a divine appointment. The drug addicts were continuously interrupting us as we were trying to share the gospel with 'normal' people. The addicts figured we were soft touches, and were hoping we'd give them some money. But they were the only people who were at all responsive to our street preaching. It took a long while – months – before the penny dropped. We were praying, 'Lord, give us normal people, ones we can build with. Lord, normal people...'"

Elliott was growing increasingly frustrated with the spiritual hardness of the nation. It felt as if they weren't getting anywhere with the church plant. The only glimmer of hope was the contacts with the addicts. One day, Cheli asked for help. Could Elliott and Lindsay take her to a Christian drug rehabilitation center in the north of Spain? The missionaries consented.

They returned to the rehab two months later to visit her, and were profoundly impacted by what they saw. In such a short space of time, God had graciously rebuilt much of her ruined life.

Relationships with other addicts deepened. Nearly every week, the missionaries would take a desperate addict to one of the centers.

On a return trip from a rehab, Elliott was praying about their calling to Spain. Something turned in his heart. He had come from a vibrant and dynamic missionary church in Latin America, and he longed to see that same fire and passion in the lives of men and women in Spain. Hope and expectation rose up in his spirit.

When he got home, he shared the stirrings with Mary. Standing in the doorway of his kitchen he said, "If we're willing to work with outcasts and addicts and prostitutes – the worst – God is going to give us a church, a big church, and He's going to give it to us fast." As the words came out of his mouth, both he and Mary felt a supernatural visitation – they were overwhelmed with an immediate sense of the power and the presence of God. "It was as if a 'YES!' broke through from eternity, and rose up and shouted in our spirits."

The Teppers drafted a proposal requesting support for an outreach to addicts, and presented it to the Spanish Field Conference. Their WEC peers turned it down, saying, "That kind of ministry is too hard, too costly, and you lack the necessary skills. Besides, it's impossible to mix a rehab with a church. If you want to do it, we'll pray for you."

The Teppers, Lindsay, and another WEC missionary, Myk Hall, found themselves drawn to the addicts more and more. As part of his field placement, Lindsay lived with the addicts in the rehab residence at REMAR for seven months, and said of the experience, "I came back to San Blas a different person." He was very persuasive, and talked Myk into a five-month residence in the women's home. Their time at REMAR turned both their lives around.

In the first two years, Elliott and Lindsay took sixty addicts to three different Christian rehabs – Teen Challenge, REMAR, and RETO. The addicts' mothers were so grateful for the missionaries' intervention, and the concern shown to their children, that they joined the fledgling church for Bible studies. One day, an addict's mother, Maruja, was diagnosed with cancer of the uterus. The church held a special prayer time for her. In the pre-surgery examination, it was discovered that there was no longer any evidence of the cancer. Word of the healing spread, and her friends started coming to the church.

That was the good news. The bad news was that the addicts

didn't stay at the centers. They'd cause problems, and they'd disappear, only to surface again in San Blas. "We'd drop the addict off, stay the night with the local pastor, and on our arrival back in San Blas, there would be the addict, on the street where we'd picked him up. He'd run away from the center, traveled through the night, and arrived back home before we did!"

One day, Miguel Diez, from REMAR, phoned and said, "The guys you bring from San Blas are different from the guys we get elsewhere. Yours are hard and mean-spirited. We can't take any more for a while. Give us a break." Ray Pollnow, the Director of RETO, made a similar observation, but with a twist: "The San Blas guys are a breed of their own. Send us more. I want to discover the spirit behind these guys."

In December 1985, Ray phoned Elliott and said, "I think I've discovered the spiritual 'strongholds' over San Blas. I believe there are two – lies and deceit." That resonated with Lindsay and Elliott and the other missionaries with whom they associated. Two addicts, for instance, were coming to the Friday night prayer meetings. Their names were Raul and Angel. Both were gang leaders and drug pushers. They both had street names. Raul's was *El Tocho*, a nickname which had a double meaning: "The Stocky One" and "The Stubborn One." Both fit. Angel's was the counterpoint to his real name: *Angel El Veneno*, "The Poisoned Angel." He got the name because of his personality, and because he stank. He never bathed. The two of them only came to the meetings because they hoped for a handout. But any money they were given was turned into heroin.

One Sunday morning meeting, Raul came with another addict, "Hippy." They were both high. They'd been up all night committing a burglary on a bar. Having stolen all the coins out of the poker machines, they had then made their way to the gypsy camp to buy heroin before making their way to the meeting hoping to get something to eat. Elliott was encouraging people to join in an open prayer time and Hippy surprised the gathering by praying: "Thank you, Lord, that while we were burgling, You didn't let the police catch us."

Lies and deceit perfectly characterized not only the addicts, but many of their parents as well. One father said of his children, "They're so successful. I'm so proud of them." At the time, there was inter-generational incest in the family, the eldest daughter was a prostitute, the son-in-law was in prison for armed robbery, the middle boy was on heroin, and the youngest in the family had raped a neighbor when he was thirteen.

"Lies and deceit" became a focus of the church's prayers. They spoke the Lord's blessing over San Blas, and prayed for a spiritual turning over the neighborhood. Three weeks later, New Year's Eve, 1985, the single missionaries were getting ready for a big supper party. While out shopping for some last-minute groceries, Lindsay met Hippy on the street. He was miserable, strung-out, and desperate.

"I accompanied him to his house," recalled Lindsay. "I'd never seen anything like it before or since. There was wall-to-wall rubbish, and used, bloody syringes lying strewn on the floor, from the kitchen to the lounge. He'd long since vacated the bedroom as it had become unliveable. Hippy said he really wanted to go to a rehab center, and I told him that I would pick him up the next morning at 7.30 a.m.

"I returned to our New Year's Eve dinner with all the others and recounted what I'd found. Suddenly none of us felt very festive. We thought about inviting him to join us, but figured he'd be too embarrassed to accept. We decided to prepare 'dinner-for-one' and take it to him. It's Spanish custom to eat twelve grapes on the twelve strokes of midnight, so we even placed twelve grapes in a small container. I got to Hippy's at 10.30. He was embarrassed to see so much food. I just left it for him on the coffee table next to the sofa-cum-bed and returned home.

"We were up very late; at 7.00 a.m. my alarm woke me from a dead sleep. I suddenly remembered why I had set it so early. I rushed to Hippy's house and knocked, but there was no answer. I pounded away for fifteen minutes, until the door slowly opened and a dazed Hippy wanted to know what was going on. I reminded him of his request for help. Through his drugged fog, he recalled something of our previous night's conversation. I packed his bag for him while he dressed himself in slow motion. Then we raced at break-neck speed to the bus station.

"I paid for the ticket and saw him seated on the bus, and then waited until the bus was out of sight. We were getting wise. Too many addicts had tricked us, getting off the bus just before its departure. They'd then cash in their tickets, and use the money for their next fix!

"I prayed a rather faithless prayer: 'Lord, please, may Hippy stay in the center.' Nobody in San Blas expected him to stay, but he surprised us all. He was a model resident, and eventually became one of the RETO center's main leaders.

"Hippy phoned his family each Saturday and told them how he was doing. Eventually his sister, Begonia, decided that it was time for her to have a second try. Her first stay was a negative experience, and lasted only a matter of days, but she was impressed with the changes she saw in her brother. She also did well, and that inspired another San Blas girl, Toni. We took her to the same center, and soon there was a wave of addicts appearing at our regular church meetings asking if we would take them to a rehab."

Early in January 1986, Angel came looking for Lindsay. "Raul wants to talk to you." Lindsay wasn't sure if this was good news. Raul and Lindsay hadn't exactly hit it off. The missionary had recently walked in on one of Raul's drug deals. On the other hand, perhaps it was taxi time – a year before in September, Elliott had taken Raul up to RETO but he had only stayed for three weeks and then left to return to drugs. Maybe he was ready to give it another try.

Angel took Lindsay to Raul. He was strung-out and desperate. "I need help, but there's a problem. I have a court case in two weeks." That meant there was no point even trying to take him to a center – Raul would only just be through the hardest part of his withdrawal in two weeks. "We both knew that it would have been counterproductive to send him four hours north, only to have him return to Madrid at a very crucial time in his withdrawal process. He didn't want a second failure.

"Raul and I were not friends. I really don't know why I did what I did. Part of it may have been shock – this was the first time he'd ever been civil towards me. I know that I really wanted to help him, and I couldn't simply walk away and leave him without a satisfactory solution.

"Why don't you come to my flat – detox there, and then we'll get you to court." As the words came out of his mouth, Lindsay wished they hadn't.

While he was thinking, *"What have I done?"* Raul asked, "When?"

What could Lindsay say?

"Tomorrow, 9.00 a.m."

The next morning, the apartment buzzer rang at 9.00 a.m. sharp. When Lindsay opened the door, there was *El Tocho*. Such punctuality was unusual. And he wasn't stoned. That was really unusual.

Lindsay set a few ground rules: "I can't just stay here for two weeks, baby-sitting you. I'll stay with you through the worst of your withdrawal. Then, if I go to the bank, you come with me. If I go shopping, you go. When I go out evangelizing, you come with me." It was a deal.

The next four days, Lindsay stayed up with Raul through the nights, made him tea and soup, and cleaned up after his vomiting episodes. Myk was alongside too. She even mended his ripped underwear on her sewing machine. That really impressed Raul. Towards the end of the first week, the worst was over. Raul became Lindsay's shadow. They did everything together.

"Raul had heard the gospel many times in the other centers, he'd been to some of our meetings, and he had overheard us preach on the streets. Now, he was handing out tracts with us – and telling people about Jesus – and he wasn't even converted!"

Raul had to accompany Lindsay and Myk to a mission outreach, at a church south-west of Madrid. It was a poorly organized event, and Lindsay felt it was a disaster for Raul – an embarrassment for the gospel. On the drive home, Lindsay and Myk were chatting, and Raul blurted out, "All this talk about love. I don't understand it. I don't think that anyone has ever really loved me." Myk, from the back seat, reached up front, put her arms around him and said, *"We* love you."

Later Raul said, "It felt like Jesus wrapped His arms around me."

It was late when they got home and Lindsay wanted to go to bed. Raul was rambling away about wanting God to change his life. Lindsay told him to go to sleep; they'd talk some more in the morning.

"The next thing I knew was that it was as if God shouted, 'Listen to him!' "

Lindsay asked, "Do you want to give your life to the Lord?"

"That's what I've been trying to tell you for the last two hours!"

In the dark of night, 20 January 1986, they knelt, prayed, and Raul gave his heart to the Lord.

"There was a remarkable peace that seemed to fill the room. A holy silence. It was wonderful."

Raul didn't go to bed that night. He sat in a chair, whispering, *"Dios, Dios, Dios..."* "God, God, God..." The next morning he told Lindsay that he had made contact with Someone very real. He knew that God was personal, and he was part of Him.

Lindsay was struck that Raul seemed markedly softer. Now he laughed ... and he didn't sneer nearly as often.

A few days later Raul said, "Look, I know that our agreement was for two weeks, but do I have to go? Can't I stay here?" Lindsay consented. There were no conditions; it just seemed like the right thing to do.

Raul had only ever read sports magazines. Now he was devouring the Bible, and asking lots of questions. Raul and Lindsay and Elliott spent many late nights, talking into the small hours.

Raul's court case was annulled, a small token of the forgiveness and new life he now had in Christ. His love for Jesus seemed to grow daily, and his old drug friends were quick to see the changes in him. Many of them started to come to the prayer meetings because of Raul's compelling testimony. It was evidenced in seemingly insignificant ways, but they were huge frontiers for a recovering drug addict. One day, Lindsay gave Raul money for bread and sent him out to the grocers, alone. Raul came back with both bread and the change. Lindsay's trust and Raul's faithfulness marked a decided breakthrough.

Three months after his conversion, Raul said to Lindsay, "Hey, why don't we take in another guy. What you've done with me, why don't we do it with someone else? We have a spare bed." It was the "we" that struck Lindsay the hardest. He agreed, as again it seemed like the right thing to do.

Raul knew an addict from another neighborhood, Javi, and Lindsay knew his mother. She had started coming to the church. Together, the three of them convinced Javi to live with Lindsay and Raul, but he only stayed for six weeks, and then left. Javi was hooked on everything – when he could get nothing else, he would chew coffee grounds to get a high.

Shortly afterwards, Paco and his mother showed up at the door of the church. He had failed a rehab in the north, and they wouldn't take him back. His mother knew of the San Blas church, and came pleading for help. They agreed to receive him, and Raul immediately took over his care. The two of them shared a bedroom, and one night Lindsay overheard Raul saying, "What God did with me, He can do with you." That was "the program." There was no methodology; it was all relationship.

After another three months, Raul and Paco brought José home. He was thirty-two years old, and had been in prison seventeen times for armed robbery. José was mean, had a raging temper and, because of his paranoia, he was frequently out of control. Over the weeks of his stay, they watched his bitterness turn – instead of cursing, he awoke with a grin from ear to ear. He started singing worship choruses, and became teachable. He was marginally literate; José joined the others for Bible study, and slowly began to read and write. Lindsay noted, "They spent a lot of time in the Book of Revelation. The visions, the beast and the battles fascinated these recovering addicts."

Word quickly got around about the care the addicts were getting – and that there was a big change. Nobody had to leave the neighborhood. Lindsay, however, wasn't sure that this kind of ministry was what he was supposed to be doing. It seemed that they were breaking all the rules – the other rehabs were a long way from the city. That forced the addicts to leave the area they did drugs in, and live on a farm. While it got them away from their influences, it also put them in a very foreign environment, because the average addict is a city boy. It was no wonder that they didn't do very well when they returned to their cities.

In a prayer conversation with the Lord, Lindsay was asking for direction and confirmation. He felt the Lord ask him, "How big am I? Am I big enough to change these boys in the middle of their war zone?" Something happened in Lindsay's spirit; something was settled that day. All the criticisms that they were receiving were suddenly silenced in his heart. It no longer mattered that the neighbors didn't want drug addicts in their building. Nor did it matter that concerned friends and their spiritual leaders misunderstood the call – they were *not* being distracted from real evangelism, and sidetracked into social work. This was the call of God on their lives.

The addicts genuinely wanted their help. Myk took in a girl, Isabel, then Ana, and later Mari, and helped them through their withdrawal periods. Mari's husband showed up at Lindsay's flat with a garbage bag of clothes – his. Manolo, *Majara*, "the Crazy One," wanted to move in. That would make five in a three-bedroom flat: Lindsay, Raul, Paco, José, and Manolo. The neighbors were already upset. Rather than have a scene that would further antagonize the other tenants, Lindsay said Manolo could come, but had to spend the first night in the church. Lindsay slept with him on the floor of the church. This gang leader seemed genuine. The five men started entering and leaving the apartment as quietly as possible.

When José and Manolo joined the group, things shifted from one on one, to two on two. Raul had discipled Paco; now Raul was discipling one, and Paco was discipling the other. These were the early origins of the role of the shadow, the 24-hour care and supervision that a newly arrived addict receives at Betel.

In Lindsay's apartment life together had its moments, for only months before the guys were macho gang leaders. One night Paco and Manolo had a very violent, verbal argument over who'd watch what on TV. Lindsay intervened, and separated them so he could talk to each of them alone. It sounded as though Manolo had been in the wrong. Lindsay told him that he had to go to Paco and apologize.

"Apologize! If I were in the street right now, I'd run a knife through him!"

"It's up to you – we're not going on unless you do."

Manolo realized that if he didn't apologize, he was back out on the street. He walked out of the room, and into the lounge.

"Paco, I'm sorry," he snapped through clenched teeth.

It was the first time he'd ever apologized to anybody, for anything. He walked back into his bedroom. Lindsay went in to encourage him. "I'm proud of you – you did the right thing."

Manolo was sitting on his bunk, facing the wall, and wouldn't turn around. He was crying, and didn't want Lindsay to see.

"What's wrong?"

"Nothing..."

There was a long pause.

"You know, that was the hardest thing I've ever had to do."

Manolo had stabbed, shot, and punched people, and had received the same. Forgiveness required a new kind of toughness.

The Teppers, Lindsay, and Myk were feeding the guys, but as their health returned, they ate like horses. The addicts' mothers were contributing supplies, but the men needed to work. Once they were through their heroin withdrawal they were bored and Lindsay was busy inventing work for them. Every day, they spring-cleaned the flat. They painted the walls. They painted the radiators. They painted the covers on the radiators. A month later, they changed the color scheme, and repainted everything!

They received a request to help move a friend, and it was their first paid job. They got other contracts, laying ceramic tiles, doing small plumbing jobs, and some general carpentry. As they completed the work, it was obvious that their vocational successes were building dignity back into their lives. This was especially the case as they became self-sustaining.

Lindsay taught the guys how to keep their own books, and they were soon responsible to make everything balance. From the start, they were taught to tithe. Starting from zero, they accepted giving as another aspect of their life together.

It wasn't all success, however. Lindsay recounts the other side of the story.

"A man called Gonzalo came for a few days and left. Another man called Moky stayed for ten days. He left, and took the church offering with him. I had put it on top of my desk, and even a bit of money in plain view was too big a temptation.

"The following day, Moky's family phoned to tell us that he had used the Sunday offering money to buy heroin. He had overdosed and was rushed to hospital where he was pronounced clinically dead. The doctors were able to resuscitate him, and sent him home.

"Very late that night, Elliott, Raul and I went to see him. We told him that we forgave him, and cautioned him that he should not take lightly the fact that God had spared his life. We never saw Moky again. I learned later that he died of AIDS."

In December, eleven months after Raul's conversion, two street guys showed up at the apartment on the same day. Both were disgustingly filthy. Their names were Luis Mendosa and Vidgi. Having met them on a street outreach, the others had talked them into coming to the flat.

Lindsay knew that they were more than the neighbors could manage. There had already been several tenants' meetings, and it was unanimous – the neighbors wanted the men out. The ladies wouldn't get into the lift with the men – their tattoos and scarred faces scared them too much.

With these two street guys, Lindsay knew they were in trouble. To minimize the damage, he and the other men took them to the church and showered them there. They cut their hair and had them shave. They got them new clothes, and come nightfall, in the dark, they snuck them into the flat. There were now seven men living in an apartment which measured 800 square feet.

Luis Pino was the next to join them. He'd been addicted to heroin since he was eighteen years old and the drugs had taken their toll. His health was so poor, he had fought a lady for her purse, and lost.

While on the street, in the rain, trying to sell tissue packets at the traffic lights, he noticed a muddy flyer in the gutter. It advertised a free drug center: Betel. Luis peeled the flyer from the ground and carefully folded it and put it in his pocket. Later, he showed it to his wife, Lola. She phoned the number, and after making sure that the center was indeed free, asked if her husband could come. They were told to come in the following day.

They were late for the appointment. Lindsay, who needed to leave to do a pickup job with José, told them to come back tomorrow. Lola and Luis were disappointed; for Lindsay, it was a test to see how serious they were. The next day they were on time, and after a short interview it was felt Luis should be allowed to join them. He moved into the apartment that afternoon.

There was no bed for him, and no place to put one. Raul gave up his bed, and slept on the floor. Luis said later, "I'd never seen anything like it – that a street guy would do that. It made me want to stay, because what I saw was real love."

A few months later Luis Pino had to go to court to face a previous shoplifting charge. Lindsay went with him. They were late, and Lindsay couldn't find a parking space. Lindsay let Luis out in front of the courthouse. It was the first time Luis was on his own since joining them.

Lindsay told him, "I'll find you as soon as I can."

When he drove away, Luis thought, "Great, now I can get a cigarette."

He was just about to bum one when he thought, "These guys are trusting me. No one has ever done that. I don't want to let them down." He walked straight into the courtroom and, from that moment on, never touched a cigarette or drugs again. The power of a momentary decision played itself out.

In December 1986 Lindsay left the guys for two weeks. He had become engaged to Myk, and went to Barcelona with her when she had the opportunity to do some recording with musician friends. Raul was left in charge of the men, and on his return Lindsay realized that he couldn't take back what he had released.

The apartment had become unusable. Lindsay promised the irate neighbors that they would be gone by the end of February. He had no idea where.

On 11 February 1987, Lindsay and the seven others moved out of the apartment and into a four-bedroom house that Elliott had found to rent. That move marked an important transition for the community. No longer were they in Lindsay's flat; now they were in their own house. And the sense of "house" rather than "rehab" meant the world to them.

One Saturday, their day off, the guys were out in their backyard in their underwear, sunning themselves when a missionary family arrived, unannounced. They wanted to see the "trophy" converts.

Raul became enraged. "This is *our* house. We are not apes in a zoo!"

The missionaries left, offended that the "fruit" couldn't be tested.

When Lindsay married Myk in April 1987, it meant that the direct, 24-hour responsibility for the Betelitos had to be fully born by the senior men themselves. Elliott, Lindsay and Myk were still directly involved in daily affairs, going to market with the men, fixing the vehicles with them, evangelizing together, but the Betelitos were maturing, and spiritual giftings were emerging. Without title or official roles declared, they were serving as pastors, even prophets. All the while, character issues were being constantly refined, humility forged, and servants' hearts imparted.

The first women's house was opened in June 1987. Estrella had just returned to San Blas from the RETO women's community, and was asked to be the house leader. Lola, Luis Pino's wife, was the first resident. She was jealous of the changes she saw in Luis. "I was living with my parents, in their comfortable home. I had my son, and my job. But I was so depressed. Luis had nothing, yet I'd never seen him so happy." She decided to accept Myk's offer to bring her son Luisete and start a new life. It took a week to quit her job, settle her affairs, and get rid of their dog.

In November 1989 Betel's first spiritual "daughter" was born. Lindsay, Myk, and their baby Rebeca left Madrid with Tomas Lopez, Juan Capilla and two other men. They set off for Valencia in an old van filled with used furniture. Over the next two years, new Betels were planted roughly every six months: in Cuenca, Barcelona, Almeria, and Cueta. Young leaders were sent out with God's blessing, and an old van filled with used furniture. They found a house and a shop to rent, and as they began befriending local addicts, the proceeds from the thrift shop enabled them to be self-sustaining.

In May 1991 Raul was ordained as Betel's first indigenous pastor, and with his wife Jenny became the first WEC-Betel ex-addict church planters. He was also a passionate spokesman for Betel. At a regional clergy gathering, a local pastor accosted Betel for starting churches: "Why don't you do what you do best? You do the rehabilitation; we'll send you our guys to get off drugs, and when they're straight, you send them back to us."

Raul stood to his feet. "'*Your* guys?' You want us to do all the dirty work, so you can have them back all clean and tidy, sitting politely in your church? You can call them *your* guys when you've picked them off the streets, and you've bathed their dirty sores, when you've cleaned up their vomit, when you've stayed up all night through their withdrawals, when you've put up with their rebellion, and seen them mature in Christ. *Then* you can call them '*your* guys.'" Typical Raul.

In 1993 the work spread beyond Spain to New York City, and Naples, Italy. In 1995, centers were started in Germany, Mexico and Portugal.

So many of Betel's distinctives were defined during those first few years. The dynamics of practical love in action; peer care, testimony and discipleship; trust, forgiveness and grace; free entrance, free exit; work, dignity and self-sustaining employment all grew out of relationship. The Teppers, Lindsay and Myk didn't implement a program, or follow a church-planting strategy. Rather, they received those whom the Lord sent them, and built structure around the needs as they arose. In Elliott's words, "The ministry to the drug addicts and the marginalized was a spontaneous expression of love, mercy, and faith. We had no idea of where we were going, what we were doing, or how we'd do it. We just tried to respond to what we felt God was calling forth. We chose the name 'House of God' – *Betel* in Spanish – because that's exactly what we experienced on the streets of San Blas, caring for the addicts: '*Surely God is in this place and* [we] *knew it not*' (Genesis 28:16).

"We weren't psychologists, or trained rehab specialists. The only thing we had to give was the presence and power of God. Living in Betel's houses brings them under the supernatural covering of the Kingdom of God. A bed and clean sheets, a shower, clean clothes, food, and a friend who will bandage their abscesses, and help them through their withdrawal are all practical ways of showing the addicts God's love. It would be the love of God, and that love alone, that would restore their lives."

Such a glorious redemption costs. The Teppers had their keys stolen on their arrival in Madrid. That was but a beginning. Their home and vehicles have been robbed twenty-three times. The thefts at the church are even more numerous. Sound systems, tools, generators, vans and thousands of dollars of cash have been stolen over the years.

In 1991, the Teppers' son Timothy was killed in a tragic car accident. It could have taken Elliott and his other three sons as well. There were other griefs to come.

Luis Mendoza and Manolo died of AIDS. Raul was the first of the pastors to die of AIDS. In August 1990, Raul, his wife Jenny, and their baby Sefora had gone to Barcelona, and pioneered the second of Betel's church plants. The work grew quickly, but Raul had to return to Madrid when his health began to fail. He continued to give pastoral care as he could. Skin and bone as he was, *El Tocho* had an uncommon authority to speak into the lives of those who were suffering. When he preached, he was too weak to stand. He talked a lot about heaven and about radical discipleship, and everyone hung on his words.

Miguel Angel Jambrina, *Jambri*, followed a similar track. The tenth addict to join the growing community, he also came from San Blas, from the same street as Raul. When they could no longer fit all the men in the first house – there were twenty-five of them in the small farmhouse – Jambri was first in line to open a 'new' house a few kilometers away. The building was derelict – it had no windows, no doors, only four walls and a partial roof. Six brave souls went with him, and they rebuilt the place. In less than a year, he handed over the thriving work, and went to a new work in Cuenca, east of Madrid.

At a *cumbre*, a pastors' summit in 1993, when Elliott put out a missionary call to open a work in Italy, Jambri put up his hand. 'My wife and I will go.' Everyone took a deep breath – it was one thing that someone wanted to go – it was another to consider someone as sick as Jambri was. He was in the terminal stage of AIDS. He was losing weight and suffering high fevers. Because of his weakened immunity, he was constantly plagued with opportunistic diseases. Yet he was so excited, and so convinced that this was the call of God that he talked the leadership into releasing him. No one had the heart to stop him.

He pioneered the work in Naples, and in three months the work was financially independent of Madrid, for Jambri had quickly won the heart of the Italians. His commitment to Jesus, his determination, discipline, passion, and pathos inspired, challenged, and convicted all those whom he met.

Despite the fact that he was in and out of hospital, the work continued to grow. Twenty to twenty-five recovering addicts were in residence; the thrift store was financially viable; leaders were being raised up: Betel's reputation in Italy was well established. As his health failed, Jambri directed much of the work by phone from hospital. The nursing staff grew accustomed to his bedside leadership meetings.

By October 1995, he had to be taken back to Madrid to receive hospital care that was unavailable in Naples. Within days, he won the respect of the other AIDS patients on the ward. From his hospital bed, Jambri continued to give direction and heart to the work in Naples, again by telephone.

Jambri died in a Madrid hospital in August 1996. His example of total commitment, one in which physical limitations were in no way limiting, set an imprint, a benchmark that is still spoken of in Naples and around Betel.

Raul died on 1 September 1995, almost a year before Jambri. Shortly before his death, Raul spoke a word that was fully evident in Jambri's life, and has steeled the spirit of Betelitos ever since. He slipped off his oxygen mask and declared, 'If we do not surrender, we will conquer.'

This chapter has tracked the amazing growth of Betel-Madrid's early ministry and development. The following chapter from Betel-Birmingham is a detailed look at the kind of life that is redeemed and transformed. It traces the spiritual distance one man has traveled in a very short space of time.

Chapter 4

Accelerated Grace

"Those who rebuild you make better speed than those who pulled you down." (Isaiah 49:17)

Sean Davies is missing the tip of his left thumb.[1] He mashed it with a lump hammer when the chisel he was pounding slipped. At the time he was working on a safe in the basement of the fast food restaurant he and his mates had broken into. It was the first big job he had done without his father alongside. He was fifteen years old.

The boys were having a great time, smoking joints, and snorting coke. It was a "safecracking party."

Sean had deftly peeled back the outer steel jacket with a sledgehammer, and was starting on the concrete liner. That's when things went wrong. He was working in cramped quarters; his thumb was too close to the jagged steel, and the blow of the mis-directed lump hammer tore a chunk off his thumb. After the stream of profanity, he looked at his mates. "I'm in trouble."

They wrapped up his thumb with towels from the toilet and finished the job.

"I remember the buzz, the adrenaline as we left the restaurant. I was smoking a great big joint, covered in concrete dust and blood, a big wad of money in the bag; wow, man."

Driving away, Sean held up fistfuls of cash, and said to his pals, "The first of many!" And it was.

But Sean had been previously arrested for football violence, and the police had taken a DNA sample. That's why he knew he was in for it. It would only be a matter of time before they came calling. They knew where he lived.

"I grew up in an extremely strange family. Not strange to me, because I grew up around it. But now, looking back, it wasn't a very good start to life."

There were always drugs around the house – his dad was always smoking dope with his friends. Sean started at an early age. Father and son would roll joints together, tossing them into the fruit bowl on the side table, "for later."

Sean was soon taking amphetamines. One night, his mom was at his bedroom door. "Got any of that hard stuff that keeps you up all night? That speed stuff. I want to do some cleaning, and I can't smoke any dope; it just makes me fall asleep."

"Wow, Mom."

A few months later Sean's father met him in the hall. He was holding a bag full of pills and a roll of cash. "What's this then?"

"It's ecstasy, Dad."

"That new dance drug that everybody's takin'? Stayin' up all night? Fair enough."

A casual conversation about drugs. Most parents would have freaked; Sean's father just wanted to know what his cut was. "You're still living in my house; what's my percentage?"

But it wasn't just drugs that made for a strange upbringing.

"When I was in school, I wasn't like other kids. I was deep in myself and very withdrawn. I found it really, really hard to learn. I tried, but things didn't sink in, and I used to get picked on because of it. I got put into a remedial class, and once you're in there, you get ridiculed all the time. I got loads of stick, and because of it, I didn't like school at all.

"What I did like was time with my dad. I used to sit and watch him set up the newest burglar alarm systems in the living-room. He'd set up motion sensors and work on them until he could keep them from going off. When he'd finished, I'd set them up and try and remember what he'd done. Surprisingly, it came pretty easily to me. I couldn't remember any of my schoolwork, yet I could sit and watch my dad for three hours doing something complex and remember nearly every single thing he'd done.

"Dad came home one day, and my younger brother told him, 'Sean's in the shed. He's playing with your tools.' Dad came out, and found me working on an alarm system he himself hadn't tried. I showed him how to break it. He asked how long it took me to figure it out. I said, 'About an hour.' That was it. From then on he began to teach me his trade.

"It went from alarms to safecracking. We'd work away in the garage, with hand grinders, and sledgehammers and chisels – breaking into safes that he and his gang had stolen."

Sean got on-the-job training. "Dad took me out with him, and he taught me how to break into big countryside manor homes. He liked to specialize in antique jewelry and guns. We'd either break into the safe at the house, or we'd pry it off the wall and take it home.

"All I wanted was for my dad to love me. If this was the only way I could get any recognition – a pat on the back – then I'd do it."

Soon Sean was out committing burglaries on his own. He would bring home his spoils, and his parents would pick through it admiringly. "Oh, I like this. I'll have that. Give me that for your mother." His father would ask, "Do you want me to sell that for you? I know a guy; I can get a good price."

"My dad had contacts everywhere. He had his fingers in all the pies that were going. If money could be made at it, he was in.

"I was fourteen years old; I was getting in at 5 o'clock in the morning. I had to take cocaine to keep myself awake at school."

One morning, when Sean's teacher was going on at him, he looked at her and said, "You know, I'm not that good at being good, but I'm really good at being bad."

A few months later, Sean came home from a snatch – he had waited outside a bank night deposit, and given the bloke who was making the drop a good slap, and grabbed the money. Four hours later, he was having a drink with his dad, who said, "As soon as I heard the police helicopters, the sirens, and the cruisers charging up the motorway, I knew you'd been at it again." Sean wasn't angry; instead, he changed the subject.

Having discovered that Sean had recently started using heroin, his father was full of questions: how much Sean used, how often, what it was like, where he got it from, and how he dealt it. "Dad knew that there was a lot of money to be made and he wanted in on it."

"My father taught me how to burgle; I wanted him to teach me something else. He ran a bouncing business. He's a big guy, 6ft 3in; he'd go to the gym three times a week. A fight would break out, and he'd walk straight in and start throwing punches and the next thing, guys would be laid out on the floor. I wanted to be just like him.

"I asked him to teach me how to fight. I was always getting bullied for being dumb. I'd come home with black eyes. He said to me, 'I can teach you how to break open safes, that's easy. But only you can teach yourself how to fight.' "

The lessons began.

"At school, there was a big guy named Tank. He'd been slapping me about, stealing my joints, making me look like a fool in front of his girlfriends, and making me cry. He'd been at it quite a while. I had had enough of it, so I went into the woodworking room at school and got a wooden mallet. I walked up behind him. Tank didn't see me coming, but his friends did. What struck me was the shock on all the faces right in front of me. They were all staring at me. It was a massive turning point in my life.

"Tank turned round, and I smashed him in the forehead with the mallet. Split him open from hairline to eyebrows. I remember the sound it made when I hit him.

"My life changed after that. You know, I was the talk of the school. When I was in the police station, one of the officers said to me, 'You've got some swing on yer, Daviesy.' And they all knew my dad. When word went round what I'd done, they'd come up and say, 'So, you're big Ben's son?'

"I liked all the attention and the recognition. After that, no one in the school messed me about. Suddenly I was the one with the girlfriends, and I was the one who was out when everybody else was at home."

Sean had entered the fast lane. It would get faster.

He was arrested for shooting a bus driver with an air rifle. "I was living in a neighborhood that everyone knew as 'The Zoo.'

This place was *bad*. I took aim on a bus that was coming down the street. The policewoman that arrested me said that it was quite an amazing shot because the driver's side window was only open a few inches, and he was doing about forty miles per hour. I was about sixty feet away, and I shot him in the temple, right through the gap in the window. I didn't kill him, but the bus ran into a lamppost. I was the talk of the East End for about a month."

Sean was frequently arrested for fighting, or for "being cheeky." "Me and my buddies would be hanging out, and a policeman would come and ask, 'What are you up to now?' I'd light a joint up in front of him; he'd ask me for it. I'd say, 'Take it.' Sheer arrogance.

"From the time I was fifteen, I couldn't keep my hands to myself. I got busted for fighting so many times. I got in a fight outside of the Odeon Theatre. I was standing in the queue with a girl and some black guys starting giving me hassle. I got scared because there were a few of them and they were bigger than I was. So I just wrapped myself around this one guy's head, and got his nose in my mouth and just held on. He was screaming, and his mates just backed right off. I hung on to his nose till the police came. I got three months in Kirk Levington, a detention center for juveniles.

"I was heavily into football violence, a devoted Leeds United supporter. I was hanging around with the guys that organized things. I even wrote off to America to become a member of the Ku Klux Klan. I sent them $75, and they sent me a membership certificate. I hung it on the wall in my bedroom.

"While I was in the detention center, I got into a pretty serious fight over football. The other guy was a Newcastle supporter. We were brawling in the toilets and we made a lot of noise. He wouldn't give in, and I wouldn't give in, so we beat each other up pretty badly. Because we were at it a while word got round, and the detention officers came running in.

"Me and this guy just looked at each other and smiled, and started fighting the officers together. We both knew that we were going to get a beating anyway. We figured we might as well give them a bit of it too."

✌

"All that mattered was drugs, money and girls. If trouble came along with it, a fight, all the better. I wanted people to be scared of me, and I accomplished it. If people were afraid, they'd stay away. That's what I wanted. I'd walk into pubs and people wouldn't even look at me. The guys left me alone, and the girls joined up with us. They liked me; at least, they liked my lifestyle. Blokes would be sitting at the bar buying beer for the girls; I'd walk in and order three or four bottles of champagne.

"By then I was taking a lot of acid, and experimenting with ecstasy. It had just come on the market in England. We were trying a drug called pharmacy, which was a really weird drug. I liked ecstasy though. I was taking cocaine every single day. It was my drug of choice. I loved it. I was spending $750 a day on cocaine, just putting it up my nose.

"If anybody wanted me, they knew where to find me: at the Cherry Tree. It's a wine bar. I was there, full time, drinking, taking drugs, plotting things to do, and sorting things out. I was eighteen years old, and had my own gang, Donald, Bill, and Steve. We were together twenty-four hours a day. Everything we did, we did together. They're dead now.

"We made big money. I discovered that walking into places with guns and demanding money was a lot easier than breaking into places and cutting safes open. It was a lot faster. Really fast. We'd charge into a nightclub just before it closed. I'd shove my shotgun into the owner's face and scream, 'Open the safe or I'm takin' your head off.' Most of the time we didn't get as much money as safecracking, but we'd do two or three robberies in a row, and we'd do all right for the week."

"I wasn't superman when it came to fighting. I took my fair share of beatings, but I had no fear. I learned that in prison. Fights in prison could get very dangerous, because nobody cares about anything but their reputation. I got into a football brawl and was stabbed in the eye with a flint knife. The surgeon had to perform microsurgery on it. The socket got sliced open, and my eyeball was hanging out on my cheek. The rest of my face was a bit of a mess. The side of my nose was all smashed in, and most of my teeth were pounded into my lips. I was in hospital for about a month, and then went straight to prison when the doctors deemed me healthy enough to go.

"My face was still in a state; my hands were in a state – I'd broken several knuckles in the brawl, and I was hurting. I smoked a lot of heroin to ease the pain.

"A couple of the guys on the wing were looking at my face and the mess, and they figured this was their chance. I always had a lot of drugs, even while I was in prison. I've swallowed balloons full of stuff and brought it in. Now, with a simple slap, my face would be split wide open again, and anything I had would be theirs for the taking.

"Four of them came into my cell while I was smoking heroin. They were carrying socks filled with batteries and were going to do me up right. I learned a long time ago that if somebody is coming towards you, 'Run at 'em, run at 'em, just run straight at 'em.' Even so, I got smashed up pretty badly. We had a roll about, and with all their whacking they opened the stitches in my head. So, I was back down to the hospital wing, getting sorted out again.

"All I could think of was, 'Four guys against one, look at 'im, he can't even see out of one eye, what chance has he got?' I knew who had set the whole thing up."

Sean got quiet. After a long pause he said, "Let's just say, I hurt him bad. *Real* bad. He'll never forget me."

Once released, Sean went to live with Elizabeth who was by now seven months' pregnant and had moved into a little house. She didn't take drugs, but she enjoyed Sean's party lifestyle. According to Elizabeth, he was a fun guy to be around.

But he wasn't around long. He was high all the time, and forever in need of cash. A friend told him of a guy that had five pounds of cocaine and a big bag of collection money in his wardrobe. "I never questioned the guy's integrity; he'd given me things before, and never let me down. You know, he'd always done his homework. It seemed like a really easy touch.

"I was high. I'd done just over a quarter of an ounce of crack cocaine, which is a lot. I rapped on the guy's door. He opened it, and I busted him on the nose with the butt of my gun. His wife was screaming, so I put the gun in her face and told her to shut up. My mates, Donald, Bill and Steve were with me, and we had a policy: 'If you terrorize them, you're gonna get what you want. Don't just scare 'em; terrorize 'em.'

"That's how far gone I was by that time. I look back and I think to myself, wow, that's awful.

"I had backed the guy's wife up against the washing machine. I stood there, all relaxed as if this were a natural thing. The guy was crying, and I said to him, 'You know why we're here. Go upstairs and get it. I know exactly what's there, so if there is anything missin' I'll blow 'er 'ead off.' He was crying, she was crying, and I was laughing."

There was $15,000 in the stash, and $7,000 in Maltese money, plus the cocaine.

"I don't want to talk about the next episode in my life. All I'll say is that some guys did something wrong to me. They messed a deal up for me, so I messed a deal up for them. I lost about forty-five grand on my deal. The deal I messed up for them was worth about $400,000. They weren't happy.

"I should have seen it coming, but because I was stoned all the time, I got 'laxidaisy.' One night Bill took my shotgun home with him to clean it. That was the night thirteen guys came straight through my house. Some came through the front door, some smashed all my windows out.

"Elizabeth was sitting on the sofa. Flying glass cut her, and someone hit her on the head with a baseball bat. The guys who smashed the front door down squirted ammonia in my eyes, but I was so full of cocaine and heroin, I didn't feel a thing. I just couldn't see. I was in a pair of boxer shorts, barefoot, standing in glass, fighting with guys who were hitting me with baseball bats. It was a very small room and it was pretty crowded, so no one ever got a really good swing in.

"Because of the drugs, I went berserk. I fought them right across the room, and into the kitchen. I knew there was a big knife on the counter. I slashed one of them straight across his arm. I stabbed another one through the cheek. Once I had the knife, they all started to scatter in different directions because no one wanted to get stuck.

"When the police got there I was in the street, blind from the ammonia, covered in blood from rolling around on the broken glass, red welts all over my arms and back from getting baseball-batted. And I was the one that got arrested!

"The police were after me for thirteen charges of burglary and robbery. They didn't know I was living with Elizabeth, so they didn't know I was there. They took me to hospital, got me fixed up, and then took me to prison on remand.

"Elizabeth thought I was going to jail forever, so she started divorce proceedings. She was the one who was unfaithful though. I had helped a family friend get a business going – I'd given him $7,500. To thank me, he jumped in bed with my wife."

Sean was sent to Dartmoor prison. Because he had been a juvenile for most of his previous arrests, he had done his time in detention centers and minimum security prisons. Now, he was with the "big boys." He was led out of the prison van handcuffed and manacled. The welcoming officer showed him the sign above the gate, and translated the Italian: *"Abandon hope all ye who enter here."* [2] The officer got in his face: "You're in our house now."

"I've been in a lot of big houses, mate."

"Ya, but here, we don't care."

"That's good mate, 'cause neither do I."

He was in Dartmoor from 27 November 1991 until 27 March 1998. He would have been out earlier, but for the additional eighteen months he received for assaulting a prison officer.

"It was in the Servery. I had just gotten my food, when an officer reached his hand through the bars and yanked my ponytail, banging my head against the bars. 'What have I told you about pushing in, Daviesy?'

"I turned and stared at him, bending my metal tray back and forth until it split. He looked at me like, 'You wouldn't dare,' and I just looked back, 'Don't tempt me.'

"I flung hot stew on him, and he bent over, screaming. I yanked the tray up and the split edge of the tray cut off the end of his nose. Eighteen more months."

Because of Sean's "self-destruct" attitude, he was considered a subversive prisoner, and was upgraded to Category A.

Twenty-three hours of every day, he was locked in a six-by-eight-foot cell. He was let out for one hour of exercise in the morning. There was no toilet in his cell; only a slop bucket that was dumped three times a day. In addition there was a bed, a desk and chair – and it wasn't long before he lost the table. The prison got fed up continually having to replace what Sean kept smashing up. Once destroyed, he would take a leg, wrap strips of bed sheet around the end, and use it as a torch that he'd stick out the window of his cell. It served as a marker for inmates using mirrors to look out their windows, searching through Dartmoor's fog for his signal. Once located, drug caches fixed to the end of bed-sheet ropes were swung skillfully, window to window. From the outside, his brother kept him well supplied with cannabis and heroin. On special occasions like Christmas or his birthday, he'd get crack cocaine. His brother would get prostitute-addicts to bring it in on visits.

"When I got out in March, the first thing I tried to do was get a gun. I phoned Donald, Bill and Steve, and told them to meet me at the train station. I wanted to kill the guys that smashed me up, and then I wanted to kill Elizabeth's boyfriend, and then just go to jail again. I didn't care, 'cause I didn't have nothing left in life. All the lust for robberies and money was gone. I just wanted to stay stoned.

"Instead of gettin' me a gun, you know what they did? They brought my mom. She had only one thing to say: 'Sean, you've *got* to change.' It stuck in my mind."

"I was only out two days when I went to a secular rehabilitation center. I was there for about eight weeks. A judge had ordered it. I ended up chasing a lot of Scottish lads around the house with a carving knife because they were having a go at me. The rehab threw me out. For the next six weeks, it was heroin and burglaries.

"One afternoon, I was blasted, and really off me 'ead. I was talking to this guy, and all at once I started crying. 'I can't take any more.' I had a needle in my arm. 'I can't take no more. I've had enough. This is it, man. It's getting to me.'

"My mate looked across the road, and said, 'Let's go in here.' It was a church.

"He took me to the office, and the secretary rang the pastor. His name is Andrew Lancaster. We talked a little, and then he prayed for me.

"He showed me a flyer and asked, 'Do you fancy trying this place?' It was about Betel.

"I said I'd give it a go. He phoned, and I spoke to Jenny. I remember speaking to her, because I was off my head before Andrew prayed for me, but after, it was like I knew everything that was going on around me. She told me to come in the next day.

"I spent the night with my pals, the three lads that I used to hang around with. I told them that I was going to this Christian rehab in Birmingham. 'I want to try and sort myself out, 'cause at this rate I'm gonna be dead by the end of the year.' I didn't want to die. They said, 'You ain't gonna last two weeks.'

"I wanted to give it a try, so I arranged a time to meet Andrew Lancaster again. He purchased a ticket and he put me on the coach for Birmingham. I was in the toilets the whole trip, shooting up. Jason and a few others fetched me at the train station. I can't remember much, but Veronika said I just sat there with my head in my hands, looking really gone, not at all well. They helped me into their car, and the first thing out of someone's mouth was, 'Sean, Jesus loves ya.'

"The first thing I thought straight away was, 'As soon as I get out of this car, I'm gonna do you in.' I think Jason knew what I was thinking because he saw the startled look on my face. He just smiled at me.

"I remember the evening I arrived at Betel, 18 September 1998. I remember walking through the front doors, and – just talking about it, I can feel it now – you know when you walk in somewhere, you can sense something? Even though I was high, I sensed it as soon as I walked through the doors. I *knew* there was something there. Something that I wanted. You know when you know that there's something there, and you know that you want it, but you don't know what it is? That's what I knew.

"I remember how nice people were to me. Even in the state I was in. Everybody was happy. Nobody was growling at each other. You could feel the love – you could see it in their eyes. I wanted it. I didn't know if I'd get it, but I wanted it. I knew there was something there, because I knew these guys were just like I was. So if they've got it, why couldn't I have it?

"As that first night wore on, and the drugs wore off, things got a bit blurred. Sitting at table next morning, I must have looked a right state. My legs were shaking; my 'turkey' was just comin' on. Eduardo and Antonio came over, and told me that it would get better if I only just stuck it out. My legs were bouncing so much that the table was shaking. They each took hold of a leg while I tried to eat something.

"My 'turkey' *really* set in, and once I'd gone through that first night, awake, I knew it was going to be the first night of *many*; of sitting up, watching the sun come up, and watching the sun go down; sun come up, sun go down.

"But for some reason, I know now – it was God – it couldn't have been anything else – I knew that if I left Betel I *was* going to die. I mean I was virtually dead anyway. I didn't want to die. I didn't.

"Monday came. I spent a lot of time on the sofa with a quilt pulled up around me, and everybody showed me so much love. These guys had just been through the same thing I was going through. I remember carrying on with them, and the more I carried on with them, the more love they showed me. I remember screaming and shouting at people, *really* screaming and shouting. They just smiled at me and asked if I wanted a cup of tea.

"Darlene, and Elaine, and Joye prayed for me. They didn't say, 'It's too late.' They were so kind to me.

"Jenny came in. She was the one who had spoken to me on the phone, so she knew all about me. She didn't care. It didn't matter. It didn't matter where I'd come from, or what I'd left behind. It was what was in front of me.

"This was the first time that I've walked into a place and people have loved me for who I *am*. Not for what I can give them, not for what I've got, but just for me. It was, 'Let's gather round Sean. He needs our help.' I'd never experienced that kind of love before. It was alien to me. I liked it; and I wanted more of it."

❧

"My 'turkey' was the hardest two weeks of my life. I had done a *lot* of heroin just before coming to Betel so it didn't surprise me. I was awake for two solid weeks, with not a minute of sleep. I was in pain all the time. Part of me wanted to run away, but it was like my feet were glued to the floor. All the time I was thinking to myself, 'Sean, you could cure this in an hour and a hit of heroin.' But there was another thought: 'Sean, if you're gonna leave, you're gonna die.' I just held on to that thought, 'If you're gonna leave, you're gonna die.'

"After a few days I was put to work with Jason, helping him landscape. He says he killed my 'turkey' with flagstones! I was totally exhausted, but still couldn't sleep. My eyes felt like baseballs and my head was pounding because I'd been awake for so long.

"I had come to the end of myself, and I no longer wanted to be the Sean that I had been for so many years. I never wanted to be that way again. I wanted to live. I wanted to start enjoying myself. I wanted to feel a happiness inside, to be content with my life. I was willing to open myself up to hope to get that happiness.

"That's what I did – I opened my heart up to Jesus.

"I was sitting in my bed, and at 3 o'clock in the morning I picked up the Bible that had been given to me. I thought to myself, 'Right then, if they are all getting something out of this book, then why can't I? There's got to be something here.'

"I went down to the living-room in the early hours of the morning, on my own. I started reading the Psalms and I fell asleep. That was the thing that said to me, 'God is real.' Because He answered my prayers – He gave me rest.

"Jesus said, *'Come to me, all who are weary and whose load is heavy; I will give you rest.'*[3] And He did, man. I cried out to Him, and I slept. Downstairs, in the middle of the living-room floor, with a Bible in my hands.

"Those first days were so hard, but the guys at Betel loved me through it, even though I was nasty to every one of them. I carried on with them, screaming and shouting and threatening 'em. Wow, I remember the anger that used to well up within me. But the more I'd growl and threaten and carry on, the more love they'd show me.

"It was amazing, because I'd try turning the table on them.

I'd switch on these guys, and try to show them love, to disorient them and catch them off guard. But it didn't work that way. When I'd start showing these guys love, they were over the moon."

On 13 November 1998, Sean was ordered back to Leeds to appear in court. He had previously been charged with theft; what complicated matters was that when he was arrested, he had smashed up the furniture in the interview room at the police station. On the day of his arrest his solicitor told him that because of his past record, there would be no leniency. He would probably go back to prison until the year 2000.

When he met with his solicitor a month before his trial Sean had been at Betel for only eight weeks. She said, "Wow, look at you! The last time I saw you, you were a wreck. What's happened to you?" He told her about Betel.

In court, Sean was not particularly encouraged. Neither was the magistrate. It wasn't their first meeting. By this time, Sean had a prior record of thirty-eight charges. Many were for armed robbery; twenty-five were burglary charges. As Sean put it, "The magistrate was sick of my face."

Sean's solicitor told of all the changes that had occurred since his arrival at Betel. She then turned to Victor, one of the Betel missionaries, and asked him to speak on Sean's behalf. When Victor had finished, the magistrate's face was totally different. He didn't have that 'I'll-get-you' look any more. The scowl had turned to a smile.

"Sean, you are thirty-one years of age, and it is time that we stop sending you to jail. You have come to a point in your life where you can choose one of two roads to travel. The first road you know all too well. It leads to destruction. The other road is the one that you have just recently begun travelling. You can keep on that road, and become somebody.

"Sean, I am going to give you a chance. I am going to give you a conditional discharge, and set you free to go back to Betel. You can walk away from Betel if you want, but I hope that you will stay and make something of yourself."

"I couldn't believe what I was hearing. Neither could my solicitor. I left the courtroom feeling that I had been given a chance by God. It felt like the Holy Spirit climbed into that magistrate and spoke through him. I felt that all of my past life had been cut away from me, and that my new life lay ahead."

"Through the fourteen months I've been at Betel, I've persevered. I've tried my hardest, but I know I can't do any of it without Jesus. This is just how it is. I need Jesus. That's the top and bottom of it. God is the Father of my life, and Jesus has given me true happiness, true meaning in life. I'm happy and content with nothing, as long as I have Jesus. He's done what nothing and no one else could do. He's given me a meaning and a purpose in life in so many ways.

"When I left school at eleven, I really couldn't read or write. In the last year of prison I tried taking a few classes but didn't take it seriously. At Betel I went through a Bible course and worked hard at it. At the end there were two exams. I'd never written an exam, and it rattled me. It was really hard to study. It was like the information just didn't stick in my brain. I prayed that I'd get at least one right answer on each of them. I didn't want to face a zero.

"When I got the exam I just stared at it for ten minutes – nothing made sense. One of the leadership team, Mary Alice, came over and said I'd do okay once I started. When the marks came back I got 75 out of 100 on both exams. Everyone else did better than me, but I didn't care. I was so excited and thankful I went up to my room and cried.

"Being able to read is no small thing. But Jesus is doing a bigger work in me still. He's using people here at Betel to break me, and build me, and stretch me.

"Last Christmas for instance, I got put on discipline. I had to wash dishes indefinitely. I had been very negative, and my anger was ripping right out of me. There were a couple of guys on clean-up with me, but they left Betel after a week. They got fed up. I just got on with it and never complained. I'd walk into the kitchen after every meal and just get on with it.

"I must have shown a bit of responsibility there by going in and just doing it whenever I was supposed to. No one ever had to go find me.

"When I came off it about three weeks later, I was asked to be one of the 'responsibles' in the house. I thought it was strange, just coming off discipline, and suddenly making decisions about the other men. But something had changed in me, standing over the sink. Something of my anger got healed.

"I handle situations a lot better now. Now when I get angry, I get angry with me, instead of at somebody else. And I've learned to cry.

"I keep praying for perseverance, because it's hard. Times do get hard. I found out that I've got epilepsy. I've had seizures that have landed me in hospital. I've developed some skin disorders as well. It's some of the rubbish I have to go through. But I'm learning to cope. I'm learning to hand it over to Jesus. I'm learning to give it over to the Lord, and find peace in my afflictions. Find peace in knowing and believing in faith that God *will* heal me; that God is there for me. God will help me, and will never let me down. Jesus is always there, and sometimes I doubt – we all doubt, but I'm learnin'.

"That's what I've learnt since I've been here – that's what I'm still learning while I'm here. It's all through the love that's been shown to me since I've been here. Now I give that same love freely to the new guys that come to Betel. That's what I want to do.

"I don't feel ashamed about telling anybody about who set me free. I know where I've come from and I know what God's brought me out of. And I never want to go back to that way. I never want to be back in the drugs again. Noooooooooo. I've never been as happy in my whole life. Sometimes I might not seem happy, but on those days, you know, I was a lot worse out there. It's hard to explain; it's like I've got a big sun inside me, glowing.

"Where else could I find this freedom in life? I didn't find it anywhere else. Only in Jesus. That's what Betel has done for me. It's given me that kind of freedom.

"I go about my jobs with a smile. I mean, I can moan and groan like everybody else. Just lately I've been through a bad patch, and I've been very angry and very arrogant, and not a lot of people have wanted to talk to me. But that's because I've been trying to take the steering wheel by myself. I'm slowly learning to give it over to God bit by bit. God tells me that I'm getting there. In my quiet times He says, 'That's it Sean, just a little bit more, a little bit more.' And I'm giving Him a little bit more, and I'm getting there.

"I really thank God for what He's done for me since I've been here – I really can't explain it all – all that He's done. The way He's quelling my anger, the way He's sorting out my emotions, the way He's torn down the walls that I was hiding behind. Only God could do these things. A lot of other people have tried doing these things for me and it's never worked. Believe me, it's *never* worked. But with God, nothing is impossible.

"He restored my family to me, my mum and dad, even though there's lots of problems between us to be sorted. Only God could restore that relationship. And my relationship with my son; only God could restore that.

"At first, it was like I was praying and getting nowhere. One day someone said to me, 'Sean, you got to give it over to Him, and forget about it. Stop trying to do things off your own back.' I did my best to give the whole thing over. About a week later, my mum phoned up. It took a bit longer with my son. Six months later, I got a phone call from my eight-year-old son, Brendan. He said, 'Hi, Dad. Are you still my dad?' "

"Since I've been here, my three best friends have died. My mum phoned on 1 January 1999, and said she had bad news. Donald, Bill and Steve were killed in a head-on car crash early New Year's morning – they were all stoned. She said, 'Sean, if you weren't at Betel, you'd be dead.'

"She was right – I did everything with my mates. I would have been with them in that car. I'd be dead. But no. God had other plans. He took me out of that situation, and placed me in Betel. God is so good.

"All I can say is 'I am here.' I am here, and I have no plans to go anywhere else. I am staying here. I believe that God has a *big* plan for me, and I'm going to stick around to find out what it is. He lets me have little sneak previews, which is fine, but I want to see the full picture. I want to see what God's got for me.

"Plus, God's told me, 'Stay put,' so I'm staying put. I couldn't think of a better place to be than here. God's presence is all over this place; it's drippin' in this place. I love this place, man. From my heart I love this place.

"This is my house – Betel is God's house, but it's my house.

"I was in prison a total of eleven and a half years. I've been living at Betel for fourteen months. It's amazing what God's done in my life since I've been here. I thank Him, and I love Him, and I'm staying."

All of that from a man who maintained, "If I can get in *one* good punch, it's worth a beatin'."

Notes

1. Names have been changed throughout this story.
2. *LASCIATE OGNI SPERANZA, VOI CH'ENTRATE.* Sean was never told of the inscription's origin. They are the words that are carved into the lintel over the gateway to hell, in Dante's *Divine Comedy*, Book I, *Inferno*, Cantos III, verse 10.
3. Matthew 11:28.

Chapter 5

Love Covers

"I was found by those who were not looking..."
(Romans 10:20; Isaiah 65:1)

One Saturday night, I joined six Betelitos on an evangelistic outreach mission. We traveled into the inner city of Birmingham to a local hostel where seventy men were in residence. Many of them were psychiatric patients who had been turned out on the street because of government cuts to health care. Most of the elderly at the hostel were alcoholics; the younger men were bottomed heroin addicts. It was all such a striking contrast to Betel.

Outside the hostel, broken wine bottles and rubbish lay in heaps around the door. Inside, the hallway floor and walls were thick with grimy filth. The reek of urine was overpowering as we passed the toilets. The stench of perpetual nicotine in the common room was suffocating. MTV was blaring away; the guys playing pool cursed continuously. What struck hardest was the depth of pathos on so many of the faces.

We chatted with a dozen of the men. One of them, Brian, asked pointedly: "Why do you bother to come to this dump?" Wayne, a Betelito, answered: "Because there's a better place, a better way to live." He then shared openly what his old life as an addict had been like, and all that Jesus had changed. Brian listened attentively for an hour. Wayne invited him to come to Betel. Brian laughed, shook his head, and staggered towards his dormitory room, his "dump."

Paul was drawn by what he heard the Betelitos share, and wanted to return to Betel with us. We left the common room, and went to collect his stuff.

He lived in a room with seven other men. When he opened the door, I thought I was going to be sick. The stench of urine and dirty laundry forced me to hold my breath. Paul's bed sheets were in a crumpled ball at the bottom of the vinyl-covered mattress. He opened his locker and, from the bottom of it, pulled out a small heap of dirty laundry. Two garbage bags' worth. His worldly possessions. That was it. He was vacated.

Paul is a "slasher." The clinical name is a "self-harmer." As we had talked earlier in the evening, I could see the healed scars all over his hands. He had pulled up his sleeves to show us his forearms, and I've never seen such a ghastly mess. Then he pulled up his pant legs to the knees. Laid over horrible gash scars were forty red, bloody razor cuts on each leg.

I could barely manage my tears.

On the drive back to Betel, the guys remarked how haunting it was to walk into the hostel, and hear the men's stories. For most of them, it was all too familiar. Two of them physically shuddered as they reflected on the evening. I asked why. Both answered the same way: "I'm so thankful Betel is my home."

Luke O'Conner is one who shares that gratitude.[1] His home is also Betel-Birmingham, but he was raised in the south-eastern United States. He loved being with his dad – when his father was sober. But the majority of his memories are not good ones, because dad was drunk much of the time. He was often physically and emotionally abusive, and typically unpredictable. There'd be times he'd laugh off seriously bad behavior but Luke has vivid memories of the other times. Once, he left his bicycle out on the lawn. His father's slaps were what woke him in the middle of the night.

Dad took "his little man" drinking at an early age – he'd pull a beer out of a six pack, and pass it to his five-year-old son. Luke's uncle told him that dad would regularly put beer in Luke's baby bottle. He certainly acquired the taste at an early age.

In his early teen years he started smoking marijuana, and experimented with any drug he could get his hands on. At university, it was predominantly LSD. On the job, it was cocaine and crack. He also drank very heavily. Life slid quickly downhill;

his marriage failed, as did multiple career attempts. His several rehab experiences were also unsuccessful.

For a time, Luke worked at his father's septic tank business. It was his job to precede the pumper trucks and locate a customer's septic tank, scrape off the dirt that covered the lid, and remove it. One day a chatty customer kept him at the door longer than Luke wanted to stay. When he finally got to the backyard, he found that the tank was already exposed, and the lid removed. On inspection, Luke saw something that shocked him. One of the family dogs had fallen in the tank. He was half drowned as he'd exhausted himself trying to claw his way out. Luke looked at the horrified owner.

"Aren't you going to get him out?"

"Uhh, uhh, I ain't getting him out. Not like that."

Luke reached down, and with his bare hands grabbed the dog by the fur. The mess squished between his fingers. He pulled the dog out, and laid him limp on the ground. The owner wanted to bury the dog before his son got home. He didn't want a scene. Luke couldn't believe what he was hearing – as they argued, the dog came round. They hosed him off, and Luke left.

The whole scene bothered him all day. It didn't matter how much he drank; he couldn't get the picture out of his mind. It bothered him all night. On waking the next morning, it was the first thing that popped into his head.

It was later that day that he realized – *he* was the dog in the septic tank. No one was there to help; everyone was saying, "Throw him away, he's no good, he's half dead anyway. Bury him." Luke knew a little bit about God from Sunday school; it felt like that day, God reached down into his mess and pulled him out, washed him off and cleaned him up.

But he kept drinking heavily. It was some time later that Luke understood a further piece of the picture – the dog couldn't get out of the septic tank because he didn't have any foundation under his feet. Luke knew there was no foundation to his life.

He was about to be evicted from his tiny one-bedroom efficiency apartment. His sole possessions were an air mattress and a clock radio. He'd sold everything else. He had stolen repeatedly from his family and his employers. Drugs had been beyond his means for some time; all that Luke had went towards the daily half gallon of liquor he was drinking. Physically he was a wreck after twelve years of drug and alcohol abuse. He wanted to die.

Luke's sister is a member of Myrtle Grove Presbyterian Church. It is also the Teppers' home church. One furlough, Elliott and Mary were visiting, and knowing something of Betel, Luke's sister told him that he should speak with Elliott. Luke was less than enthusiastic, but knowing that he was soon to be homeless, he consented. Three days later he was on a plane, heading for Betel-Birmingham. He knew he needed to get an ocean away from old influences.

"Those first weeks were hard. I was detoxing, but more than that, I went through an intense period of loneliness. I was in a foreign country, surrounded by people who couldn't speak like I do, talking about things that I didn't understand.

"I reached a point where I cried out to God in absolute desperation. It was all up to Him. There was nowhere else for me to go, nothing else for me to do. I have absolutely nothing, except what's here at Betel. The Spirit that God's placed here, His Spirit, He's the freedom that's here; He's the reality here, and it's really clear that you're not going to work your way into it, because it's all a gift.

"From the very beginning, that's clear. It's just reliance on God. You can see that in the leadership, and you can see it in the guys that have been here a while. I see it in Mary Alice,[2] when her eyes all fill with tears. You can just see the love there. I know now where it comes from. It's not something that they strain and struggle to do, and it's not because they're getting paid to do it. They're responding to the commission that they've been given. They're responding to God's presence here."

The following stories are but a few samples from the thousands of testimonies at Betel. While the details are unique to every person, two dynamics recur repeatedly. Like Luke, they tell of a stirring, a revelation, a desire, a heart's cry for something more. For many of them, it's a cry for something more than they experienced in drug rehabs and hostels.

Darrin was brought up on an estate in the slums of Blackpool. "My step-father beat me more or less every day. There were times when I got kept in bed for over a week, without being fed. It was bad. He'd bang me 'ead off sinks, things like that. I remember being at the police station when I was just a kid, showing 'em all the scars on me 'ead and all that from all the beatin's.

"I left the estate when I was fifteen. I started using drugs when I was eleven years old. Solvents, cannabis, drink, speed, LSD, anything, you know, anything I could get me hands on really."

Darrin was arrested repeatedly for shoplifting and robbery, for gang violence and football hooliganism. His friends were drug dealers and suppliers.

Tragedy occurred when his youngest brother fell out of a window, and died in Darrin's arms when he had been baby-sitting. A dealer-friend suggested that heroin would take away his anguish. "It gave me the escape that I needed from the reality around me. Too much hurt – my mum was calling me a murderer.

"He just came into my room and offered it to me. He asked me for my arm, and loaded me up. That was the first time. He knew that I'd be back to buy more.

"It took away the hurt and pain that I was feeling. Without the heroin, I don't think I'd be here today; I think I would have taken my life. The heroin took the pain away, but the first day I tried to go without it, I just didn't feel right. So, I thought, I'll just buy some more.

"After about six months, well I started putting more into each hit. It wasn't long before I was hitting about three or four times a day, and they were big amounts. I finished up injecting a sixteenth of heroin a day, a gram's worth.

"One of my friends had AIDS. He's dead now. I didn't know he was infected when I first started knocking around with him, not until a couple of months after. We were shooting up together. There were used needles lying about all over. Lots of times, I used his. When the heroin arrived, if you didn't have a needle, then you would miss out. It all got put in the same spoon. We'd all be there, drawing up at the same time, passing the needles around. AIDS didn't scare me; I was on self-destruct. Nothing bothered me at all. I was addicted. I would try not taking the drugs, but then I'd end up getting violently ill. I'd get chills, I wouldn't be able to eat, or walk, or even think. The easy way was to just keep shooting up."

In 1994, Darrin accidentally overdosed on heroin.

"When I came around in the hospital, the nurses asked me who my next of kin was. I told them, and they went to phone my mom. She said that she was sick of it and that she didn't want to know. That was after they had told her that I was DOA – 'dead on arrival.' It really got to me, that she didn't care. It was then that I knew that I had to come off the drugs.

"But I couldn't. Even though I wanted to, I couldn't. I'd have a needle in my arm, and I'd stare at it. 'I really don't want to do this.' And the plunger would go down. I'd been injecting for six years. It was an everyday thing."

"I'd been in rehabs several times while in prison. I was in a rehab in Fife, Scotland, taking morphine sulphate tablets (MST). It's a painkiller. All they would give me was one week's detoxification, one week's worth! I'd been doing drugs for eleven years!"

Darrin went back to the streets – more drugs, more crime, and back to prison.

"The day after I got released from jail, I went into a rehab called Inward House. I was there three months and they said that I had a street attitude, a jail attitude, and there was no chance for me. I left.

"I started to smoke weed again, but for the most part I was straight. I started work, and at the end of the season I got a bonus. I took it and scored heroin. It felt a little strange, putting a needle in my arm again.

"I realized that I had a big problem, so I went to the doctor's and got put on a methadone prescription. I ended up on long-term methadone – every single day for four years. I ended up on 300 mg a day; there's lads in here that don't believe that, but you build up a tolerance, just like with heroin."

"I got a sentence last year, for police assault. My probation officer told me about Betel. I rang up and spoke to Darlene on the phone.

"I was told that Betel is a Christian place for people with addictions. When she told me about the no-smoking policy, I didn't like that. I didn't mind having to be drug free; that's why I wanted to come, but I didn't like the no-smoking bit.

"I was out on the streets for a couple of days before I came to Betel. I actually had to do a graft [shoplifting 'to order'] to get my train fare.

"When I got to Betel, I was still wrecked from so much methadone. While I was in jail, I had to walk around with my name and my number on me, and when I was asked my name, I'd just pull the card out of my pocket, 'cause I couldn't speak. My brain wasn't functioning. At Betel, I had just started to get my head around. I still couldn't come out with any conversation. If someone said something to me, and left me for about five minutes, yeh, I might be able to think about what I was going to say, and then come out with it.

"I knew from going to other rehabs that the first couple of weeks at Betel would be a drag. It's like when you go to a new jail: there's no getting out of them. You just have to get your head around.

"I've started to get used to the routine; I like the worship in the mornings. The singing really lifts me. I've been here two weeks now. I'm still detoxing. I'm feeling it now; it's still coming out of my bones. But it's different here. It's not like doing 'turkey' in prison or in a rehab, all juiced up on pharmaceuticals.

"Here at Betel, you give up more than you do anywhere else – especially the cigarettes. But the worship and the meetings, they make up for the things that you've given up. It's like you're getting a drug anyway. Everyday I wake up here, I feel the security and the safety of this place."

Darrin updated his story five months later.

"Early in January, I was out with some of the guys going door to door with the Betel calendars. The police stopped us and radioed in to the station to see if there were any warrants out on us. There were some for me, which totally surprised me.

"I had come to Betel straight from jail, and when you're released, the prison is supposed to hold you under 'gate arrest' if there are outstanding warrants. They should have kept me, but there must have been a glitch in the system. When they released me, I thought everything had been taken care of. I left thinking that I had a clean slate.

"The police arrested me and took me to the Small Heath Station. When the Blackpool Police arrived to pick me up, one of them happened to be the drug officer who knew me very well – he knew the details of my past, and just exactly what I was like. He said that I looked different, so I told him and the other officer what the Lord was doing in my life. We talked the whole two hours to Blackpool.

"On arrival, I was taken to lock-up. This was the first time I had ever been in jail drug-free. Some of the prison officers wondered what had happened to me. They could see the difference in me because my photograph was still up on the wall for outstanding warrants!

"They happened to put me in a cell with a lad that I knew from the streets. He told me that he had brought some heroin into the jail, and that if I wanted some, we could do the deal when we were let out into the exercise yard. I told my friend that I had Jesus in my life, and that I didn't need or want heroin any more.

"I asked the officers for a Bible. I turned to Luke 1:37 where it says that all things are possible with God. That verse carried me through. When I sat waiting to go up to court that morning, my thoughts went back to that scripture. I had been told there was no way I would get bail – that I was looking at eighteen months in prison, because there were six outstanding charges.

"I got released to Betel on bail until the court date. The day of the trial, the magistrate read a report that Mary Alice had written about my life at Betel, and then looked at some other reports that had been written about all that's changed. Just before he pronounced sentence, a probation officer came up to me and asked, 'What's this monastery that you're in? I've never dealt with anything like this before.' We talked for a while, and he asked for some Betel literature to give to the drug addicts he works with.

"It was sentence time. The magistrate looked at me and said, 'Darrin, you have an appalling criminal record and we have previously had no option but to send you to jail. Prison hasn't made much of an impression on you, but this place Betel is truly changing you. I'm keeping you there. We were going to send you to jail this afternoon, but we release you to Betel on a twelve-month probation order.'"

As he told me all that had changed for him, a huge grin crossed Darrin's face. "I'm so thankful to be here at Betel. There were only three ways my life was going to go – I was going to die of an overdose, get killed on the streets, or do the rest of my life in prison. There are still guys out on the streets looking to kill me.

"Here, at Betel, there are guys looking to save my life."

Many at Betel have had to make literal life or death choices. The starkness of the decision is softened by the care the newly arrived receive. Over and over again, there is one reason they stay at Betel – the love keeps them.

Juana Garcia Mellinas became a heroin addict at thirteen. She had her first child at sixteen, shortly after she got married. With her husband, she robbed banks, jewelry shops – wherever there was money. At nineteen she was sent to prison.

Juana got out before her husband did, but her family had turned their backs on her, and for six months she survived on the streets. She was arrested repeatedly, and was ultimately sentenced to another six years.

As part of her parole, she was allowed to go to Betel on conditional release. She arrived in Malaga, Spain, in August 1997, and lived and worked with the community during the day, and was returned to prison at night. In November 1999, she was allowed full-time residence, and her complete sentence was served on 4 February 2000.

Juana had been given a Betel flyer while on the streets in Madrid. It read, "When you're too sick to steal, come to us, and we'll look after you." She was pregnant with her second child when she entered Betel, and was suffering badly with morning sickness. She was detoxing and craving the cigarettes she had to give up.

"My shadows [the women who took turns staying with her twenty-four hours a day] showed me so much love. They convinced me that they didn't want me to leave. Nobody's ever wanted me around like that."

Though she wanted to run, she felt she kept hearing a little voice within saying, "Look, you have to endure."

She told her house leader what a hard a time she was having. They cried together, and the leader told Juana, "You have to trust God – He's the only one who can help." She started to read the Bible she'd been given and, over the next few months, slowly began to feel that the deadness in her heart was changing.

"The thing that really convinced me of God's love was that when my baby was born, she was HIV-positive. Everybody expected her to be dead in two years. I said to God, 'If You are real, heal my girl.' Every day thereafter, I felt a greater peace. Every day, I was able to leave Rebecca to the Lord's care a bit more."

As she trusted the Lord with her daughter's future, she watched the child's happiness and strength grow. A year later, Rebecca was tested, and no trace of the virus was found. Not only was the doctor surprised that the HIV had remitted; he was astounded that Rebecca no longer had hepatitis.

Juana plans to stay in Betel, and raise Rebecca in the stability of a nurturing and honoring home.

Some of the family histories *prior* to life at Betel are absolutely horrific. Despite the frightening abuses, the need to belong runs deep. Very few addicts purposefully set out to destroy their lives. The old rock and roll song named the dynamic succinctly – they're just "lookin' for love in all the wrong places."

Callum's story marks just how wrong it can get.

His mom and dad fought a lot. When they split up he took it very hard, and went off and did his own thing. When they got divorced, he blamed himself.

By the time he was thirteen years old, he was drunk most weekends. By fourteen he was using marijuana. He liked the high it gave him. That went on for a year or so; he was lifted repeatedly by the police for under-age drinking, and causing disturbances.

His father wanted him to go to university, but he thought to himself, "What would annoy Dad most? What's the most disappointing job I can find?" So, he went off to trade school to become a brick mason. There, he and the other guys in his class experimented with the drugs that were making the rounds. He also became involved in the occult. It started as a joke, playing around with ouija boards and tarot cards. However, it became more than "harmless fun," and he became really interested in it. He bought books on witchcraft and demonology and began a serious course of study.

His girlfriend, Lynn, fell pregnant at sixteen, and Callum started drinking very heavily. He dropped out of trade school and got work as an apprentice bricklayer. Soon he was making $600 a week, and most of that was spent on amphetamines to keep him going while he was working. He'd stay cranked for four weeks at a time.

Then it was two weeks of hell on earth as he tried to get some sleep. He showed signs of psychosis and paranoia. More drink, more speed; LSD was now regularly in the mix.

"Six months after my son Callum was born, I lost my job. I couldn't be counted on. I became very depressed and was stoned all the time. But so much speed was wrecking me. Lynn wasn't happy with me because of my mood swings. We had been living together, but she told me she was moving house, and that I wasn't going with her.

"I got a flat in one of the roughest neighborhoods in all of Scotland. I had never seen a place like it in my life. I had no trouble fitting in – it was my kind of place. I had grown up watching violent videos, and being a big Glasgow Rangers supporter, I was at the front of the football brawls. Politics opened up more violence, and I began going to Orange Order meetings. In western Scotland, there is a very close association with Northern Ireland. Before long I was raising money for the UVF (Ulster Volunteer Force). I don't want to say how.

"Though I wasn't living with Lynn, she fell pregnant again. When she gave birth to Iain, she told me that he might not be my child. I was a mess.

"I started going to séances – I was hoping to make contact with my dead grandfather. He had been more like a father to me as a child, and I felt like I needed his help. That opened the door, and it ultimately led to my involvement in a blood ritual.

"I was really fascinated with the supernatural, and so I was welcoming demons into my flat, and giving them authority over areas of my life. I wanted their power so I could manipulate people and get things I wanted. I'd get out the encyclopaedia on demonology and witchcraft, and I'd leave it on my bedside table opened up. In the morning it would be opened up to a different page, the one I was supposed to read for that day. These 'dark devotions' went on for a long time."

"My mom started doing a Teen Challenge drug bus ministry in Paisley. One night I went down to visit her, and was talking to one of the guys on the bus. He asked me, 'What do you believe?' I told him that I believed in the supernatural, and that I believed there's a God, but not the same one that he worshipped. I told him about some of my séance experiences, and how I talked regularly to my dead grandfather. He basically dared me to 'test the spirits.' I had a Bible tucked away in a closet, and he told me to read 1 John 4:1 and see what happened.

"I went home, did my usual meditation, and then I read those verses. The spirits appeared – I had some incense burning, and I could see them moving through it. I decided to test them. I asked them about Jesus Christ; if Jesus Christ was the Lord and Savior. They went crazy. I have never seen anything go as crazy as that in all my life. They sent things sailing through the air, and were shrieking, 'How dare you bring that name in here after all we've done for you?'

"I wasn't stoned that night. I think that's what made it all the more real. It really scared me – I got really drunk, and blacked out. When I regained consciousness, I was in my back garden, dressed only in my boxer shorts and one sock. It was 3 o'clock in the morning, in January, and it was freezing cold. The door was locked from the inside with the key in it, and there was nobody in my house. I still don't know how it happened.

"I woke my neighbor up, and she took me in."

"I was dealing speed, LSD, and cocaine, mostly to pay for my own habit. Having been a brick mason, I was also on the 'brew,' the government dole, so there was good money.

"But cocaine and LSD do not mix at all well, and I thought I would go nuts. When you're on cocaine, it's an intense high, and when it peaks, you feel so full of energy, like you're going to explode. It's like you're super-alive. It felt like I could do anything I put my mind to. LSD was different. I took LSD because I enjoyed the hallucinations. I took it and tried to go in as deep as I could go with it. I wanted more of the supernatural.

"I wanted both experiences, so I'd take LSD with cocaine, and it always left me feeling that if it didn't kill me, I'd have to be put in a mental institution. The coke so amplified the LSD that it caused me to have really bad trips. I started seeing things I didn't want to see and I started hearing things no one should hear. I felt myself slipping into madness.

"One night I was at my friend's house, stoned, and I lost it completely. I smashed the place up. I took off, and ran all the way to my flat, where I tried to hide in a corner. It was the wrong place to run to. Because of the welcome I had given the demons, they called it *their* house. That night, the devil himself appeared. A beam of light hit my bedroom window; it bent, and then shattered.

"He started talking to me. He said, 'You're mine; you'll never be free.' His face was so beautiful. It's hard to explain, but it was like the most handsome face in the world, until he turned and looked at me again. Then I saw the other side of his face. It was distorted, and I've never seen such evil and ugly bitterness. When he said, 'You'll never be free,' I knew what he meant. I knew that I would never be free of drug addiction, and that I'd always be his."

"After that night, I stopped taking LSD. I was still drunk most of the time; I'd do a little cocaine and some speed, just to keep myself alert. A few days later I was watching Callum and Iain, and I was going through withdrawals. Lynn was out Christmas shopping, and she said that she would be gone a couple of hours. I was dying for something to drink. Iain wasn't well; he wouldn't stop crying. Lynn was away for more than a few hours, from 11 o'clock until 8 o'clock, and I was really strung out. Iain wouldn't feed; he wouldn't take his bottle.

"I got very frustrated. I picked him up and shook him. I wasn't violent, and it wasn't for very long, but it was enough to cause his brain to haemorrhage. It left him severely disabled.

"I got him to the hospital, and the doctors called the police in. They interviewed me for about three hours. I denied everything. But I was going crazy, so the doctors put me on Valium, to calm my nerves. I was allowed to go, pending further inquiries.

"A few weeks later I was at the pub with a couple of my friends. We were drinking and watching football, having a good time – until I got a phone call from my neighbor saying the police had just left my house. I thought they had come up to arrest me for hurting Iain. (It was for another offence, a breach of peace that I had committed.) In my panic, I went back to the flat, took my full bottle of Valium, some paracetamol, and three months worth of co-proximal, crushed the lot into powder, and drank it down with a bottle of whiskey.

"Soon everything went black.

"My neighbor found me about forty hours later, and she took me to the hospital. I was drifting in and out of consciousness, and I was asked if I would let the doctors intervene. They wanted to inject me with a drug to combat the paracetamol poisoning. I refused. I told them that I just wanted to die. They told me that liver and kidney failure is one of the most agonizing deaths possible. I still refused.

"I think this was the point when the Lord intervened, because I wasn't feeling like vomiting at all. It was as if He reached inside of me and pushed everything that was in my system out. I was violently sick for five minutes.

"The nurses phoned my mom, even though I told them not to. She came and visited me. I was very nasty to her, and she left the hospital crying. She came back the next day and left me the phone number for Teen Challenge. I looked at it, and figured I had nothing to lose.

"I phoned up, and a guy called Fin came to see me. He spoke to me about the Lord and asked, 'Do you want to change your life?' We talked about Teen Challenge, and I told him I wanted to go there. He said, 'Right. There's a six-month waiting list.' I said, 'I'll be dead in six months.'

"He gave me the number of Victory Outreach in Wales. I phoned them, and they refused me, because of my pending court case. They gave me Betel's number. I gave them a go, and I spoke to Jenny. It was a Friday; she told me to come in on Monday.

"I left Glasgow, headed for Birmingham, and really started on a journey in life."

"I arrived at Betel in January of 1998, and as soon as I got in the door, I wanted to leave. I couldn't handle it; the place was too immense. Obviously, the spirits didn't want me to stay. But, I believe the Lord put His hand on me, and it was His strength that kept me from running. Two days later, at the Wednesday night meeting, Kent preached, and came up to me after the meeting and asked, 'How are you doing?' I blurted out, 'I've got demons inside me, and they're not happy.'

"He said, 'Right, we'll pray for you.' "He went and got a couple of guys, and as soon as he left, I ran from the Chapel to the front door. But something drew me back. I walked back and sat down, and the guys asked me if I was OK.

"Then, they started praying. Eduardo, the Spaniard, was very loud and boisterous, shouting in Spanish, and praying in tongues. I remember thinking, 'These people think that *I'm* crazy!...'

"I felt freer after that, but two weeks later, some other things had risen up. The leadership prayed for me again, and during that deliverance session, I saw a vivid vision of a demon burning in a lake of fire. He was trying to grab bits of paper that were covered with curses. These were the records of the curses that had been spoken over my life, over my sons' lives, and over my brothers' and my father's life.

"Kent could tell that I was seeing something. As I was telling him about the vision, Eduardo was telling Kent the same thing in Spanish. (Kent is bilingual.) As I was describing it, he was describing it in Spanish. At the time, Eduardo's English wasn't very good, and with my thick Scottish accent, there was no way he could have described it the exact same way I was describing it.

"As they continued to pray, the demon sunk under the lake of fire, and the bits of curse-papers burst into flames.

"They prayed with me as I rebuked the devil, and asked Jesus into my life as my Lord and Savior. That night I smiled for the first time in a long time. I'd obviously smiled before, but it had always been a smirking smile, laughing at somebody's misfortune. This time, it was pure joy and happiness. At the next meeting, I was able to lift my hands and worship the Lord."

"Through the first year at Betel, it felt like I was under attack constantly. The devil just never let up on me at all. He said that I would go to prison for what I had done to my son. That thought terrified me. I told Mary Alice, Kent, Eduardo and Jenny all of the details, the whole truth, and the weight just lifted off my shoulders.

"A couple of days later, my head was messed up from telling the leaders my story. 'What are they going to think of me?' I thought they would condemn me and look down on me. More accusations. I left Betel.

"I disappeared into Glasgow, and stayed drunk for a week. But I knew that I had to come back. Betel had become my family. I had friends that knew me, and loved me. I knew I didn't have to put on a show or wear a mask for them. That meant so much to me. It's what I've wanted my whole life.

"I came back to Betel, knowing that it was the best possible place to get my life sorted. Kent and Mary Alice assured me that God had forgiven me; their acceptance overwhelmed me. After I'd met with them, two of the lads, Jason and Matthew, came up and wrapped their arms around me and told me they wanted me at Betel. But it was very, very hard for me to accept forgiveness from anybody, even God, because I couldn't forgive myself. I thought I deserved punishment – even if it was just what I was putting myself through, re-living that night, over and over again.

"I thought that I deserved it – I did deserve it – but now I know that Jesus has cleansed me of all my sins. I've got a clear revelation of God's forgiveness, and that set me free to forgive myself. He took the punishment for what I had done.

"As soon as I accepted God's forgiveness, it was like taking a giant leap, instead of baby steps. I wasn't just smiling, I was laughing and joking, and I am a much nicer person to be around. I've never experienced such peace and happiness and joy in my life as I have now. I can't really express the gratitude I have towards God for pulling me out of the deep dark pit that I was in, and bringing me into the light.

"That someone like me should be allowed to enter into His presence, after the things that I have done ... but that's the revelation of forgiving grace."

"When Iain's case was tried, the court released me to Betel on probation, but that conviction doesn't really matter, because it's God that has called me here, and I'm not going anywhere.

"Recently, a close relative appealed the case, and I could do five to fifteen years. I'd like to stay out of prison, obviously, but if I have to do time, it's only four walls; I'm free on the inside. I know that the Lord will be by my side wherever I go. Confinement in prison used to be one of my big fears. But the Apostle Paul spent a lot of time in prison, and God used him mightily while he did time. If I go to prison, the Lord's got something for me there – but I believe that the Lord wants me to work with Betel.

"I've been a responsible for about eight months now, and I hope someday that the Lord will use me to open a new Betel center in Scotland. I can see the guys in Betel impacting Britain in a totally new way. That's because the Lord has done so much in our lives. The power of gratitude is amazing!

"Jesus went to the cross in obedience to the Father, and didn't compromise in what He had to do. He's done *everything* for me – forgiven me, cleansed me, delivered me – and now, all I want to do is obey Him in everything and not compromise in what He has for me to do."

One of the principles at Betel is "free entrance, free exit." There is no charge for Betel's ministry, and one is free to leave whenever one wishes. Approximately half of those presently in residence stayed for a time, went back to the streets, and hurriedly returned to Betel.

The dynamics of call and compromise, success and regress, forgiveness and resolve are common to the human heart. The following stories, one from Hamburg, another from Malaga, and another from Marseilles point the way.

Johannes Plath, of Neumünster, Germany, was four years old when his father died. His mother suffered a severe nervous breakdown, and wasn't able to take care of Johannes and his two brothers. The family was split up; he was sent to live with an aunt, and then to another family. To cope with the grief and dislocation, he began building emotional walls to protect himself from pain. He also became very independent, suspect of authority, and rebellious by nature.

"By the age of six, I was doing what I wanted – even when I was returned to my mother. Over the next nine years, I was in four different schools, and through all the changes I had one best friend. His name was Volker. His family were Christians and I really enjoyed being with them. I felt like Volker's father considered me an extra son.

"In 1974 we moved to Hamburg, but I kept close contact with Volker and his family, until he was killed in a car accident. We were both fifteen at the time.

"Until then I never had anything to do with drugs. My reality was a dream world that I created in my imagination. I read a lot of comic books growing up, and they fed the fantasies. When Volker died it hurt so badly I could hardly stand it. It was like I fell into a deep dark hole and didn't know how to get out of it. Fourteen days after his death, I took drugs for the first time in my life. They opened more of my dream world, and if I took enough, they kept me from feeling the pain.

"A year later, I had become a big-time drug dealer.

"Over the next few years, I was in and out of prison. I'd 'recover' while doing my time, but as soon as I got out, it would all start again. Deep in my heart I knew that I was running away. I knew where my problem was but I didn't know how to handle it.

"In 1989 I had another time of 'recovering' – while in prison I spent six months in psychotherapy. When I got out, I went straight back to drugs. The next nine years, till March 1998, I was constantly being arrested for robbery and drug-dealing, and was in and out of prison.

"A year earlier, 1997, while in prison, I went to the library to borrow a book. I was just browsing, and what caught my attention was the title, *A Man Named Jesus*. As I read the book I realized that I couldn't do anything to change myself. I also realized that my desperation was a gift. I cried out to God to help me – and He did. There in prison God started little by little to transform me – transforming my thoughts and attitudes.

"Soon after, my mother died in a car accident. The bricks in the wall around my heart went higher. My first girlfriend died of cancer, and the second girlfriend overdosed. Their deaths actually didn't bother me too much emotionally – the wall was too high.

"I intentionally misbehaved in prison, so that I had another eight months added to my sentence. I was afraid to go back on the street – I knew I couldn't live out there by myself. When I was released, it was straight back into the drugs, and then back to prison.

"Before I came out of jail I prayed, 'Oh Lord, show me which way to go – I don't know what to do when I get out of here.'"

A friend in prison had given a Betel flyer to Johannes. He took it with him when his sentence was finished.

"As soon as I was released, I went straight to the Hamburg train station to buy drugs. I spent fourteen days on the street, stoned. I knew I needed help, so I thought I'd give Betel a try. I stayed for two and a half months, but was always fighting with the leaders. I didn't like them telling me what I could and couldn't do.

"I spent three weeks on the street and thought I'd try Betel again. I knew that if I stayed by myself, I'd always be in drugs. The second time I stayed in Betel for ten weeks, and then left. I thought that I had sorted out enough of my life and that I could make it on my own. Two months on the streets more than proved me wrong. I was straight back into the drugs. It was a very difficult time – there were stronger temptations than I'd ever faced before.

"Through it all, what I realized was that a dirty cloth is only good to spread more dirt. Being together with 'my friends, the junkies,' I felt that I didn't belong to them any more.

"I returned to Betel for a third time. When I entered the *Rastro* in Hamburg I was willing to do anything – all I wanted was to stay with Betel. That was 8 October 1999. I got put on two weeks' discipline washing dishes. Once in a while I had the feeling that the other guys were joking about me, but I didn't care. I was back where I knew I needed to be."

"I am getting to know God better and better. I was a drug addict for eighteen years. I am infected with the hepatitis C virus, but I am no longer afraid of dying. I can see how God has always held His hand over my life – I survived prison violence, severe car accidents, and six heroin overdoses. God's grace has always been strong enough to keep me.

"I have received lots of inner-healing through the Holy Spirit, and the walls in my heart are coming down. To know God as my Father is my healing. I have learned what it means to love and to be loved. That huge change took place through love and humility – His love to me, and my humility before Him. The key for everything is humility; without real humility, everything is just show.

"When I am humble and receive the love of God, then it is paradise. Betel is a wonderful place to learn about humility.

"The most difficult thing for me here in Betel is to give the love I already have to 'everybody.' There are guys here that I don't really like. Especially in difficult situations, God is showing that I don't have enough love yet. I am slowly learning to let things go, and not take things so seriously. Because He is so patient with me, I am learning to wait as other people change.

"My main desire over all is to grow constantly in Jesus, and be able to confront every temptation victoriously."

José Manuel was raised in Sevilla, Spain. He described himself as curious by nature. He experimented with any drug he could get. By the time he was eighteen years old, he was fully addicted to heroin. For a while it seemed that money and heroin solved all his problems. But not for long.

"I think of the nine years of addiction as bath bubbles. My life seemed full and frothy and fun, but it didn't take long for it all to burst, and all that was left was a dirty film."

José knew of Betel through his brother, who was also an addict. They had both tried other community drug rehabs, but kept returning to the streets. The word was that Betel was different. In June 1995, José arrived at Betel-Malaga from Sevilla, having been told that 90 per cent of addicts return to their old life if they don't make a break with their friends. He told his employer that he needed fifteen days off to do his "turkey," and then he'd return.

He had no intention or desire to join the community – in fact, the thought repulsed him. He thought it was like volunteering for prison! He only wanted to kick his addiction and get on with his life.

"'Fifteen days, and I'm gone.' Attitudinally, I came with full bags packed. But day by day, it was like I stripped."

At the end of the fifteen days, he felt that life at Betel wasn't as bad as he feared it would be, and so asked his employer's medical officer for another two weeks' leave.

"I had never cared for anyone but myself. After my two-week detox, I was put to work at the *Rastro*, the thrift shop. One day I overheard a woman asking another Betelito for help. Her husband had abandoned her and her three young daughters. She wasn't a drug addict – she wasn't so much asking for help for herself, but for her daughters. I started to bawl. Someone else's need had touched my heart. It was the first time that had ever happened."

During the evening meeting, the preacher called forward anyone who felt any unrest. José stayed seated, but kept thinking about the woman all through dinner.[3] After lights out, José's inner commotion kept him awake. Suddenly, he jumped out of bed. The responsible looked at him and said, "What's wrong with you?"

"I want to receive Jesus."

He expected something dramatic to happen after they prayed together. It didn't, though he realized that something within him had changed – the inner turmoil was gone. He crawled back into bed. "I had the deepest sleep of my life."

José stayed at Betel for four months, and then left. His mother was to have surgery and needed his care. Within days, he was sucked back into the drug vortex. For two weeks he totally forgot about the Lord, and then one night while stoned, a non-Christian friend said, "We're both losers. Our only hope is God." José couldn't stop thinking about those words, and five days later, 27 December 1995, he returned to Betel-Malaga.

The guys welcomed him back with open arms. "Their acceptance and forgiveness felt like it was straight from God Himself. The loser mentality and its condemnation lifted, and love, peace and freedom took their place."

Not long after, he was made the house leader. "Being like one of them, I know how they feel. Sometimes things get a little crazy here – guys get mad, and feelings get hurt. I know that in order for them to forgive, they have to be forgiven first; only then can they come to forgive others.

"One night, two guys were arguing in the dining room, in front of all the others. I came in, split them up, and took them into my office. As we talked, I told them, 'Look, we have to love one another. There's no other way.' I don't know exactly what I said next, but they both started to cry.

"All on their own, at breakfast the next day, these two stood up, and in front of all the men, asked forgiveness from the rest of the guys. Then they turned, and publicly forgave one another. It was so unexpected, the other *chicos* were stunned into silence."

The power of acceptance and forgiveness brings a healing all its own, and unconditional love restores the irreparable. At Betel, these graces continuously bring restoration as the sincere are freely given as many chances as they need to overcome failure.

After over a decade of addiction, Francisco began to get his life straightened around in the Betel-Madrid. In the space of four and a half years, he showed himself to be very diligent, thoughtful, and a hard worker. He became the house leader in Mariblanca, and from there went to be the leader of the Betel chicken farm in Toledo.

Regrettably, it was too complicated an operation for Francisco to manage. He and the men working for him really didn't understand the technology that controlled the feed, water, heating and ventilation systems. There was a three-month period when he didn't disclose the problems he was facing. As it was a time of rapid growth for Betel, the pastors were extremely busy, and quickly believed Francisco's reports that everything was fine. Every Monday he'd attend the leaders' meeting, and never once asked for help, or shared any of his difficulties. In hindsight, he was given too much freedom and responsibility.

He ran into serious technical difficulties, and chickens started to die. Then, Francisco got a bad batch of feed and more chickens died. He began to panic, and started to sell off Betel's pigs privately, supposedly to pay bills that were mounting. He stopped paying the rent for a number of months and he didn't pay the feed bill. The pumps in the wells burned out, so he attached city water to the farm, and ran up a $7,500 water bill. Then one day, he just left.

Francisco later confessed to stealing $45; through mismanagement, he left Betel with debts and equipment repairs that totaled $45,000. It was Betel's biggest economic failure.

"I left because I wanted to do things my own way. I wanted to solve the problems, and be the hero. When I couldn't, I didn't know what to do but run. I knew I had a call on my life – in the four years at Betel, I had felt God's presence on me in very strong, even heavy ways. But I put the things of God aside, to return to the drugs. I looked to heroin for comfort.

"I hit bottom – further down than I thought possible. I was completely alone, and 100 per cent dependent on heroin. I was living worse than an animal – they take care of themselves."

He spent the next three years wrapped up in a blanket, begging on the Gran Via, one of the principal tourist streets of Madrid. He lost all but one of his teeth and became very sickly.

"I knew where I should go, and what I should do – return to Betel – but I refused to listen to the Voice that called me back. I knew I had a family at Betel that would take me back, and take care of me. But I didn't want to face the trust that I had broken."

One of the pastors, Juan Carlos, still had a burden for him. He repeatedly visited Francisco on the street, and asked him to return to Betel.

"I kept refusing, until one day, he called me from across the street. As soon as I heard his voice, something in my heart leapt – that day I went with him, and not long afterwards, I came with him to Marseilles. It was important for me to make a break. I needed to move away from my drug life."

They had difficulty getting him across the border from Spain into France. He looked like a mad man.

"Over the six months I've been in France, everything has been restored. I feel so very privileged. I've touched God, and I've handled the things of the world. Now I have chosen to hang on to God. I know I will never let Him go. This is where I will stay.

"God has forgiven me, and released me from condemnation. I had failed Betel badly; I was afraid of seeing Elliott. That's not quite right – more ashamed than afraid. But God has taken forty-five pounds of condemnation from me, and I feel free.

"I am so thankful to God for Betel. I never had a family – no love, no care. In Betel, the reward is not material – it's belonging, and it's so strong, it's like a stamp on my heart. This is where I know I belong."

Paul, the self-harmer from the hostel, left Betel the night he arrived. He said that he felt "overwhelming separation anxiety" from his government-funded therapist whom he had been seeing three hours a week, for the last seven years.

His parting words: "I don't want to interrupt the progress we're making."

The Betel house leader asked Paul about the fresh bandages on his arms and legs. He'd slashed himself four times the previous week.

Notes

1. The names of the addicts whose stories are told in this chapter have all been changed..
2. Kent and Mary Alice Martin are the Directors of the Betel-Birmingham.
3. Spaniards eat very late; at Betel, it is customary to eat after the church meeting.

Chapter 6

Jealous Conversions

"Why should we stay here and die?"   (2 Kings 7:4)

While visiting the Betel in Naples, Italy, we spent Saturday morning in *Pinetta Mare*, "Pines by the Sea," a piece of land measuring five acres which was reforested thirty years ago. A well-worn path traverses some wasteland that joins the forest to the road. From the fringe of the forest into its heart, there are used syringes everywhere. "Everywhere" is no exaggeration. The ground is covered with a blanket of used syringes and their wrappers. The government Health Department offers addicts free needles. The old ones are not required in exchange, so they are just dropped after use. Cigarette boxes and coke cans add to the rubbish.

We were in the woods almost an hour, wandering through the front edge of the forest, handing out Betel flyers. I counted over a hundred men that came to score. Nine women wandered in. Only a few of the addicts refused the literature we were offering. The takers looked carefully at our faces – the Betelitos with me got much longer looks than I did. The addicts knew that those guys were now clean. They wanted to know how. Many stopped and talked engagedly. No one threw the flyer away.

I spoke with Mario for twenty minutes. He has been a heroin addict for thirteen years. As his high was wearing off, he was quite lucid. He had taken one of our flyers, and, leaning against a tree, he read the tract, *Lo Sono la Droga*, "I Am the Drug." He had lots of questions about Betel. As his English was very good, I spoke to him while the Betelitos chatted to other addicts in Italian.

Mario knew he had to change his life. His parents had just told him they never wanted to see him again. He didn't go into details.

He had practical questions about Betel – "Is it free? What are the rules? How long can I stay? Do they let Catholics in?" It all seemed good to him. He carefully took the flyer, wrote Armando's name and phone number on it, folded it, and even more carefully put it in his wallet. Armando is the Director of Betel-Genoa, eight hours to the north.

Mario said he was serious about getting free, and knew he needed to leave local friends and bad influences. He said he would call Armando on Monday.

I asked, "Why Monday?"

"I have to go and see my parents tomorrow. I need to tell them that I am sorry for all that I have done. I need to tell them what I am going to do, and where I am going to go. They will pray for me."

The tract "I Am the Drug" is a graphic personification of heroin. Part of it reads:

> "It's me who, in the beginning, makes you live beyond this present world full of problems. But with time I am the very thing that you cannot live without. After you have tried me, you're mine for the rest of your life...
>
> I am purposely destroying your life in every area – physically, morally and spiritually. It's me who has destroyed your family ... It's me that has caused you to go to prison...
>
> I have you trapped."

Whoever wrote it could well have been thinking about Josh's life story, 950 miles away, in the north of England.[1]

From high-rolling drug dealing, his life crashed hard. A couple of deals went bad, and he became a marked man.

"I had nowhere to go, so I was sleeping in a garbage dumpster. On Christmas evening, I walked all the way up to my mother's house. I was stoned and drunk. I hid in the bushes outside her house so I could look in through the front window, through the little snow-sprayed Christmas trees. My family was laughing and joking. They were all there, from my youngest nephew to my oldest aunt, my stepfather, my mother, my brothers, my sisters-in-law. There was a big table with a nice turkey in the middle, glasses of red wine, fancy candles and streamers and a roaring fire and a big tree with fur on the top. It was a beautiful Christmas and I remember seeing them all laughing and smiling and joking and pulling crackers. I looked down at myself. I was covered in dirt. I had fresh needle marks in my arms.

"I started crying my eyes out, 'cause I was nothin'. My family wanted nothin' to do with me, and I was all on my own. I was paranoid, and all I wanted to do was kill myself.

"When everybody turns their back on ya, you start thinkin', 'What sort of person am I?'

"One night I was in a bail hostel, waiting to go to court. I had no address that I could give the police because all the addresses I had were prostitutes' addresses or drug addicts'. I was full of heroin and methadone, I had been drinking cider all day, and I was smashed; I was off me 'ead.

"I started to think, 'Where am I going with my life? How can I get out of where I'm at? How am I gonna change it all around? I've always been a drug addict, and I'll always be here, in and out of jail. I'm just going down deeper and deeper. My family don't love me, and the girls don't love me. I've hurt them all before; they'd be better off without me ... '

"I got a razor blade and I sliced my wrist. There was blood everywhere.

"Somebody came in, got an ambulance, and took me to hospital. I had passed out, and when I woke up, there was nobody there. My family wasn't there, my mother wasn't there. I had thought, 'If I do this to myself, she'll come and see me,' but there was none of it. I was just on my own and that made things worse.

"Another night, I was sitting and thinking, 'What's the use, I'll do it this time. I won't slash my wrists because there'll be blood everywhere ... ' I injected just under a gram of heroin, which should have killed me. I woke up in a hospital. When you take an overdose to kill yourself and you wake up and you're still alive, it's really depressing. I felt like such an absolute failure.

"That second suicide attempt got me put on 'section,' in a psychiatric hospital, under constant observation. They filled me with diazepam; I was tripping on 600 mg a day. They don't know what else to do with you. You're a heroin addict, and they're filling you with sleeping pills and tranquilizers!

"The psychiatrists were telling me, 'The problem you've got is something terminal; it's something in your mind. Something must have happened to you, something you're not dealing with.' They want you to talk about all your problems. They bring them all to the surface, get them good and raw, and then they just leave them all there. They'd sit me in a room and draw things out of me, all of my personal problems, but there'd be no solution. It's just like, 'Deal with it.'

" *'I'm in hospital, having tried to kill myself three times because I can't deal with it!'*

"Their solution was more diazepam. They had me so stoned, I'd just flop over. Basically I was so numb I couldn't move. All day. Day after day. For about three months. They slowly reduced the dosage, and in some bright spark's assessment, they felt I was ready to 're-enter the community.' They felt I was all right to go out and get on with living again. But they'd not solved anything.

"It was just like the two rehabs I did to detox heroin. I came out empty, with nothing there to fill what I needed filling. They got rid of the drugs, but that was the easy part. The drugs are nothing. Coming off drugs is easy; two weeks and you're clean. But it's the problems in the heart. It was the void of life, just completely no life. I was like a shell. The only thing rattling around in there was self-pity – it was all 'Me, Me, Me,' and it was enormous. When I was younger, I used to believe that the world revolved around me. Now it didn't. I was on my own, and it looked like I'd always be on my own. I never felt love, I never felt joy, I never felt peace. There was always something raging in my head.

"I did something really stupid, and did a bit of time. When I was out of prison about six months, things got a little bit worse. I was involved with a gang in Glossop who basically controlled all the heroin. When I got out of prison, I got a loan of three ounces of heroin, worth $3,000. I was supposed to deal it, but basically I smoked a lot of it. What I did sell, I spent on more heroin. The people who loaned it to me wanted their money, but it was gone, so it was time to either get out or get a serious beating. I was too stoned to get out fast enough. They got a hold of me, punched me around a bit, and threatened my life. It was bad enough that one of them got ten years for violent assault.

"That rattled me pretty badly. I went to a local church drop-in called the Glossop Christian Community Centre. I'd been there once before, but just for a cup of tea. This time I was looking for my friend Andy, to see if he could help me. We talked and he gave me Betel's number, and told me to call them. I rung up and I spoke to Jenny. Two days later, I was at Betel.

"As soon as I walked through the door, it felt like I'd found somewhere that I'd be loved. Some of the first people I met were Kent and Mary Alice, the leaders of Betel, and I knew right off that they were genuine. I just knew it.

"I saw something in Mary Alice which made me think, WOW. She was so peaceful; something in me wanted to know what it was she had. It was like I could talk to Mary Alice about anything, and I knew that Kent wasn't going to turn against me. They didn't want me for something, they didn't want something from me – there was no threat there. I felt I could tell them anything, and it would be safe.

"It wasn't like the psychiatrists were. They would sit me down, ask all kinds of nosey questions about my personal life, and get me all angry. But at Betel, it was different. They'd ask me something so they could help me. There was a genuine love and a care that I'd never felt before. It was something new, brand new. It was a new emotion, the first hint of joy.

"I could also see a difference in the guys. One of them – Dave – knows the same people I know in Glasgow. I know the lifestyle he had lived 'cause I was livin' it with him. I thought, 'Well if you've been a drug addict and you've been an alcoholic and you've been a violent person, you've done this and you've done that, and you're no longer violent, then why? I want to know.'

"Seeing guys like Dave gave me hope. I saw peace and I saw joy; I saw a release from fear and I saw happiness; I saw a purpose, you know. Take Matthew, for instance. He was one of the house leaders. He had been a crack addict for many years, but he didn't talk like a crack addict, 'cause I know crack addicts. They are very selfish and mean and violent and angry and paranoid and depressed. But looking at Matthew, I saw a person I wanted to be.

"Every time I asked the guys about what changed them, I got the same answer: 'Jesus.'

"After a couple of days in Betel, at the Wednesday night meeting, I went forward for prayer. Kent and Eduardo and Jenny prayed for me. I got laid out in the Spirit.

"Up to that point, I had withdrawals from heroin. They stopped. I just didn't sleep for nine days. I didn't get the sweats, I didn't get the shivers, I didn't get the diarrhoea, I didn't get the cramps, I didn't get the serious stomach cramps that you get, I didn't get the aching limbs. Just nine sleepless nights, and I was free from drugs. I was free from heroin.

"Because I started to change, I thought I was all right. I thought I had made it, and I could leave and I'd be all right. I thought that life would be OK again. I figured I didn't need to be at Betel, so I left.

"Straight away, as soon as I left the covering of God in the building, I started sneezing and my nose started running, I started yawning, my legs started to ache, I got cold shivers, and I got cramps. I got as far as Birmingham and then I walked halfway back to Betel. I rung them up, two hours after I'd left and said, 'I've made the biggest mistake of my life. Can I come back?'

"They said, 'Yes, you can.'"

The tract, "I Am the Drug" concludes with heroin stating:

> "You are in love with me. There is nothing in the world that can break our love affair. My only enemy is Jesus Christ. Whatever I destroy, He goes and restores. He has snatched away so many of my followers, and now I see them living so happily with Him..."

It's almost as if Betel has made jealousy a spiritual gift. "Holy covetousness" is at the root of conversion after conversion. The details of the stories change; the heart's desire remains the same.

Julia's conversion succinctly demonstrates this dynamic. Thomas, the story after hers, is a study in contrasts.

Julia's father was an alcoholic. She began taking drugs when she was fourteen years old. At eighteen, she was mainlining heroin. Over the next five years of addiction, her family begged her to get help. She entered Betel in June 1990, desperate.

"I had come to hate my life as a club girl. There was absolutely no future in it. I felt as if I was sinking into a deeper and deeper hole. My brother-in-law told my family about Centro Betel in Madrid, and they put a lot of pressure on me to admit myself. I only went along so they'd leave me in peace. When I went for the entrance interview, I met people I had known on the streets. They looked as if they were doing really well, and I felt like there might be some hope for me. The people at Betel said I could either stay in Madrid, or go to a new work that had recently opened in Valencia. I owed money to some pretty rough crowds in Madrid, and I was afraid that they would find me and give me another beating. Valencia sounded like a smart choice!

"My family put me on the train, and as soon as they left, I shot up. When we arrived in Valencia, I was so stoned that the conductor had to drag me off the train. He left me slumped over on one of the station benches. It wasn't difficult for the Betel leaders, Trini and Milagros, to figure out who they'd come to collect."

The women in the house helped Julia pass her *mono*, the two-week detox. "The care that I received kept me there. I loved the love." When the worst was over, the girls taught her the Betel routine. At first, it felt too much for Julia. She packed her bag every morning for weeks, but stayed because of the kindnesses she received through the day.

"It was a difficult time because when I came to the center, I was pregnant, though I didn't realize it. I thought the sickness was just part of my *mono*. When I found out two months later during my medical check-up, I was sure that Betel would make me leave. I decided that rather than getting kicked out, I'd just disappear on my own. But that thought made me miserable. It was a horrible time because I didn't know where I'd go, or what I'd do.

"Eloisa had taken me to the doctor's, and she convinced me to come 'home.' Later that day I finally told the house leader, Trini, that I was pregnant. We talked for a little while and then she left. I spent the rest of the day in tears.

"Trini told the other girls about my pregnancy, and they came in and said, 'You're blessed.' That's not what I was thinking."

After the evening meal later that night, Trini appeared in Julia's dorm room. She was carrying a bouquet of flowers, and a note from all the women that read: "Keep going forward – we'll help you, and be with you, because God loves you and your baby." Nine and a half years later, Julia still treasures that note.

"It was Trini's life and the love I saw in the other women that made me want what they had – Jesus. He filled the emptiness I felt inside." [2]

Trini died of AIDS in July 1994.

Thomas is a good-looking, polite, witty young man. [3] He is one who carries about him a sense of destiny. I met him at Betel-Birmingham, and it was a defining moment in my life. After hearing his story, I am looking at people differently. An echo, a stirring, a word resounds somewhere deep within: *You may never know the secrets that person is carrying.*

"My dad was pretty frustrated with his life. When he got angry, he used to take it out on me. He'd knock me around, even when I hadn't done anything wrong. I lived in fear, never knowing what kind of mood he'd be in when he came home from work. I started to think, 'Why should I try and live the way he wants me to live, when he's not living up to the expectations that I have of a father?'"

Thomas started drinking when he was eight years old, and smoking cannabis when he was eleven. His friends were five years older than he was; they just passed to Thomas whatever they were using. A few years later they were into ecstasy and speed.

"The drugs took away my fear. When I was high, my worries

got pushed down so I didn't have to think about them. I could be happy ... what I thought was happy anyway."

Thomas got involved in the dance music scene, going to house parties and big clubs. He was fourteen. "We were doing a lot of ecstasy, and when it wore off, we felt awful. My friends were taking heroin to help the comedown, and they offered it to me. I didn't want to get into drug use that deeply though.

"One night I was really, really sick from the ecstasy tablets, and my mates insisted that a few lines of heroin would solve everything. It did make me feel good. Heroin pushed my fears so far down, it seemed like they were almost gone. It was a great escape. What I was searching for was a non-existent state; I didn't want to deal with any of my problems."

Thomas was fifteen years old.

"Within a few years, I was DJing in the clubs, and using heroin two or three times a week, to come down from the ecstasy and speed. I'd been out with a girl named Debbie a few times. She was a good friend. Like all my friends, she was injecting heroin and taking ecstasy. I was injecting ecstasy, and she was on and on to let her inject it too. I knew that if you happen to be allergic to just one of the chemicals in ecstasy, it could kill you. However, she was very persistent, and I finally gave in. By then I'd had three injections myself, and I was so out of it that I didn't know what was going on.

"But I can still picture it in my mind; it is so vivid. It's very hard for me to talk about.

"I gave her an injection, and then I went off to talk to the club manager. We were dealing ecstasy together. When I got back, Debbie was having trouble breathing. She was shaking. I tried to hold her – she stared straight forward, right deep into my eyes. She started convulsing, and I started panicking. The harder she shook, the tighter I tried to hold her. It got really violent, and when I couldn't hold on any longer, and pulled back, I saw that foam was coming out of her mouth. That was it. She died.

"I freaked.

"I got up and looked around; it was only the two of us behind the stage. Over a thousand kids were out front dancing ... I just

walked away, and left the club. I didn't know what to do. I just
started running.

"The police called it 'accidental death.'

"I started using heroin every day, all the time, to escape, to
run from the memory. I thought if I took enough, it would
blank it out.

"My family knew that I was taking drugs by now. I'd
repeatedly stolen money from them, and sold a lot of their stuff
to pay for the drugs. They tried taking me to psychiatrists and
drug counselors, but no one knew why I had to stay stoned."

"My dad had an affair, and my mom had a mental breakdown.
Later, she tried to kill herself. She overdosed on tranquilizers.
I'm quite sure that she did it because she was so lonely. She
wanted attention, because after she took the pills, she phoned
up my auntie, and she came and rushed mom to the hospital.

"When my father saw me, he blamed me for her overdose. He
said, 'Do you know what you're doing to your mother?' I yelled
at him, 'Look what *you've* done to her!' We had a huge shouting
match. It was hell. Over and over I blamed him for my
miserable life.

"I went to see my mom in hospital. She started screaming as
soon as she saw me: 'Get out! I never want to see you again!
You're not my son. Get out of here – I never want to see you
again. I hate you!'

"I left the hospital in a daze. I bought some heroin and shot
up. Those last words, 'I hate you,' undid me. I thought, 'Why
am I living? How much worse can this pain get?'

"I know now that it was the devil that put the words in my
head: 'Why don't you kill yourself?'

"I got a razor blade and cut my wrist. I did it in a little park
in the town center. There was a guy who watched me crawl into
the bushes. I guess he thought that I was going to use drugs,
because he came around to see what I was doing. Blood was
pumping out of my arm; he peeled off his shirt, tied it around
my arm, and then ran and phoned for the ambulance.

"He was there when I woke up in the hospital. 'Are you all
right, Thomas?' he asked. I said, 'Yes,' and he was gone. I never
did find out his name.

"If he wasn't an angel, then God sent him to me because He didn't want me to die. But at that time, I didn't have any comprehension of God. I'd heard a bit about God creating the world, and about heaven and hell, but I didn't believe any of it. Life was the evolution theory, death, burial and rot. I didn't believe in spirit or soul. I just thought that you are what you are and when it's over, that's it."

"My heroin usage was increasing. To pay for it, I used to 'shoplift to order.' I'd go around to a buyer's house, and ask what he wanted. He'd give me a shopping list, and I'd go out and steal it. Then they'd pay me for the stuff.

"Soon, I needed more money for more heroin, so I burgled pretty much every flat in the immediate neighborhood. Mine was the only one that didn't get done. The police put it together and came around one morning, smashed the door in, and dragged me out of bed. The next day I went to court, and the court remanded me to jail.

"I had never spent a night in jail, and it scared me. Because I had been beaten up by my father so many times, I was scared of getting punched. I'd heard the stories about prison – the raping and the violence. When I went back up to court, the magistrate said that they couldn't find any evidence that I'd done the burglaries. As I had a number of outstanding shoplifting charges, he gave me twelve months.

"I'd been in prison about a week, and the guy that I'd done most of the burglaries with got sentenced to the same prison. They let us stay in the same cell. He had been in and out of prison for a number of years, and was my exact opposite. He was a guy who had no fear in him. He was a fighter. If anyone even said 'boo' to him, he'd give them a thrashing. He basically ran the drugs in prison, dealing and stealing, and as his mate, it meant I got looked after pretty well. I did as much drugs in prison as I did on the outside. But he scared me too, because he was a nasty piece of work. If he was really out to get someone, he'd take a big metal teapot, and squirt jam packets into it, and pour in loads of sugar, and some boiling water. Then he'd throw it in their face. The goo would be like hot tar, and they'd be horribly burned.

"I used to think, 'I don't want to be like this guy.' He was getting involved in vendettas and turf wars, and I used to think, 'If things don't change, I'll probably end up dead with him.'"

"When I was released from prison, I had nowhere to go. For eight months I slept in a corner of a big multi-level car park. Every night I'd go up to the roof, stoned on heroin, and I'd stand on the very edge, and lean way out. I wanted the pain to stop. I can't really explain how, but I know it was God keeping me through this time. I knew it because I just couldn't jump.

"In the city center, there's a Christian café for the homeless. You could get a cup of tea and some soup. It's called 'The Missing Piece.' I went because I was hungry. I met two ladies, Ann and Linda. They lead worship there on Thursday nights, and they started telling me about the love of God and how I didn't have to live this way. I gave them a hard time. 'What has God done for me? If God loves me, why has my life been like it is?'

"These ladies just wouldn't give up on me. They just kept saying, 'Come back next Thursday for the worship meeting.' I went back, and they asked if they could pray with me. I said, 'You can if you want to, but it won't do anything.' They prayed, and I just broke down in tears.

"Ann asked, 'What's the matter?' I said, 'I can't go on living like this. It's just too much for me.' She came over and she gave me a hug. I'd been on the streets for eight months. I was dirty and smelly and covered in blood from the heroin injections. I couldn't believe that she could love someone as filthy as me.

"Several weeks went by. I was still going out and shooting up. Thursday nights, I'd go to The Missing Piece. Ann kept checking in on me, and she knew I was still using. She said, 'If you're serious about changing your life, I know a place called Betel. You've got to stop smoking straight away; no drinking; no drugs, and you'll have to work after you've done your 'turkey.'

"She told me more about Betel. 'They have a sauna, and a Jacuzzi, and when you go through your detox, the staff give you massages.' When I heard that, I thought I would give it a go.

"They drove me to Birmingham, and when I got to Betel I thought it looked pretty nice. I handed Ann my syringes and cigarettes and said, 'I'm going in there with nothing. I'll give it my best.'

"John Kav, one of the leaders, checked me in. I went downstairs and sat down beside another new guy, Paul. John came by a short while later and asked, 'Well, are you ready?' I thought I was going to get a sauna or something. He said, 'Come on, you can give me a hand on the grounds.' It was 5 November, it was freezing cold out, and it was drizzling. I said, 'Look, I'm not doing any work – I was told that if I came here, I had two weeks off for withdrawals. I want to get in the sauna or the Jacuzzi or something like that.'

He started laughing, and then asked, 'What're you on about?'

" 'I want a sauna.'

"He said, 'There's a golf club down the road, but you're not going to get that sort of thing around here.'

"That made me angry because I felt like those Christian ladies had lied to me. I've seen them since, and I asked them why they talked about saunas and stuff. They asked, 'Well, are you glad?'

" 'You wouldn't have gotten me there without it.'

" 'Exactly; if we hadn't said that, you wouldn't have come.'

"It was a bit crafty, but it worked, and I thank them for it.

"John kept me out in the garden the whole afternoon, building a bonfire for Guy Fawkes Day. I was freezing cold, and I thought, 'This is like an army camp. You come here to get off drugs, and they make you go outside and work. Next they'll have me digging holes in the rain! I'm off in the morning. As soon as I wake up in the morning, I'm out of here.'

"The next day, I packed my stuff. But then I started thinking, 'What are you going back to? The streets. Give this a go until the withdrawal is finished.' And that's what I did. Just a few days at a time. I'd wake up: 'Right, I'm leaving.' Then I'd say, 'No; give it another day.' "

"Everybody at Betel has to go to the worship services, and I'd sit there thinking, 'This is a bit too much.' The guys were singing and shouting and laughing. My idea of church was people sitting quietly, with their hands folded in their laps. But I could see things in the senior guys. I'd heard their stories. They came from backgrounds that were worse than mine; they'd been in prison a lot more; they'd been hurt a lot more than me, and now they were happy and free. They didn't seem to want to go back on drugs. I wanted whatever it was that changed them.

"I asked one of them, 'What is it that you lads have got that I can see in you?' He said, 'Jesus.' I thought, 'Oh here we go again, here's another one.' He said, 'Have you ever thought of giving your life to God?'

" 'I don't know what that means. Do I say, "God, I give you my life," and it's like I'm a robot, or what?'

"He started to set me right, and I told him I didn't think I was ready.

"A couple of weeks later, when I'd been at Betel three months, still saying, 'I'll stick it out one more day,' Eduardo, Matthew and a few of the other lads prayed with me. I felt like I'd give God a go. When I made the decision, I was expecting some big bang, or fireworks or something, but nothing like that happened. Instead, it was like I got my feelings back. I couldn't stop thinking about what I had done to my family. There was so much guilt working away at me, destroying me inside. Memories tortured me. I'd see my mom in hospital after her suicide attempt, and hear her screaming at me.

"The guys were telling me that now that I've been washed in the blood, my sins had all been forgiven..., but then I'd picture Debbie's overdose all over again. Inside my head I'd hear: 'There's no way that God will forgive that.'

"I knew that He would forgive me of all the other stuff, but He must be up there thinking, 'Right, when you and I meet, we're going to have some words.' The devil was firing things into my head, 'You killed that girl, and she's now in hell because of you.' It was just crushing me.

"I hadn't told anyone about Debbie's death. It could have got back to her family, or the police."

"Five months after I came to Betel, we went to a local church to see a play called *Heaven's Gates and Hell's Flames*. There's a scene where two girls are injecting drugs, and they die. The devil comes along and drags them to hell, and while we were watching the play, I burst into tears.

"One of the senior Betel guys, Andy, was sitting next to me. He put his arm around me and asked, 'What's the matter?' I bawled all the way home. When we got home, he sat me down in the Chapel and asked again, 'What's wrong?'

"I told him all about it. He said we needed to talk to Kent, Betel's Director. The next morning I told him the whole story. Kent asked, 'Do you believe that you're forgiven for this?' I shook my head. 'No way.'

" 'God forgives all sins.'

"I couldn't let it go. Kent suggested spending a longer prayer time together, and through that time I began to feel forgiveness in my heart. I know now that I am forgiven. It's not just what other people say. I can feel in my heart that I'm forgiven, and that blows me away. The devil's lies have been silenced.

"Recently, I've been asking the Lord if I should tell Debbie's family about my involvement with her death. It happened four years ago, and I know that it would open up painful wounds for them. They know that she was an addict, and I know I only gave her what she asked for, so it seems best at this time not to say anything. But it might be right in the future."

"I've been at Betel now a little over a year, and it is the family that I've always wanted. It's the love that has kept me here. To me, Betel is a bunch of walking miracles, because the people that love me were just like me, or worse. Drug addicts are known for a lot of things, but love isn't one of them!

"It's all God's doing. It's like the love-circles get bigger and bigger in my life. When I came to Betel, my family didn't know I was coming. My mom and dad didn't know where I was. They'd heard stories that I was dead, or locked away in jail.

"In the early months here, I'd hear guys tell how God restored their families, and I'd just stare at the floor. I didn't think it would ever be possible for me and my family to be reunited. I had heard it so many times – that my mom didn't ever want to see me ever again.

"When I'd been at Betel about eight or nine months, one of the leaders came up and asked, 'Have you spoken to your parents yet?' I said no. I didn't tell him that I didn't have the courage to phone them. He asked for my mom's number.

Reluctantly, I gave it to him. Five minutes later he came back and said, 'Your mom is delighted that you're here; she wants to speak to you.'

"My mom now phones me twice every weekend. She comes up to Betel as often as she can. On her first visit, I so wanted to give my mom a kiss and say to her, 'I love you.' No sooner were the words out of my mouth when she said, 'I love you, son.' All of this is the Lord's doing. To me it's amazing, and there is so much gratitude in my heart just for that one blessing.

"It's one of the things that I try to tell the new guys here, that there is nothing impossible for the Lord."

Thomas had never worked a day in his life before coming to Betel. Under Eduardo's supervision, he now manages one of the community thrift shops.

"One of the things my mom used to say to me over and over again was that she could never trust me with money – that it was my biggest downfall. I never had any – I'd run off with it, buy drugs, and get high. But now, and all glory be to the Lord for this, I have been raised up to run the shop. I'll never forget the first day that I actually was in charge of the till. It had been a really good day, and at closing, I was staring at $600. I almost heard a voice: 'Thomas, this is the most money that you've had for years. Why don't you disappear – and have a good time?'

"The temptation was really strong, but I recognized it for what it was, and I started praying about it. I felt the Lord say to me, 'Yeah, Thomas, that's what you would have done in your old life. But think about all the people that you will disappoint – your parents, the Betel leadership, but most of all, think of Me.'

"He's the person that I really want to please, and if I had taken the money and run, it would have been a slap in the Lord's face. He's saved me, and raised me up to a position of responsibility.

"Every day at Betel gives me the chance to deepen my relationship with the Lord and become a lot stronger. It's like a training ground. Trusting me with money was one small thing, and who knows what He wants from me in the days ahead. I just hope I'll be able to say, 'Whatever You've called me for, I say, YES, Lord, Your will be done, not mine.'

"Day by day, Christ continues to build His love in me. What I want most to do is reach out and touch people with that same love, the love the Lord has touched my life with. It amazes my mother. On one of her visits, she asked, 'Thomas, how can you get up and give a devotional?' She'd never seen me speak in front of a crowd. I said, 'Mom, I *am* uncomfortable speaking out like that, but if just one word out of a thousand helps one person, then it's worth it, even if the whole crowd laughs at me. If just one person gets helped in any way, if it touches them, and makes them believe in God, then it's worth it.'"

"God gave me a scripture that makes a lot of sense of my life. It's Isaiah 42:16–17. God says,

> *'I will lead the blind along a way they never knew,*
> *I will guide them along paths they have not known,*
> *I will make the darkness to become light for them,*
> *and the rough places smooth.*
> *These are the things that I will do.*
> *I will not leave my people,*
> *but those who trust in idols,*
> *who say to their statues, "You are our gods,"*
> *will be rejected and disgraced.'*

Someone read that out one day, and when I heard it, I knew that it was all about me. *I* was blind. God guided my feet to Betel, a place I'd never heard of, and He's made the darkness of my life become light. I used to worship heroin and cocaine, any drug I could get. The Lord has taken that away from me, and I know that He's forgiven me for my idolatry; He's forgiven my every sin.

"I can't say 'Thank you' enough."

Back in Naples, Betel workers return to *Pinetta Mare* every Saturday morning to meet with the addicts. Their presence is so accepted, drug deals are conducted right in front of them. That's the addicts' unspoken way of saying that they trust the Betelitos.

Three weeks after my visit in Naples, Lindsay McKenzie, the Director of the Italian work, wrote me an email to say, "It was an uncanny feeling. Claudio and I were handing out tracts, while six feet away, the dealers were handing out wraps [heroin wrapped up in white paper]. Claudio put it into words: 'Do you see the paradox? We're handing out papers offering *life*, free of charge, and they're handing out papers offering *death*, at a premium.'"

To date, Mario hasn't called Armando. He is still in the woods of *Pinetta Mare*. Pray that he doesn't lose his wallet, and the Betel flyer that is so carefully folded inside.

Notes

1. This is a continuation of his story from Chapter 2.
2. Julia became the women's house leader in Valencia. She married Juan Capillia in September 1993. Together, they direct the Ceuta and Algeciras Betels in North Africa and southern Spain.
3. Names and places have been changed throughout this story.

Chapter 7

Coveralls and a Wrench

"It was there from the beginning; we have heard it; we have seen it with our own eyes; we looked upon it, and felt it with our own hands; our theme is the Word which gives life."
(1 John 1:1)

The city of Lisbon is built on hillsides and valleys. Towards the south of the city, half a mile from the river Tajo is a *barrio*, a neighborhood known as *Casal Ventoso*. It is built on a steep hill that faces east.

The on-shore winds of the Atlantic blow past the old government quarter, the King's Palace, and one of the wealthier neighborhoods across the valley. The winds blow past Lisbon's booming financial district to the east. The winds blow past Lisbon's prison, a ten-minute walk away. Across the estuary, on the hillside a kilometer away, the winds blow past a 65-meter statue of *Christo Rei*, "Christ the King," His arms outstretched. He squarely faces *Casal Ventoso*.

All these winds funnel through the surrounding valleys, and are driven up the hill of *Casal Ventoso*, hence its name: the "Marriage of the Winds."

There is nothing romantic about the place. The area looks like a war-zone. A single word is descriptively suggestive: the place is hideous. There is rubbish everywhere. Thousands of small cardboard boxes litter the ground. They are the remains of the free needle kits provided by the Portuguese Ministry of Health. In the box are two disposable syringes, two gauze wipes, a condom, and a tiny bottle of sterile water. An instruction sheet on how to inject safely is included for the beginner.

111

The bottom third of the hill is rubble. Buildings have collapsed, or been bulldozed. In the middle third are shells of buildings, many without roofs or windows. The top third is a tired but functioning *barrio*. Children's clothes hang from the wash lines.

The population mirrors the topography. BMWs and Mercedes roar in and out of the upper regions of *Casal Ventoso*. They are driven by the heroin dealers, or businessmen in suits and silk ties who have come to score. They leave quickly.

A little lower down the hill, the taxis predominate, affording a measure of anonymity to the addict who still has something to care about. They too aren't in *Ventoso* long.

Below the taxis are several hundred pedestrians, mostly men, moving up and down the hill. Some stride, as on a mission. Others wander and stumble, mission accomplished.

There is a ludicrous order, even in this hell. Amidst the desolation and waste, the men form a lethargic queue as they wait their turn in the dealers' den. They line up for the very thing that makes an absolute shambles of their lives.

The afternoon we were on the hill there were two police officers, standing not a half block away. The line-ups, some forty men long, were easily within the peripheral view of the cops. The police presence was a farce. At the head of each line is a watchman. If a cop comes near, he warns the dealers; they immediately close the store, and disappear below into a labyrinth of tunnels that connect the houses.

Just down the hill from the dealers, we watched as a young man kept thrusting a needle in his forearm. He couldn't get up a vein. With the needle still in his arm, he bent down and pulled out the shoelace from his left shoe. With one end in his teeth, he tied it around his arm as a tourniquet. He clenched his fist and worked the needle around for ten minutes. Full addiction often requires ten hits a day – if there's enough money, more. That means 300 needle penetrations per month. At that rate, the veins don't stand up long.

On a bit of levelish ground stood two weather-beaten tents – heroin huts for the discreet. The tent landlord collects his rent – a few drops of heroin from each of his customers. A few yards away, a well-dressed young man barely managed to stay on his feet as he swayed back and forth. The syringe was still in his arm. He stared at the needle, as if frozen, for fifteen minutes. A young woman, gaunt and dirty, emerged from one of the tents. A large grimy bandage was wrapped around much of her neck. An open abscess, a suicide attempt, or a knife wound?

Towards the bottom are the destitute. They seem to be clinging to the side of the hill. They are too weak to stand. Clusters of four or five men huddle around small fires, sharing needles. One couldn't find his jugular vein by himself. He solicited the help of his friend. A hundred feet away, seated in the rubble, another addict had his shoe off. His arms had become unusable long ago. He was shooting up into the vein in the arch of his foot. Another sat with his trousers around his ankles. He was shooting into his privates.

At the bottom of *Ventoso* are those who have no money for heroin. They sit amongst the rubbish, fixated with the needle. They inject water and lemon, imagining the heroin they are craving. For hours they seem to take an almost erotic pleasure working the needle.

We saw three bodies sprawled motionless amidst the rubble. There is an average of two deaths a day in *Casal Ventoso*.

My friend Alan was with me. He knows the heart of God more than anyone I know. We'd been in *Ventoso* about half an hour when he said, "I just cried out, 'God, my heart's not big enough to take all of this in.'" There were tears in his eyes. "As soon as I said that, I felt the Lord say, 'Mine is.'"

We spent an afternoon in *Casal Ventoso* handing out Betel flyers. Translated, the Portuguese read: "Don't be discouraged. If you have problems with drugs or alcohol, or if you feel marginalized, contact us. We have had the same problems that you have. Betel offers help, FREE." At the bottom of the page were printed the church address, and both the local and international telephone numbers.

Some on the hill had no interest at all, and walked straight past us. None of the addicts were in any way hostile. Very few were cold towards us. The majority took the flyer and pocketed it. Some approached us, wanting to talk. Betel has a good reputation and is well regarded on the hill.

Fig. 1: *Elliott Tepper, International Director of Association Betel, on his "Betelephone".*

Fig. 2: *Lindsay McKenzie, Co-founder of Association Betel, and Director of Betel-Italy (image taken from video).*

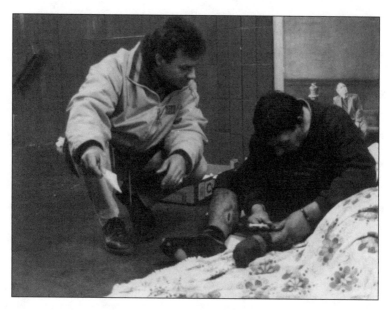

Fig. 3: *A former addict sharing his faith in a subway how his life has been changed through Betel.*

Fig. 4: *Relaxing with a game of ping-pong in Betel, Naples.*

Fig. 5: *An addict in a heroin-induced stupor in Vertedero, Madrid.*

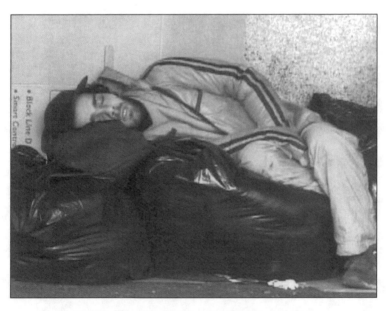

Fig. 6: *A heroin addict in a Naples railway station (image taken from video).*

Fig. 7: *Jave Gonzalez, 8 March 1989,*
on admission to Betel.

Fig. 8: *Pastor Jave Gonzalez,*
26 February 2000.

Fig. 9: *Alexis Peres,*
House Leader.

Fig. 10: *Pastor Juan Carlos Matesanz*
(image taken from video).

Fig. 11: *Shooting up in Canal Ventoso, Lisbon.*

Fig. 12: *A new life in Lisbon – looking forward to lunch at Betel.*

119

Fig. 13: *The senior pastors and spouses of Betel, Madrid,
many of whom are HIV-positive or have had sclerosis of the liver.*

Fig. 14:
The men's house in Madrid

Fig. 15: *"Break Free" – the outreach bus for Betel-Birmingham, England.*

Fig. 16: *Betel "cumbre" worship, 26 February 2000, Madrid.*

A young woman was the first to seek us out. Her eyes were badly infected. She had a jagged red scar that ran from the bridge of her nose down to the bottom of her right nostril. With desperate, sincere longing, she asked if she came to Betel, could she bring her child with her as well. She was told, "Of course." She nodded, and walked away.

A young man approached Perry, a WEC missionary who had come from Madrid to help as one of our translators. The addict tapped Perry on the shoulder, and asked for a flyer. "Betel – is it really free?" Perry nodded. The young man said, "OK, I want to go now. Please take me in now."

He had been on heroin only two years, and his wife was threatening to take their two daughters back to Angola, their family home, if he didn't get himself sorted. He waited around with us until it was time for us to leave; on the way to the van, he said, "I'd rather give up drugs than give up my family."

Later that night, at the end of the church meeting, he came forward to respond to the call of Jesus on his life. Tears streamed down his face as he prayed.

He wasn't alone. Fifteen others stood at his side. Roughly fifteen per cent of the evening's congregation came forward to give their lives to Christ. At the very end of the meeting, the same guys that only months earlier had queued for heroin in *Casal Ventoso* were now standing, waiting patiently in church. The same hands were now holding out their Bibles to us. The needle scars and abscesses were so very evident on their forearms. The men were asking us to write something on the inside cover – a Bible verse, a word of encouragement, something to mark a milestone in their walk to victory.

I spent part of an afternoon with two Portuguese Betelitos in a coffee shop near the men's house in Fonte da Telha.

José Luis is a handsome, athletic thirty-year-old, with bright eyes and a winsome smile.[1] He grew up in Curraleira, a *barrio* similar to *Casal Ventoso*, on the north side of Lisbon. By the time he was ten years old, he was addicted to hashish. His mother was a heroin dealer; he injected heroin for fifteen years. José Luis' three brothers are all addicts. One is presently in prison. Another is a member of the Bilbao Betel family, in the

Basque country of northern Spain. The third was last heard of somewhere in Switzerland.

Early in the last year of his addiction, 1997, José and one of his brothers robbed their mother. They took her drug stockpile, her jewels, and her cash. She called the police on them – but reported only the missing jewels and cash. To evade arrest, José fled to *Casal Ventoso*. Because he had family connections, he got work as a watchman. His job was to stand at the door of a dealer's house, and announce police arrivals. His pay: a quarter gram of coke, and a quarter gram of heroin. Pay-day: every four hours.

His weight dropped fifty-five pounds, and his health quickly failed.

José's brother had been in Betel for three days, and told him about the kindnesses he'd received. "If you want to stay out of jail, you'd better go to Betel too." José heeded his older brother's counsel, and joined the Lisbon family in December 1998. He was baptized seven months later. When I asked him about that decision, José Luis grinned from ear to ear. "That was the smartest thing I've ever done with my life, and the happiest day."

I asked, "Do you think it's going to last?"

He looked me squarely in the eye. "Yeah; it's going to last."

In the past year, José Luis has also returned to the *Ventoso* on evangelistic outreaches. "All of my old friends are either dead, or in prison." Every time he walks the hill, he fights feelings of revulsion. "I've wasted so much of my life."

With the addicts, he fearlessly and passionately shares all that Jesus has done for him. "I know that any one of them could die right there, with their next hit."

Paulo Barao is thirty-four years old. He did drugs for half his life. "For the last twelve years of addiction, my first waking thought was heroin." Paulo was in prison three times for robbery. His family refused to see him in his last year of addiction.

I asked him about *Casal Ventoso*. He knew it well. That's where he bought his drugs.

He first met the Betel guys while they were handing out flyers on the hill. They asked him, "Do you want to get off drugs?"

"Of course. Every addict wants out. It's just that there's no hope. It isn't possible."

He took the Betel literature, put it in his pocket and forgot about it.

Several nights later he took the flyer out – he was desperate for drugs but had no money. He felt that his only option was to phone Betel. He knew the Betelitos were ex-addicts, but he thought they were crazy, talking about *"quitar el mono"* – "getting the monkey off your back", "cold turkey" – without methadone. He didn't believe it was possible. Nevertheless, he called Betel and they came and picked him up the next morning at a pre-arranged rendezvous. (Of every ten that call Betel, only one keeps their appointment.) Paulo arrived in Betel in February 1998.

His first impression of Betel was that of shock. "My life was drugs, violence, robbery and prison. Suddenly people were *giving* me food and clothes. I couldn't believe the kindnesses. No one had ever given me anything before."

He described what happened over the next few months as a process in which he drew near to Christ. In his room he proudly displays the photograph of his baptism in the Atlantic Ocean eight months after his arrival at Betel. One year after his arrival at Betel he was made a house leader. He now extends care to seventeen guys, and oversees one of the *Rastros* – the thrift shops. He regularly preaches both to the guys in his house and at the church. He frequently returns to *Ventoso* with the other Betelitos on outreach missions.

"I feel two things when I go back there. The first is gratitude to God for Betel, and the way He has used them to rescue my life. The second is an overwhelming sense of impotence – so many guys are still so lost. Even though I was one of them, it's still difficult to talk to them. Once in *Ventoso*, there's no escape. No one ever escapes the grip of *Ventoso* in his own strength. Only God can open the eyes, and give the desire to leave."

The reason Paulo responded: "In one special moment, God intervened and opened my eyes. I realized – there's no other way."

Paulo was one of our guides at *Ventoso*. He took us to *o muro de vergonha*, "the wall of shame," the retaining wall of the railway tunnel at the bottom of the hill. Two years earlier, he was one of the shells huddled against the wall.

Betel is full of remarkable stories of radical life-change like those of José Luis and Paulo. I asked Kent Martin how transformation of such magnitude takes place. In answering the question, he spoke of one of the key leadership positions in Betel's ministry.

"The house leader must be the most mature, committed, organized, loyal, spiritual and sacrificial servant-member of any communal Betel household. Hopefully, he or she has also got some business sense!

"Because the house leaders live with the Betelitos, they are the senior leadership's 'eyes' and 'window' into the spiritual and relational health of the households. They are also probably the first genuine Christian role model most recovering addicts have lived with, making their role as peer-discipler indispensable. House leaders' changed lives model faith and freedom without equal. I've observed something remarkable, even mystical, at this level: they serve not only to sow the first seeds of hope in broken lives, but their example seems a vital ingredient to spiritual germination."

Jorge Rato is the house leader in Mejorada del Campo, the largest of Betel's men's houses in Madrid.

"I usually spend most of the day working in one of our used furniture stores. No one at Betel gets paid; customers often ask why I am willing to work without earning anything. Before I answer, I call some of the guys around me.

'My "salary" is to take a guy near death, someone heroin has destroyed, and see him changed over time. When there's a smile on his face, and a different look in his eyes, that's my salary.

"When a broken antique is repaired, what's it worth? What's a reconstructed life worth?"

Jorge's face is covered with scars. He has a raspy, gravelly voice, and bright eyes. Big, frequent smiles spread over his whole face.

He proudly flashes his false teeth. For three years, until June 1997, Jorge lived in the train tunnel at the base of *Casal Ventoso*. (The train that uses the tracks is a day-liner, so many of the addicts at the bottom sleep in the tunnel at night.) He was HIV-positive, and had infections throughout his body. Candida had spread from his mouth to his eye. He eventually went blind for a time. He was covered with abscesses. The few teeth he had were rotten stubs.

When the Betelitos were doing an outreach mission, someone had handed Jorge a flyer, and talked about a free center. Jorge had tried other centers, but always ended up back at *Ventoso*. The *chicos* talked him into trying Betel.

On his third day in residence, one of the senior pastors, Juan Carlos, was visiting Betel-Lisbon, and befriended Jorge. They spent the afternoon together, and Jorge felt he had found someone he could trust, someone who understood him. When Juan Carlos was leaving Lisbon to return to the Madrid center, he said, "I have space in the van for one more. Anyone want to go?" He looked straight at Jorge. Jorge crawled into the van.

"Those first weeks at Betel weren't easy. I was a diligent communist and a committed atheist. I didn't believe in God, and everything here was new. But though I didn't understand what they were talking about, I felt good. It felt right. Sometimes.

"Sometimes I'd hear the testimonies of the senior guys, and I'd think, 'They have to be lying. There's no way. I don't believe it.' But little by little, I started opening the drawer of my heart, and pulling out things I'd hidden in there that I didn't want to live with. Things about being adopted. About being unwanted. All the reasons I started taking drugs.

"I started to think about the things I did while I was on drugs ... Feelings buried down deep started to surface. Part of my communism caused me to deny my feelings, and to disregard anything spiritual. All of that was turning. The hard exterior was cracking open.

"I had tried to be the guardian, the controller of my life. That took me to the bottom of *Ventoso*. I thought, 'I've always tried everything; I better try what these guys have.' I knew I had the AIDS virus, and I figured I better try Jesus before I had to face death. I accepted what was being said about Christ, and I began to see miracles – one of the first was reconciliation with my family. They had made it very clear they never wanted to see me ever again.

"That was an 'external miracle.' The first 'internal' miracle was the peace that came over me. I used to be very nervous, but not since I gave my life to Christ. Now there is a sense of hope, and a sense of victory, even with the AIDS – I don't lose sleep over it. Before, I would stare at the ceiling all night long.

"The biggest miracle was what has happened to my heart. I used to see some of the senior guys cry. I had no tears, ever. My heart was too hard. But at one *cumbre*, someone prayed for me, and I started to weep. Old tears from way back in my past suddenly broke through to the surface in a flood. It was only a few days afterwards that the Lord showed me a verse, one that just kept ringing in my ears for weeks – it's in Joel 2:13: *'Rend your hearts and not your garments.'*

"I used to be tormented by past memories – especially of life with my alcoholic mother. I had been praying, 'Lord, whether I cry or not, please heal these memories.' As soon as I asked for that, a fight started in my heart. All sorts of fears and doubts got stirred up, and there were decisions I had to make.

"Part of me wanted to keep certain areas in my life a secret from God. There were things I didn't want to yield. In the *cumbre*, the tears flooded that stuff out. They opened the areas I'd shut off, and I let God have it all."

After a year and a half at Betel, Jorge was made the senior house leader in Mejorada. He presently oversees twenty-five guys. The Spanish name for the position is the *responsable*, "the responsible one." It is up to Jorge to co-ordinate the functioning of the house, and organize the shops and the vans. He is the one who must keep the balance between work, and the men's spiritual growth. Jorge is remarkably tender in the care that he extends to the men.

When I was in Madrid in September 1999, I took a team with me. Some of them stayed in the Mejorada house. In their dorm room, there were five bunk beds, for ten men. Just before lights out, Jorge came in to check with the guys to make sure everything was okay. He went over to the guy on the top bunk across the room. He was having his devotions; he and Jorge recited a few of the Scripture memory verses the *chico* was working on. Then Jorge joked a while with the guy in the bunk below. He crossed the room again, and spoke with one of the new guys. He was detoxing, and he was not at all sure where he wanted to be. When Jorge had finished encouraging him to stay, he reached out and tousled the guy's hair. It wasn't in a tap, tap, tap, patronizing way, but like a loving father with his kids at bedtime.

Jorge is a huge-hearted pastor. "I came from a town where people threw me out of the taverns. People would cross the street to get out of my way. My family wouldn't have anything to do with me. The police were always after me. They frequently beat me. Now people phone Betel, and ask, 'Is Jorge there – the Portuguese guy?' The same people who would have nothing to do with me now ask, 'Can you get my son into Betel? Can you look after him? What do I have to do to get him in there? How soon can we get him there? We can get him in there now? We're on our way.'

"Months later, I send them photographs of the same guy, so that they can see how much he's changed."

Jorge is also a passionate evangelist. After he'd been at Betel eighteen months, he returned to Lisbon to visit his family. The second day he was with them he told them he was going out. They asked where. He told them, "To the *Ventoso*." Jorge said their hair stood on end.

"No, no! Not for drugs – to hand out Betel literature!"

On the hill, some of the addicts remembered him. They had a single question for him: "What's happened to you?"

"Where I once went with shame, now I go with my head held high."

In eight return visits to the *Ventoso*, Jorge has brought between thirty and forty guys back to Betel-Lisbon. He's even spoken with the dealer that gave him his first shot of heroin. Jorge talked *him* into coming to Betel.

To understand further how life-change is imparted, I asked Jorge to describe what a day at Betel looks like for a house leader.

"The two men who are to prepare the breakfast have to wake up an hour before the rest of the house. They have to start the generator for the power, and they put on the coffee. They set the table, and put out the breakfast. Then, at 7.00, they knock on the door of each of the dorm rooms, and turn on the lights.

"The men have fifteen minutes, from lights on, till breakfast. They've all showered the night before, so all they have to do is go to the bathroom, and make their beds. The difficulty lies with the new guys, who are going through their 'turkey.' They're the slow ones. Breakfast – cookies, rolls, and coffee – only lasts fifteen minutes.

"The men then have half an hour to do their teeth, shave and wash. As we have devotions in the dining room, the breakfast tables have to be taken down, and the chairs are put in a circle. At 8 o'clock, the devotional starts, and everyone has to be there. On time.

"If a guy is in the worst of his detox he and his shadow will miss a few days, but as soon as he's able, he's expected to attend.

"We have devotionals five days a week, and three or four of those we do ourselves. One or two will be done by one of the pastors, or by a leader from another house. Guys who've been with us for four or five months sometimes testify and share a scripture verse or passage that has changed their lives. When we take the devotional, we usually preach for fifteen or twenty minutes. As house leader, I preach once or twice a week. That's my biggest challenge: to make the gospel real and practical for the guys. Most of the new men are hearing about Jesus for the first time, so it has to be interesting and it has to mean something to them.

"Good devotionals have an immediate effect. We get encouraged, both from the Word, and in the worship that follows. They help us deal with the day. The guys discuss the devotionals in the vans and at work. They give us a chance to talk about real problems, and God's solutions, with guys we're living with. Work, health, community friction, clashing personalities – it's not hard to come up with sermon illustrations!

"For instance, the house is often divided into two groups. There are those who are griping and complaining about everything, and there are those who see the house as their family, their home. We're always trying to draw the complainers into the family.

"Then there's the chief, practical problem we have: *el chibato*, the 'honour among thieves.' The guys won't tell the truth because there's a code on the street that outlaws ratting on one another. That means that we never know, for instance, who stole food from the kitchen. We ask, and all we get are dumb looks. Someone's smoking. No one knows who. *El chibato*.

"The lying is so destructive, because covering over sin is also sin. To get guys to tell the truth is the hardest part of community life. Without it, we can't work. If we don't have one guy on a work team that's conquered *el chibato*, we can't trust that team to go out by itself. Without it, truth can't flow, and we have no idea what the guys get up to. Conquering *el chibato* is one of the first steps towards becoming a *responsable*.

"We talk about *el chibato* in the devotionals a lot. I continually challenge the guys to take a public stand for truth, because I want them to be able to be strong against temptation. Once you take that stand, the guys doing wrong will no longer include you, because they know that you no longer honor *el chibato*.

"After the devotional, everybody heads to the work board. There the day's jobs are posted. Every night I meet with the older *responsables*, usually about midnight – it's always too late – and we plan who's going to do the next day's jobs. We work through the list: who has to be taken to the doctor or dentist, who has to go to court, or social services. With twenty-five men in the house, somebody's going somewhere every day. We plan who will do the devotional. Then we work through the different jobs we have, and mix the new guys with more experienced men. It's a challenge to strike the right balance.

"Once everyone knows their assignments, the vehicles are checked for oil and water. The drivers are supposed to do it every morning. We've learned the hard way – too many motors have been burned out.

"Then it's off. Some are in the *Rastros*, or in the dispensary (the food bank), the carpenters' shop, the brick masons' shop, the junk yard, or delivering Betel calendars around the neighborhood.

"On the job board is also the pairing of the shadows. Every day, we leave responsible men in the house who will supervise the new guys. They help the newest arrivals through their withdrawals. When a new guy comes in, he is assigned a vacant bunk; the guy above or below him is a *responsable*, and knows that he now has a shadow. He's the first to stay with him and help him twenty-four hours a day. If the new guy wants to go for a walk, you go for a walk. If he wants to talk, you talk. If he's in pain and needs a massage, you do it. New guys are never left alone, not even to go to the toilet. We all know how vulnerable an addict is in those early days and weeks.

"Once a guy is through the worst of his *mono*, he works alongside a *responsable*, cleaning the house, and preparing the meals. It is so important for the new guys to clean the house. I myself came from the *Ventoso* – I lived in a cave. I was always hungry; I ate out of a dumpster behind a restaurant, if I was strong enough to fight off the street dogs. I never showered.

"To shave and shower daily, and to take responsibility for your bed, to have clean sheets and clothes, to sit at a table that's neatly set, and to care for the house – the value of these few simple acts makes you feel like a person again. It begins to restore something of your human dignity.

"We don't have to ask a new guy how he's doing – we just look at his bunk and closet."

"Shadowing is the hardest job at Betel. It's much harder than working in the *Rastros*. That's why we now take turns. With the brand new guys, it's a 24-hour job, so we take it in shifts. Someone has to stay up all night with the guys doing their *mono* – both to care for them, and to keep them from stealing everything in the house! One night the *chico* on watch fell asleep. A new guy took one of the wheelbarrows, filled it with all our power tools, and disappeared.

"The guys who come to us having been on methadone have to be watched very carefully, because if they've taken it with cocaine, there is the possibility of a heart attack. Three guys have died that way in the last two months.

"Shadowing is hard because there are so many tensions, disappointments, heartaches, and frustrations. One of the first times I shadowed a guy, we were working at the car-parts shop. He was through the worst of his *mono*, but said he wasn't feeling well. I made a mistake – I left him alone while I went to get him some tea. While I was gone he jumped into a customer's car and drove off. We never saw him, or the car, or the customer, ever again!

"One of the next guys I had to shadow drove me nuts. It was so bad, I wanted to strangle him. I'd ask someone to give me a break, and I'd go behind the house and cry out to God. 'Why did You have me with *him*. I'm not getting anywhere. What more do You want from me?'

"Every morning, I'd check the job sheet, and there I was again, having to shadow the same guy. I'd disappear behind the house. 'I know You don't want me to leave, Lord, but this guy won't leave either, so what am I supposed to do?' That guy drove me to read the Bible as never before. I started to see how the Lord was slowly molding the guy's character, but the bigger work was how *I* was being changed. I even got to the place where I wondered if he wasn't assigned to shadow *me* – it seemed that the Lord was using him to do more in me than I did in him.

"I had to swallow a lot of things I didn't want to deal with. It was very hard to humble myself, and serve him. I had to make myself very small. One day I had to ask him to forgive me for my attitude. I had to surrender my feelings of superiority. I realized that it really didn't matter how long I'd been at Betel or how well I knew the routine. I had come from the same place he had come from. We were exactly the same. I just got to Betel before he did. That was the only difference.

"We teach the *responsables* that the main job of the shadow is not to lay down the law continuously. For every one thing they tell a new guy he *can't* do, they need to tell him five things he *can* do. What we have to do is teach a new mathematics – the new guys need to stop counting what they can't do – they can't shoot up, they can't smoke, they can't curse – all the things they've 'lost.' Instead, they need to start counting the good things they're gaining – how their health is improving, how they're getting stronger. How they have good friends who look after them. They have a clean place to live, and decent food to eat.

"A lot of these guys have come from prison, and they have real troubles with authority. If we don't stay on their level, there will be problems. For instance, I never tell a new guy he can't go anywhere alone. He can't – that's one of the rules at Betel. But if

I *tell* him that, we might have a fight. Instead, I ask him to go somewhere with *me*. I tell him that *I* don't want to go alone. That helps make him feel significant.

"Every week, I meet with the *responsables*, and talk about how they're relating to the new guys. We all know that the way we put things, the tone – it means everything. If we don't show grace, there's a good chance a new guy will take off. So, we're constantly saying 'we', rather than 'you,' reminding ourselves that we're drug addicts, just like the new guys.

"The men return from work between 8 and 9 o'clock. They shower, and once everybody is home, we sit down to eat. We wait for everyone, because that's what good families do. All we ask is, if a team is going to be late, they should phone and let us know.

"After dinner, it's dishes. Everybody in the house is on the dish list. We all take turns. The only exception is the guys on the *mono*. They get time off until they've passed it. What changes the rotation is *platos*, 'dishes.' If a guy gets caught smoking, or drinking, or disrespects authority – it's a discretionary call – they get put on dishes. They can get *platos* for a day, or two, or, indefinitely.

"For a guy with a bad attitude, I'll say, '*Platos* until you change things around.' The longest I've ever known someone to be on *platos* is eight or nine weeks. For most guys, it's a war on pride. *Platos* will either drive them away from the center, or make them a new man. They get to choose. A good leader knows how delicate a balance *platos* is.

"Normally the generator is turned off at midnight, so the men have a couple of hours most nights to talk or read. We'll watch only the really important football games mid-week; otherwise the TV is on only on Saturday and Sunday afternoons.

"They don't call a guy a *responsable* for nothing. Wednesday and Friday nights there are meetings at the church. We eat very late on those nights. After church, and after the meal, the *responsables* meet and plan the next day's duties. It makes for a short sleep. On Monday nights we have the central leaders' meetings. And if an addict phones in the middle of the night, or just shows up, it's the *responsables* who go and pick him up and look after him.

"It's certainly not in me to do all of that. I often don't know how I manage it all. Even though there's lots of stress and problems and responsibilities, I have peace.

"I'm also learning how to pray! Very often when things are getting to me, I go to the New Testament and read the words of Jesus. They're not just something He said two thousand years ago. I take them as His words for me today. I pray, and ask the Lord to give me the capacity to do what I have to do. I ask for strength, but it doesn't come like a formula. He always surprises me.

"The Lord and I still have our debates, and He's constantly turning me around. I'm still learning to do things His way."

Betel's globalization keeps life interesting. Luis, a Spaniard, was checking a new guy into the Betel in Jackson Heights, New York. He had read him Betel's rules.[2] Though very stoned, the man said he understood them, and wanted to do whatever he had to do to change his life.

Luis recorded the man's name, and the fact that he had no address or next of kin. No infectious diseases. No drugs, prescription or otherwise. No weapons. The man had checked his money and valuables, and the last of his cigarettes. Luis asked him to empty his pockets, which the man did.

Luis' English wasn't very good, and the new guy spoke no Spanish, so working through the check-in had been a bit of a challenge. Luis had something in his eye, and was rubbing it. He asked, *"Alguna cosa mas?"* "Anything more?" Luis was asking after anything else in the man's pockets, all the while, rubbing his eye. The new guy paused, shook his head, and pulled out his glass eyeball and put it on the table. *Luis'* eyeballs nearly fell out on the floor!

Those visitors to Betel who know their church history often comment that the Betel communities have a quasi-monastic feel about them. Kent and I spoke at some length about this while I was in Betel-Birmingham. The men are living the five classic monastic vows – poverty, chastity, obedience, conversion of manners, and stability (commitment to a local community).

Kent was so engaged by the discussion, I bought him a copy of *The Rule of Saint Benedict*. He says that the guys now regularly expect him to quote Benedict in the midst of his sermons!

Salvatore Lerro has been the house leader in Betel-Naples since March 1999. He is one who well knows both how hard and how transforming it is to live with Betel's rules. Salvatore stayed in the Naples house from December 1995 through August 1996. He left after eight months, stating that he wanted to get on with his life. He didn't do well on his own.

"Those first eight months at Betel were enough to make me feel like I was part of a family, and I really missed it. My business was going reasonably well, and I was working on my marriage, but there were problems, and it wasn't long before I returned to the heroin. I couldn't get free of a twenty-year habit. My marriage broke up, and my parents closed their doors. I slept at work until I lost the job, and then lived on the streets. I missed my Betel family so much that I came back to where I knew I belonged.

"I returned to Betel in December 1997. I'd been gone sixteen months, and I had lost so much weight, and was so filthy, Lindsay didn't recognize me. It was only when I told him my name that he recognized my voice.

"Being part of a family was so important to me, the rules that had been such a hassle the first time I was at Betel were different now. In terms of Betel's rules, all the guys go through three stages: first, there's contempt. Second, we get used to them. Third, we come to see them as useful for our lives.

"During my first stay at Betel, and the first months of my return, I was in a rebellious state. 'Who do they think they are, telling me I can't smoke?' I didn't like the rules, and I didn't like the leadership. What made me stay was the other guys. They were from the same background as me, but they were coping with the rules. I saw such a change in them, and I wanted what they had. I'd look at a guy I knew on the streets. 'We both came from the same place, only he's done worse. I never committed armed robbery ... yet look at his life. He's changed so much, maybe I can change too.' Because he quit smoking, I figured I could too. The guys were happier than I was, so I figured there must be a point where you can get used to the rules, and even like them.

"But it was hard. There were lots of times when I wanted to wipe the lot. I'd swear under my breath all the time. It wasn't just the rules that made me growl. All of the spiritual talk, the devotionals, the singing; it really got to me. The thing that kept me going was all that I had suffered on the street. The thought of returning was unthinkable. There was no other way. I gritted my teeth and put up with the lot.

"In one meeting, God broke me, and I started to cry. The floodgates opened and I bawled and bawled and bawled. It was more than just a normal crying. It felt like a cleansing, a purging. All of the pent-up anger and the pent-up suffering got washed away, and I felt free. I got up from the floor a different man. The hardness was gone. I didn't feel stuck, or bound up inside.

"I had tasted something so different, something I had never experienced before. No drug had given me anything like it. It was the 'something' that I'd always looked for, always searched for. That's why I did all the drugs. I used to think that everybody always talking about Jesus was ridiculous. From that point on, I felt a huge hunger to know more about Him.

"And I had been such a selfish person, all I thought about was myself. That changed. I was a solitary kind of person. I didn't like being with others. The inferiority I felt inside lifted. I wanted to be like the other guys, sociable and open, and that desire grew. I relaxed and started liking the guys. Instead of going off to be by myself, I joined them in the lounge.

"There was a guy named Aniello, and he was having a hard time in withdrawal. He was very sick, vomiting a lot. I could never deal with that – I always thought I was going to be sick myself. Any other time I saw or heard someone being sick, I'd leave, fast. Watching Aniello, I had a most surprising desire to help. I brought him a blanket, and pulled the heater over closer to him. I made him some herbal tea, and gave him a back massage to help the pain he felt in his kidneys.

"I was amazed to see that my kindnesses brought a change in him. It was like he suddenly had a will to fight. We were two fiancés – our hearts were joined together in this thing.

"When I saw him smile for the first time, it produced in me a wave of joy that I had looked for and ached for all of my life. I had looked for it everywhere – it was the joy I'd hoped to find in marriage, in my children, in the drugs – but it produced the very opposite, because I was too selfish to know it.

"I found it the very moment that I reached out and helped someone else. I know it sounds like an overstatement – but it really felt like it was the first time I'd ever really helped someone else. I had lived life like a turtle covered with a protective shell. I was so defensive, and looked only after myself.

"Now I felt useful, and finally felt that I'd become someone who had a purpose, a mission. I had tried to put so many things in my hands, but they always ended up empty. But this time, I felt that this little sacrifice was life.

"When I saw guys changing because of a little bit of help I was able to give them, it gave me strength to do more. Aniello was the first, then Pasquale, then Giovanni . . . And a day or two later, they'd come up, give me a hug, and they'd say, 'I love you. Thank you.' Life then made sense.

"After that, the rules really weren't a problem. They were rules for life. They were rules of the house, and Betel was my home."

Life's counterpoint is never a distant horizon at Betel. A recent e-mail from Kent reads:

> "We learned just yesterday that Robert died early Sunday morning. Ten days ago, we had to put him out for a week for fighting and his poisoned attitude. We received him back last Friday night, but he walked out Saturday morning, saying he wasn't able to abide by the rules. His family found him dead in his sleep Monday morning – methadone overdose they think. It's a sad but alarming wake up call for everyone here.
>
> It was his sixth time with us.
>
> We trust God for mercy . . ."

Rules alone certainly do not bring about life-change. Experiencing the power of the Spirit, and knowing the intervention of a loving Father are more persuasive than any discipline. Alexis Peres is alive today through the power of healing prayer, and because of that experience, he has come to know a vibrant faith in Jesus Christ.

One afternoon, while at the Madrid Betel, I locked myself out of Elliott's office. No one with a key could be located, but Alexis happened to be in the office. When he understood my predicament, he walked over to the office kitchen, picked up the bread knife that was on the counter, and walked over to the office door. Fifteen seconds later, after a bit of deft wiggling of the knife, the door swung open. A quiet smile broke across his broad face, and then he winked at me. In most churches, Alexis' skill set would be considered unusual. But not at Betel.

Alexis is a big, stocky man, with thick, black, curly hair. He is quiet, almost shy. His gentle eyes are quick to sparkle with life. Since July 1997, his responsibilities include care for over seventy men, four men's houses, the Zulema mechanics shop, and the Mariblanca chicken farm.

With five other mechanics, he keeps the greater Madrid area fleet on the road – fifty-seven vans, and twelve cars. When they can, they attend to the twelve vans from some of the smaller centers nearby. Nearly all of the vehicles are tired. Alexis and his crew continuously and unashamedly practice vehicular cannibalism. They glean three quarters of the needed parts from the Betel junkyard. He spends $2,300 a month on parts that he is unable to scrounge.

Alexis was in prison five times, for robbery and trafficking heroin. For over a decade, he was addicted to cocaine. His end-use drug was heroin. On his last prison visit his father told Alexis, "Because of what you've done, you are no longer my son. As far as I'm concerned, you're dead."

Alexis tried a couple of rehabs, but both times only stayed a day. When he returned a third time, the Director told him he wasn't welcome; if he wanted help, he should try Betel. He arrived in Betel Madrid in 1990, and stayed for a year. Thinking he was ready to lead a normal life, he left, and was soon back into the cocaine and heroin. Nine months later he returned to Betel a sick man. He was taken to hospital, where he started vomiting blood. He had bronchitis, and it was discovered that a kidney had burst. He also found out that he was HIV-positive.

One of the oldest Betelitos, Antonio *El Abuelo* "the Grandfather," came to visit Alexis in hospital, and prayed for his restoration, body and soul. Alexis felt forgiveness for the first time in his life. Because he so felt the power and presence of God, he also knew he wasn't going to die just then.

After hearing Alexis' testimony, I asked him a question: "When a new *chico* gives his life to Jesus, how do you disciple him?" A puzzled look came over Alexis' face. Surely it was obvious. I asked him again, and he put the obvious into words.

"I put him in coveralls, and hand him a wrench. While we work together, I pray, 'Holy Spirit, what would You have me speak into this man's life?'"

I looked at the team that was with me. Now we had the puzzled looks.

"What about the notebooks? How can you disciple someone without a notebook? Where do they fill in the blanks?"

Slowly we realized – at Betel, it's not so much filling in the blanks as it is filling in a life.

I asked Alexis to tell us some discipleship stories. His huge pastor's heart quickly became evident.

"The first thing, the most important thing a new guy experiences is the love he receives from us. From guys that are just like him. I don't hide my past – I tell them, 'I was like you. I was a drug addict, and did the same things as you did. Maybe worse.' And simply, what God has given to me, I give to them. They can have hope.

"We want the new guys to know that God is real. One of the ways we do that is by challenging them to challenge God. 'Put a test before God – see if He really does love you.' I tell them about the way I came to trust God. My leader, Juan Carlos, challenged me to test God. At the time, my mother had had her fifth heart attack. I asked, 'God, if You really exist, please help my mother to cut back on her medication. It's making her sick.' A few days later my mother called, and she told me that the doctor had taken her off all of the medication. God had my attention!

"We encourage the *chicos* to challenge God for both big and small things, but what the guys usually put before the Lord is the restoration of family – parents, wives, children. I've seen so many guys start to cry when they ask God to turn things so that their children will forgive them.

"José, for instance, asked God to heal the bitterness in his family. He prayed that the broken relationship with his parents would be restored. Not long afterwards, his mother started phoning. Next, his father came and visited him, and in the course of the visit dad told his son that he forgave him for robbing them, and bringing disgrace on the family. Two months later his sister called and invited him to her wedding. She hadn't spoken to him for four years.

"Until José had put these challenges before God, he was inattentive at devotions, never read his Bible, and never showed any interest in God. He was always contentious, and made little effort to change his street attitude. But after the first phone call from his mother, he began to seek God.

"During his early months at the center, José was called into court for a crime he had committed before coming to Betel. He had stolen a car, and he knew he would be facing both jail and a fine. We joined José in asking God for mercy, and he went to the hearing in peace. José felt he had to tell the truth, so he confessed the crime. He told the court about Betel, and showed the judge a letter written by the Betel lawyer who spoke of the process of his rehabilitation, and evidenced life change. The lawyer asked that he stay in Betel, rather than go to prison. The judge showed mercy. He was set free; not even a fine. The whole experience put something underneath José, a foundation. Ever since, he's solid in Christ.

"I had a particular *chico* in mind when I answered your discipleship question earlier. Some of the guys have done so much drugs, they come to us completely wiped. They know nothing about nothing. I was thinking of Miguel Lavapies – he was so wrecked he couldn't even tie his own shoelaces! I made both a mechanic and a Christian out of him. Making him a mechanic was the greater challenge!

"When he arrived at the house, Miguel's heart was very wounded. He and his girlfriend were shooting up beside a railroad track. He left her to get some cigarettes. When he came back, he found her dead. A train had come by, and she was too stoned to get out of the way. He blamed himself for her death, and felt tremendous guilt and condemnation.

"Miguel was my first disciple. Surprisingly, his suffering made him very tender and open. A couple of months after he arrived, he asked me point blank, 'What can I do to fix my heart? How can I feel better? How can I get free from this condemnation? How can I open my heart to God?' We were travelling on our way to the Betel in Albeceta, to work on their vans. We spoke more about his dead girlfriend, and I told him that I believed she was already in heaven. I told him, 'What you need to do is fix your life, so that one day, you can see her there.'

"Miguel started to cry, right there in the van. The tears looked so funny as they ran down his cheeks, and dropped onto his mechanic's overalls. He turned to me and said, 'You know what, I'm going to seek God.'

"We prayed together as we drove, and from that day, he became a Christian. He's since become a mechanic; he's part of the Madrid worship team, and he and his new wife, Merche, lead the couples' home."

In the eight years he's lived at Betel, Alexis estimates that he's led over a hundred guys to the Lord.

There is presently a great deal of debate over the legalization of hard drugs. In thoroughly secular societies, drug use is considered one of numerous lifestyle choices. On many fronts, the European Community no longer talks in terms of curing drug addicts, but rather of "damage reduction." They have come to this conclusion after years of disappointing experience with ineffective rehabilitation programs. The question for them is no longer how to stop drug use. Rather, it has become a twofold issue: how to improve the incurable addict's "quality of life," and at the same time, make drug usage less damaging to the general population. Alternatively, the state needs to take control of both the supply and the quality of street drugs. This in turn would diminish the illegal side of addiction, the thieving, dealing, prostitution, and violence that goes with it. Depending on the country, between four and seven of every ten in prison are incarcerated because of illegal drugs, trading, buying, selling or stealing. To put this in some perspective, illegal drug trafficking represents eight per cent of all international trade – $390 billion annually – exceeding global trade in cars, textiles or steel. In Britain, heroin addiction alone accounted for $2 billion of property crimes in 1997.[3]

Kent Martin reflected on some of Betel's distinctives. "The most significant reason conventional rehab programs have failed is that they are based on the premise that an addict is sick. That then makes them a 'patient,' and the professional care-giver is the one who has all the answers and solutions. There is an implicit passivity imposed on the addict; not insignificantly, the costs of his or her rehabilitation are covered by some external source, typically the tax-payers' dollars. This passivity means that there is little that can be demanded of the addict. As a care-giver, you can't 'cut across their will.' You can't make them do anything they don't want to do. You can offer counseling, or medication, and the only responsibility the patient has is perhaps a few household chores, or some therapeutic gardening.

"Betel turns all of that on its head. Betel is a self-supporting community of faith. It is not a funded rehab. The men and women, the Betelitos, are not 'residents' or 'patients,' but 'family.' The issue is not so much 'care,' but life lived with one another in Christ. The men and women are most definitely cared for, but not on a psychological basis where they engage in systematic counseling week after week. It's not 'Right, we have an hour – let's talk about why you're angry all the time.' Anger management happens when issues are dealt with at work, on the job, when somebody's frustrated, when they're impatient, when they've flown off the handle. In that moment, work is put aside, and things are dealt with.

"In terms of Christian discipleship, the process is far more incarnational than it is straight Bible memory work.

"Many drug addicts have never held much of a job. Some have been on welfare, the dole, all their lives, as were their parents. Some have never worked a 'legal' day in their lives. 'Work' was burglarizing, dealing, or prostitution.

"Everybody at Betel works. The new guys are usually around the residences for the first two weeks. They are going through detox, and they need constant supervision. Even so, they help with the household chores at the residences – washing floors and bathrooms, meal preparation, washing up, and working around the property. Even this poses a challenge to some. In the New York Betel, the house leader handed a new guy a broom.

Believe it or not, the man looked at it from top to bottom and asked, 'What's this?' He then asked, 'What's it for?'

"Most of the community's members work somewhere else, distributing Betel calendars and flyers, or picking up used furniture for the thrift shops. Some do gardening or painting. Some restore and reupholster furniture or repair used appliances. Others enjoy job-security: they maintain Betel's beat-up fleet of trucks and cars!

"There's a work maxim that says '15 per cent of what we do, we love; 15 per cent of what we do, we hate; and 70 per cent is unmemorable and mundane.' If the Betelitos don't come to terms with that truth, they'll always return to drugs, ever looking for an out, or the next 'high,' because they can't cope with the unexciting realities of life. That can't be taught in group therapy, or gleaned from a self-help book.

"The 'tools' of healing at Betel are simple enough – they are wrenches, shovels, steering wheels, paintbrushes, washcloths and ladles. It's only at work that you learn the frustrations of having to work; of sometimes doing what you don't like to do. But at the end of the day, there is the simple joy and satisfaction of being a productive person who has contributed something to the community.

"One of the questions Betel leadership is most frequently asked is, 'How do you motivate the guys? How do you get them to do *anything*?'

"Work is part of the Betel ethos. It is a non-negotiable – '*If* Betel, *then* work.' But like so much of life, this is more caught than taught. The newly arrived catch it from living alongside the more senior residents."

As I was speaking to Kent about these very dynamics, one of the guys passed by our open door, singing praise: 'Thank You for saving me . . . ' He was carrying a bucket and mop. There is such a pervasive and heartfelt gratitude for what God has done in the lives of the Betelitos.

Kent continued. "Visitors who work with addicts and alcoholics are typically amazed at how industrious Betel is, and at how little co-dependence there seems to be evidenced. To survive, the heroin addict has learned to be a master manipulator. There's the standing joke at Betel: 'How can you tell if an addict is lying? His lips are moving.' The guys that come to Betel know that they have come from an extremely destructive lifestyle. As they are introduced to Jesus Christ, the issues of their pride and rebelliousness and manipulative behavior are radically contrasted and confronted. Most of them need to have the word 'humility' defined.

"The definition comes by way of demonstration. Often the very first day at Betel, a new guy is introduced to servanthood, and shown what it is to humble himself. It's done very gently and lovingly, as their 'shadow,' the one looking after them that day, asks them to help with the house chores. They are not assigned a chore; rather, they work alongside someone. 'Give me a hand – I have to clean the toilets.' Detoxing eyes pop wide open, and a willful heart is challenged.

"After two weeks, more is expected of them. They've typically passed through their 'turkey,' and are more physically capable now. They may be moving furniture, or working in a garden. The larger dynamic is that they are learning to come under someone's authority. That's a brand-new world for most re-covering addicts.

"Over-reaction is a road that leads right to a wound, every time. When emotions are not congruent with the circumstances, you have a 'situation.' So, when a Betelito gets frustrated at work, or fed up taking direction, or he's made a mistake on the job and is self-conscious about it, issues of pride, or intolerance, or insecurity give rise to anger; the dynamics of work peel back the layers of the heart and lay bare the issues.

"Leadership is constantly trying to discern the deeper wound that generates the behavior, and then apply a bit of truth, often from one of the week's morning devotions or evening meetings, and then cover it with forgiveness and love. There are thou-sands of Betelitos who are walking miracles of 'grace lovingly applied, over time.'"

While at the Betel-Birmingham, I spent a day with Jason and Paul in a furniture truck, on pick-ups and deliveries. Both these lads have horrific drug and crime pasts. On our return to Betel for lunch and another load, we took a short cut, down a very narrow country lane. A camper van approached us. We pulled over as far as we could, and stopped, burying the left-side mirror in the hedge. As the van passed by, his mirror smashed the truck's driver-side mirror. Neither of the guys said a word. I had the sense that they didn't even swear silently to themselves! Just a raised eyebrow from Jason, and a dropped jaw from Paul.

Being able to bridle your tongue is no small thing. The following testimony demonstrates how Betel 'works.' William came to Betel-Birmingham on 9 February 1999. His is a story of a telling transformation of character.

William was hyperactive when he was a child. He had convulsions and was on Phenobarbital to calm his erratic and demanding behavior. He grew up with the impression that he wasn't really wanted as a child. His parents used to tell him, "You weren't born into this family; we found you." William was constantly told that he'd never be any good, that he'd never become anything or amount to anything. He was constantly compared to his brother, and told that he didn't measure up.

William worked hard to fulfill their expectations. "I wanted to get away from my natural family, but I so wanted to belong somewhere. I'd be with Rastas one minute, and with bikers the next. I'd be with skinheads, then with football hooligans. And whatever was going on, I had to be in the front of it. I had to take things to the limit, so people would be talking about me. There would be six guys having a fight in a pub – I'd get beat up the worst, or inflict the most pain, or be the one arrested. The front guys got the attention."

That spilled over into the drug scene, and very rapidly and frighteningly, into crime.

"When I was eighteen, I got into the motorcycle scene. We were staying up all night, taking LSD and speed. I'd do speed for three or four days, and go totally psychotic. I was working construction at the time, so I had some money. A dealer I met through the bike scene introduced me to heroin. I remember the first time I smoked heroin. It instantly took all my fears away. I felt like I'd found what I was looking for, because it took all the inhibitions, all the paranoia. I just went to sleep and had these dreams, these warm comfortable dreams. Speed would fix that, but then I'd get all psychotic again, and so it was heroin to come down. It was up and down, up and down, up and down, for about two years. The heroin took over my life, and I just kicked the job in the head and ended it."

But William needed more money than petty theft yielded. "I used to steal motorcycles and sell them to the Hell's Angels. I started robbing people outright, mugging them on the streets. But the money never lasted long. I used to pinch $750 or $1,500 a day, and my mates and I would smoke that much crack in a night. Then I would have to go out the next day and do it all over again.

"As I got to know the drug dealers around, I ended up robbing them. All juiced up on heroin, guns pulled, I'd kick their doors off and take whatever they had. I used to hit people with baseball bats because they wouldn't tell me where their drugs were; I've threatened guys' girlfriends – knife poised, I've threatened to cut a woman's throat if her husband didn't sort me out with drugs.

"I was living on 'self-destruct.' I knew there'd be repercussions to the lifestyle I was living, but I just didn't care. The drugs and – I know now – the enemy, the devil, had totally taken over at this time. I just thought, 'If I die, then at least the suffering will be over.'

"I got convicted of street robbery, and went to prison for the best part of three years. My family visited me, but it didn't go well. I said, 'You've told me that I was bad ever since I was a kid. This is how your son has turned out. You were always calling me the black sheep of the family; now, is this as black as you want me to be, or do you want me to get worse? How bad do you want me to be? Do you want me to kill someone next time?'

"I'll never forget the look on my parents' faces. The resentment and hatred and the blame that I spewed on them – they refused to come and see me after that.

"I did a lot of drugs in prison, and when I finished my sentence, I went straight back to the street. The only people I knew at that time were drug dealers, prostitutes, and criminals. Unfortunately, when you're put into prison, you learn how to commit crimes better. I got good.

"I went flat-out into drugs again, robbing and thieving, and that got me another two years in prison. On my release, it was right back into the lifestyle. I was walking around, a shell, not a man at all, just a shell with nothing inside. I hated it. I knew that if I didn't die from an overdose, someone would end up shooting me, probably in the back."

"I had tried a couple of methadone programs and rehabs before, but it was easier to score in there than it was out on the streets. I tried another methadone program, then another rehab. I stayed there for three months. That didn't work out either. We'd get up, have breakfast, then have a counseling session from 10 o'clock to 12. I used to feel worse coming out of the counseling sessions than I did before I went in. The psychiatrists would bring up all the problems and pain in me, and then they'd say, 'There, that's it. Now deal with it.' They wondered why I threw chairs about.

"'You're only feeling like that because you're feeling vulnerable,' they'd say. I'd say, 'No, it's not that at all; I want to punch your head in! You're just winding me up; all you're telling me is things that I know already. That's why I do drugs! To forget. What is this place all about? I *know* that I have a problem with drugs; I *know* I have a problem with anger. You clowns are getting paid $200 an hour to tell me this?'

"We'd have dinner from 12 to 1, and then we'd have another counseling session in the afternoon. The time was ours for the rest of the day. We'd smoke and watch videos – basically, sex, drugs and rock and roll, provided it wasn't too much over the top. It didn't do us any favors at all. I used to watch cops and robbers films and fantasize about being the robber.

"I was miserable, and I didn't get along with people in the house. I thought, 'Is this what my life is going to be, in and out of rehabs, getting sorted out for a couple of months, then going back to the drugs, and then to jail? How long is this going to last?' I packed rehab in and went back to the drugs.

"It was heroin 'twenty-four-seven;' twenty-four hours a day, seven days a week. So much heroin, my arms were knackered. I had serious trouble finding a useable vein, anywhere in my body.'"

"I was living on the streets, and all I can say is, I heard a voice: 'Go – you're hungry.' I argued with myself 'I'm not hungry.'

"'Go, have a cup of tea.'

"I went into the 'Missing Piece Cafe.'"

William smiled a huge grin. "This is where my life changes." He crossed his arms over his chest and rubbed his upper arms – "I've got goosebumps talking about God's love for me here.

"The one serving the food was a lad named Matthew, a long-time friend. I said, 'Man, I thought you was dead.' We talked for most of the night. He had become a Christian, and at the end of the evening, I said, 'I want what you have. I'll give God a chance. I've had enough of this crap life. I'm thirty-five years old and have nothing to show for it.'

"The people running the cafe took me to Betel in Birmingham. My first weeks there, I was in major defense mode. That was how I had to live – 'What do you want from me?' It took a while to learn that I didn't have to be 'William with pockets full of drugs and money.' They just loved me for being William. They love William with all his faults. I've been here nine months, and I've just got a full sense of security in that. Betel is not a rehab; this is my home.

"Before, something would go wrong, and I'd say, 'That's it, I've had enough, I'm off.' If I didn't like it, I'd move on. There are people at Betel I don't like, but I'm not moving on 'cause of any of them. I'm staying because God's bringing these things out from in me to be dealt with. He's doing it to make me a better person, and I thank Him for that. There are always people who we won't get on with, and I'm learning that God will put these people in our paths so that there will be 'iron on iron' at work, like it says in Proverbs. Let's be honest – there are guys here at Betel that I don't get on with particularly well, guys I struggle with. But I'm living with them, and working alongside them every day, and the iron on iron effect means that God lets the rubbish in my life come to the surface, so that He can scrape it off. It's like He says, 'Thank you; I'll have all of that.'

"I see new guys, right off the street, and I see me. That's what I tell them. 'I'm no different than you; I've just been here longer.' No matter what happens, I have to remember that the guy beside me is my brother and that I love him, and that he needs the same grace I do. There might be rebelliousness in him, but I *know* what that's like. So, if I delegate properly and show him true leadership, rather than just tell him what to do, there's a chance that the rubbish in his life can get dealt with.

"It's not been easy. I was trying to do so much of it in my own strength. Still trying to do things 'William's way,' which is like, erratic, irrational, all over the place. But the pieces of the jigsaw are coming together because I'm going deeper into God and asking Him, all the time, for guidance and His strength.

"I'm one of the guys on the gardening crew, and a while ago at work I was trying to organize the tools, and get addresses and directions we needed for the day's job, and I found myself under extreme pressure. One particular responsible was on my case. Him hassling me brought up the rubbish – anger, and frustration, and impatience – and I ended up swearing and cursing and stomping around and throwing tools about. There was a lot there to work with, and the Lord was at work in him too – through that incident, he's learned to show more grace towards people.

"It is a learning process and it goes both ways. I'm learning to be a servant, and also to be able to delegate properly. I'm learning to lead by example. I know I can't ask someone to clean toilets if I'm going to sit around drinking a cup of tea. 'Don't ask them to do anything you won't do' is the way it works around here. I used to be such an impulsive follower. I used to be such a people pleaser, I'd give in to peer pressure all the time. Now I'm learning to become something of a leader.

"I know my way around a building site and a gardening site and a kitchen, but through my time at Betel, I've learned that I'm working because I want to work, not because I have to."

"It's been a lot of fun to witness to my customers. They're always very happy with the job we've done, and they say, 'Oh, what a polite bunch of guys.' We start talking to them about Betel, who we are, who we were, and where we've been, and then, it happens all the time: their jaw just hits the floor. The next question is usually, 'How long were you on drugs?' I tell them, 'Seventeen years,' and there comes this look on their faces ... It's only by the grace of God that I can stand in the garden and tell them how my life has changed.

"Standing before them are a bunch of ex-addicts, ex-alcoholics, ex-down-and-outs, people who they wouldn't have given the time of day, and they see them at their front door. They've watched TV programs on drugs and addicts, but now they have actually seen what God is doing in the lives of the guys that have been working around their home the last few days. They thought that the very best that could happen to us would be that we got locked up somewhere and drink methadone for the rest of our lives.

"I like to think that when they see their gardens being transformed, they see that the lives of the men working are being transformed."

"I get up at 6 a.m., not because I have to, but because I want to. That's something I've learned here, though. One morning, coming down for breakfast, I remember saying to one of the senior guys, 'Oh, I don't have time for God.' He said, 'If you put God first then the day will just fall into itself.'

"He was right. Now I get up at 6 o'clock and I pray, and read the Word, and my daily reading, knowing that within a half an hour, it's going to get pretty hectic. Guys will be running all around doing this that and the other, but my morning time helps keep me settled.

"We have a quick breakfast, and then our corporate morning worship. Then it's off to work. As we drive to the day's job, I try to pray continually, speaking in tongues, asking for guidance and asking for strength, because I know I can't do it on my own. I ask for help in situations at work, especially if the guys are clashing, and the iron on iron sparks are starting to fly. I ask the Lord to speak to these guys through me; I pray for wisdom, so that I can show them where the rubbish is coming from and where it's going.

"I spend a lot of time on my own, praying, but if I see one of the lads struggling, I try to come alongside them. Allen and Darren, not so long back, had a row right in the cab of the truck while we were driving to work, and it carried right on to the job. I split them up in different parts of the yard for a while, and then I called them back together to help me. I was on my own, weeding a border. I told them about the 'iron on iron' effect, and said, 'God put you two together on this team, because He wants to deal with some of the rubbish in your lives.'

"I told them to look at the border. To my right, where I'd been working, the border was clear and all the weeds were on the lawn. 'That's what God has done in both of your lives at the moment. The Lord is gradually taking the weeds out of your lives; now, look to the left. You've still got a long way to go, lots of weeds. If you give Him a chance, He'll clear out the lot.'

"I just try to keep focused all day, praying and putting on worship tapes. We are very fortunate that most of the people don't mind having music on while we work. Customers often come up and say they like what we play, that they've never heard it before. That opens up all sorts of conversations. Even when the guys are new and they don't necessarily listen to the words, the music is very uplifting and makes them mellow out. Depending on who I am with, I know which tapes to put on. Some of the guys who have been around a while, they get their own tapes. They choose to worship, because they know it's not sending their heads out the door.

"Usually, I let the other guys use the lawn mowers and trimmers. I like weeding the flower borders, mostly because I'm on my knees. It's the best place to be, asking God to make me humble all day long while I work. I can't wait to go to heaven and work in God's garden."

Notes

1. The names of José Luis and William in this chapter have been changed.
2. See Appendix II for Betel's "Community Rules."
3. Patrick Dixon, *The Truth About Drugs* (London: Hodder and Stoughton, 1998), pp. 2, 6, 22.

Chapter 8

Pushers to Pastors

"There is none like the Lord our God...
who sets His throne so high,
but deigns to look down so low;
who lifts the weak out of the dust
and raises the poor from the rubbish heap,
giving them a place among princes,
among the princes of His people." (Psalm 113:5–8)

At the pastors' luncheon during the *cumbre* in Madrid, 20–22 February 2000, we went round the circle and surveyed the number of years the leading men and women of Betel had lived as addicts, and the number of years they'd spent in jail. There were fifty-two senior leaders present. (Betel considers both husbands and wives to be pastors.) As they gave their answers one by one, there was no evidence of either shame or pride. Telling the number of drug years was rather a matter of fact. What broke the group into repeated gales of laughter were the ways in which the pastors assessed their incarcerations.

"Prison? None. As a boy I stole some avocados once." Everyone knew that this pastor had spent most of his adulthood in prison. Another answered, "Twelve years, drugs; years in jail ... how many prisons are there in Spain?" He started to list the ones he had "visited." A third smiled broadly, "Years in prison? I spent my *life* in reformatories and prison."

As we continued around the circle, however, it became evident just how smart these men and women are. The majority of them were only ever detained. They were never caught doing the things they had to do to buy their drugs. Their cumulative total of years in jail was eighteen; the number of years of addiction, 437.

In May 1998, the WEC International Co-ordinating Council held their annual meeting at Betel's Betania conference center in Ciudad Real. Elliott was sitting with Jonathan Chamberlain, the Deputy International Secretary. Jonathan had recently conducted a survey of 1,800 WEC missionaries in more than sixty countries. He was studying the development of national leadership, and was particularly interested in Betel's ability to take very rough uneducated men and women, from very dysfunctional backgrounds, and raise them up through conversion and into leadership in a very short period of time.

Jonathan asked Elliott: "On our questionnaire, we asked for a list of materials, books, and former professional preparation you had found useful in training your workers. I thought that you would have surely mentioned some of your earlier work as a Cambridge University economist. Instead, you cited the Bible, and the *Life of C.T. Studd*. Those two I can understand. But the *Chronicles of Narnia* by C.S. Lewis? How do they serve in leadership development?"

Elliott answered, "They're essential. In the *Chronicles* one finds all the virtues and qualities of character that make for great leadership: courage, nobility, sacrifice, loyalty, honesty, endurance, long-suffering, obedience and love for the King. If we can inspire men and women to seek these things – and if we can provide the impartation – they will be great leaders."

When asked him for an example, Elliott cited a passage from the sixth book in the Narnia series, *The Magician's Nephew*. Aslan the Great Lion is giving the cabby his kingly charge over Narnia. He asks,

> " 'If enemies come against the land, and there was war, would you be the first in the charge and the last in the retreat?'
>
> 'Well, sir,' said the cabby very slowly, 'a chap don't exactly know till he's been tried ... I'd try – that is, I 'ope I'd try – to do my bit.'

'Then,' said Aslan, 'you will have done all that a king should do.'"[1]

Elliott commented: "God chooses humble men for kingship. He looks for hearts, not background or education. All we ask of Betel leaders is to be first in the charge, and last in retreat – and to *try*, not in their strength, but God's."

This truly is the spirit of Betel's leadership.

Tito Lorenzo Herrera grew up in San Blas. After Franco's death in 1975, when a tidal wave of drugs hit the streets, San Blas was one of the neighborhoods affected. For Tito, drugs were a way to make good money. His friends were Raul, Hippy, José and Angel. For nearly a decade he lived drugs, robberies, and discos.

Once he robbed a winery with José. They held the employees at gunpoint until they had them tied up, and then they broke open the safe. Though surrounded by the police, they managed to escape with 870,00 Pesetas – $4,500.

Nearly every day, Tito passed Elliott on the streets. "It was pretty tedious. Every day, he had the same word – 'Jesus could change our lives.' Drug addicts really do want to change their lives, and we wanted out – no one wants to sleep on the streets, or be chased by police. No one really wants to have to walk around with a gun to protect themselves. No one wants to be looking over their shoulder continuously. No one wants to live a life of fear, with no friends, and no hope. Every human being has to have at least a bit of hope. Elliott was always talking about hope."

One night, Tito was out stealing. He broke into the trunk of a car, hoping to find tools. He was disappointed, until he saw a bottle of cognac. Tito was so drugged, he wasn't very discerning. He drank it down, thinking it must be very cheap cognac. It was antifreeze.

Before he could get to his mother's house, he had two cardiac arrests. The neighbors found him on the street and rushed him to hospital. During his two-month recovery, his friend José often visited him in hospital. He was living with Lindsay and Raul, and had become a Christian. Tito was impressed with the marked improvement in José's health. He was a big, strong guy again. Tito started to go to the church meetings on release from hospital.

There were other influences at work in Tito's life. "My wife was in a rehab in the north for a year. She was fed up living the drug life, and fed up living with drug addicts. She kept sending me letters, telling me all that Jesus had done in her life. They made me want to experiment, to see if I could experience what she was experiencing. I always had a voice inside me telling me I was going to change, and that life could be different."

Tito soon moved into Betel's first house. "It was very interesting to live with the same guys I used to do drugs and rob with. Obviously it wasn't easy living together. We all wanted to be better than the others. There was still lots of the 'old man' kicking around in all of us. We had lots of verbal altercations. Only those of us who were willing to fight, those who really wanted to change our lives, made it.

"When you've been living your own desires, rules are hard to take all of a sudden. There was a huge struggle inside. I wanted to leave. But I knew how dangerous it was back on the street. I knew if I didn't make serious changes, I was going to die.

"We see this continually. People leave Betel, return to the streets, and die. The pull is so strong. Especially heroin; it has a supernatural power. Drugs take over every sensitive area of your body. They take over the functions of your body, your hands, your feet, your heartbeat. You don't see things the same way, you don't perceive reality the same way. On drugs, the picture is all changed. Things are covered up. There's an obliteration of the problems. The dissatisfaction is covered. The greater the problem, the greater the cover-up.

"The secret is to have a relationship with God, as early as possible. It's like the light is turned on, and you can see everything more clearly. Without the light, you can't find your way. We can't change by ourselves. The guys that go to the centers, but don't come to know God, they all end up back on the streets.

"Several years ago, I was back in San Blas. I saw almost none of my old friends. I asked after them, and found out that many of them were in Betel, in some of our other centers. Others were in jail. Most of them were dead. AIDS killed most of them; some overdosed; a few were shot."

"I was only in Betel for a few months, when I sat through the deadest devotional anyone has ever been in. Everybody was bored. Raul couldn't stop yawning. Pino was staring out the window. Emilio was picking his ear. I was looking around, wondering what any of us were doing there. Lindsay was singing some chorus. Even he was bored.

"In the midst of it all, something inside me came alive. Something filled me. It wasn't heat, or cold, but a wind, a breath inside me. I suddenly raised my hands, and for the first time in Betel, I started to sing. That experience convinced me that God was real."

Tito was instrumental in the move to Mejorada when the first house became unusable.

"There's a part of Mejorada in my heart that will never be erased. I used to go to Merjorada to take drugs. I didn't 'find' the house. I knew exactly where it was. It was more of a dump than a house. It was filled with rats and other things I don't want to mention. When we first moved there, everybody said they'd rather live in an abandoned car, and they knew what they were talking about!

"As we started to fix the building up so it was liveable, it was as if the same things were happening to our lives.

"I have such a sense of God's supernatural grace there – so many times we all wanted to run away. One day we were painting the house with whitewash, and it was burning our skin. We were all thinking, 'This is stupid.' I'd been in the center a year, and I was thinking, 'That's it; it's time to leave.'

"I still knew very little about God, and almost nothing about His love. We took a break, and when I looked over to the table, there was a Bible, open at the Book of Haggai. I can't explain it, but my eyes focused on chapter 2, verse 9: *'The glory of this latter house will be greater than the glory of the former, says the* LORD.*'* There I was, all covered with paint, and the contrast seemed absolutely momentous – my past life in the dump of Mejorada doing drugs, and there, in that verse, God's promise of a greater glory. Something supernatural opened in my understanding that day, and it's given me staying power ever since.

"We painted that verse on the wall of the house."

"Betel is a missionary work. That is its essence. People who grow up in Betel grow up in that spirit.

"My wife and I had been in Betel for four years, and felt that God wanted to send us out. We'd already made the decision to serve Him forever, and we had such a strong desire to tell other addicts all that Jesus had done in us. I went down to the southern Spanish coast on a road trip with Elliott, seeking out possible locations for a new work. Nothing seemed right the first four days. That night, we got to Almeria very late.

"When we woke in the morning, we went out to get something to eat. A lady was giving away free newspapers. On the front page was an advertisement of a house for rent. We called for an appointment, saw it, and rented it. We saw a vacant storefront, called the agent, and rented it. That was our missionary start in Almeria. There was nothing particularly special; there were no voices, or visions. It was just so easy, so right. Fifty-eight men in three houses. We had a couples' house, and a women's house, and had sent off a team to open a work in Malaga. There were three thriving *Rastros*, and a good church.

"During that time, Elliott had spoken to me about going to New York City. We prayed about it, and felt directed to move outside of our country. Again, there was nothing special; it was just a feeling that my wife and I both had. A quiet sort of knowing. It was nothing about New York; we just knew we had to leave Spain. It was part of Betel's missionary ethos, 'into all the world,'[2] and we were Betel.

"We arrived in New York on 20 January 1993. Many times after we got here, I thought we'd made a mistake. Life's so complicated here. Here in Jackson Heights, we have many cultures under one roof. We live with continuous racial tension, with African Americans, Puerto Ricans, Germans, Peruvians, Latin and Central Americans, and us Spaniards. It's hard, all the languages and cultures and prejudices.

"I'm a man of faith, but there are many difficult moments. It has been very hard to remember the growth that I had seen before. But I know God, and I know He is above all things.

"We've been invited back to Spain, but we don't want to return. We know that God is working in our lives here, and we see the change in our lives. In Spain we grew in God, and it was a very beautiful time. We were set free from drugs, we left our old lives, the thefts, and the violence. We lived in a palace for several years. Here, we're living in a room with the King.

"In Spain we heard about God; I didn't feel like I was walking with God like I do here. We've had to step out. Here in New York, we have to walk with God. In Spain, there was always someone in authority who could teach us. Here we have to find our own way. We pray more in New York than we did in Spain! We've become more open and sensitive to hear the voice of God. Our relationship with Him is far more intimate than it ever was before.

"When I hear about the deaths – my brother died of AIDS a few days before Raul did – it's very sad. These are people who fought to the very end. Their testimonies have touched so many people. It's a mixture of pain at their death, and some release that they've been rescued, and are now in heaven. When Raul died, there was sadness, but at the same time, I knew that God had won. Nearly all the first guys have died. Manolo and Angel both have died of AIDS. Their testimony meant more to me than perhaps anyone else's. There is both sadness and gratitude to God, and an ardent desire to see that it doesn't happen to other people."

Betel is never short on surprises. We visited Juan Carlos and Mary Luz Matesanz, the pastors in Marseilles, France. In the course of our conversation, Juan Carlos referred to the writings of St John of the Cross. I didn't expect an ex-heroin addict to have read much of the sixteenth-century mystics. I asked which works he was familiar with. He answered, "I've read *The Ascent of Mount Carmel*, but it's *The Dark Night of the Soul* that made the greater impact." Juan Carlos had me at an advantage. He read them in their original Spanish.

The discussion turned to other sources; Juan Carlos continues to discover the roots of his Spanish spiritual heritage. We spoke of Francis Xavier, Don Quixote and El Cid. He articulately compared and contrasted the dynamics of the mystic, the missionary, the knight and the warrior nobleman. "These are my heroes. I hope to be a mystic warrior, bringing hope to the outcast."

Juan Carlos told his story in the S.O.S. Betel Cafe. Its success is simple: location, location, location. To get to it we drove down a long narrow street, into the heart of the red-light district of Marseilles. In most of the doorways sat a prostitute – women, men, transvestites – waiting for business.

As we sat at a table drinking espressos, I couldn't help noticing how colorful Juan Carlos is. I asked him about his tattoos. He has a dot between the thumb and forefinger of his right hand, a star on the back of his left, and a dot on his left cheekbone. They were the very first of his tattoos. Each has a significance on the street – they are the signs of the outcast.

On the left forearm just below the elbow is the rose of the winds, symbolizing adventure. It marks the hashish days.

Abraxis is tattooed just below the rose. As one beyond good and evil, Abraxis was a cult hero, and was famous for the line: "He who would be born must first destroy a world."[3] Juan Carlos was seventeen years of age when he had it done. Abraxis marked his acid and amphetamine phase of drug addiction.

High on his left arm is the Rolling Stones tongue. Mick Jagger was the icon in the heroin period. It lasted fifteen years, from the time Juan Carlos was fourteen years old.

Juan Carlos looked sideways at Mary Luz. She grinned, and shook her head playfully. He grinned and said, "I'd have to undress to show you the big one." A provocatively posed, naked woman, stretches over his whole back.

With every tattoo, Juan Carlos further signaled his marginalization. Two years before he entered Betel, he spent a short time in a rehab, where he discovered that he had AIDS. The news of his infection incapacitated him for two days, but after he had reconciled himself to the fact of his death, nothing mattered. He knew he was then capable of killing for his drugs. With nothing to lose, he feared nothing. For the last two years of addiction, his life was drugs, alcohol and violence.

⨑

Juan Carlos first heard of Betel from Carlos and Marimar. They had been drug colleagues; Juan Carlos had disappeared from the scene, because he owed them money. One day he got on a bus, and there they were. Carlos is a big man, nicknamed *El Bruto* – the Brute. He and Marimar came up to Juan Carlos, and they smiled. Instead of demanding money, they passed him a Betel tract, and told him their recovery stories.

"It was so incredibly strange, and it started me thinking. That moment opened the door to my future, but to be honest, the only reason I entered Betel was that I didn't want to die in the streets like a dog.

"The Betel guys really looked after me. It was so disorienting – there was nothing of the street ambience. No one was looking to rip me off. I didn't need to be on my guard.

"As I heard the gospel at devotions and in the meetings, my interest was quickened. There came a moment when I had to decide – which way my life was going to go, and who my friends would be. I heard in a devotional 'If you're going to be a friend of God, you have to be the enemy of men.' It was a very strong word, but it was the right one for me, because it meant I had to make a radical break with my past.

"Twelve days into the program, still in my *mono*, I was home alone with Carlos, my shadow. Carlos had to go to the phone, and as soon as he left, so did I. I jumped over the fence and I asked the neighbor for cigarettes. It was my first smoke in twelve days, and it was glory! Then I started walking into the city. The second cigarette wasn't as good as the first. The third was terrible. I felt empty inside.

"I had a great meal, a bottle of wine, and cups and cups of great coffee – and all I wanted to do was die. I shot up, but I didn't get high. I got some heroin from another dealer and another source, and I still didn't get high. Such an incredible desperation flooded over me.

"The emptiness I felt was a clear enough message – I shouldn't have left. I called Raul Casto at the center and asked for help. He refused. I knew he was testing me. I took the last bus of the night as far as it went, and then walked out to the center – two hours. I knocked on the door and no one answered. It was the middle of the night. I kept knocking. They finally let me in, but I've always wondered if they wanted me, or the sausages that my mother had given me!

"I was back. But I was *entre Pinto y Valdemoro*, an expression which loosely translated means 'between Nowhere and Limbo.' I was still smoking, I had hidden some money, and I was lying all the time. I also knew that Jesus was the only way. I had given my life to Him some time earlier, but it was a decision that I only made in my head. I needed something real, not just a truth.

"I started to read my Bible, and when I'd been in the center about three months, someone gave me a book about a revival in Canada. I read story after story of people changed by the love of God. Something exploded in me. I read about living water, and so much joy bubbled up in me, it scared me.

"I couldn't sleep – I read all of the Book of Isaiah that night, and for the next few days, it seemed like I was flying. In the process, I realized that I had lost my fear of the AIDS virus. The joy must have pushed it out. That, and hope. That was the first real sense I had of the power of God. Other changes took place those early months, but they didn't come as suddenly as losing the fear of death.

"I had lived a very depraved life, especially in my relationships with women, and my mind was filled with filthy pictures. I'd be in the meeting, worshipping, my arms raised, and I'd suddenly see a pornographic image in my mind. I'd look at godly women, and I'd have obscene thoughts.

"Little by little, as I studied my Bible, in worship, and as I prayed, my mind was renewed. It was a process of cleansing that took more than a year before I felt much victory. One thing was clear – I knew where I wanted to go. It was a long walk of faith.

"Another of the changes I noticed was that I started to care about some of the other *chicos*. Before, no one but me mattered."

"I know it sounds grandiose to say it, but I felt like I was predestined for leadership. It felt like that was why I was born. The suffering I endured, my street life, that was not my destiny.

"There were two street years, after I found out that I had AIDS, when I lost all hope. Even then I had a sense that I was going to be saved from it all. There was a sense that God, or something, was going to deliver me. At night, all alone, I'd call out for help. Even stoned, I knew there was something bigger than drugs – something more, out beyond me.

"The call to serve came once I knew that life could be directed and controlled by love. That's my only goal and purpose of living.

"Before, I had an inclination to evil. The drugs and the violence – the tattoos all declared it. I had an inclination to escape, to run. I was destroyed emotionally. I wasn't just possessed by heroin; I was given to evil. I mocked the weak and was openly cruel. *Abraxis* was my hero.

"What changed me from night to day was that book on revival, when the Holy Spirit flooded my heart. The transformation was so radical that my mother said I was like a sock turned inside out. It was so noticeable that within a week, my father, my sister and my three brothers were in tears, overwhelmed with joy and relief. I had abused the family for so long ... they knew that those horrible days were over forever."

Juan Carlos had left school when he was fourteen years old, but the last grade he passed was grade six. The Betel community was now his school.

"I learned how to sacrifice, how to work, how to love. I learned values by seeing them lived in the older guys, and I copied them. I learned even more from the missionaries – from Elliott, and Lindsay, and Paul Anderson. They were even further along than the senior Betelitos. The love of Christ in them spoke with greater force than any of their messages."

A year and a half after Juan Carlos entered Betel, he was leading the Mejorada house. He had responsibility for fifty men – all in the one house.

"Many of the guys that were coming off the street were so sick, so rough. I remember having to wash some of them off with buckets of water, they were so filthy. Luis and his twelve-year-old son came in together. They were both heroin addicts. The boy was his father's drug runner, but started stealing some of the heroin, and got hooked himself. The father was one mass of sores, from head to foot – he looked like a leopard, covered with spots – but the spots were abscesses. We put a tin sheet on the ground for him to stand on, and dumped buckets and buckets of water over him."

The men came with incredible spiritual hunger. Betel was doubling its size every year. "It seemed like I was living the same dynamic that I had read about in the book about revival eighteen months earlier.

"We worked on the house whenever there was any money. As it had been abandoned for years, there wasn't a single room that had any glass in the windows. There was no running water – we had to bucket-carry water from the river for showers. There was no electricity – we had a generator. There were no toilets, and no septic tank. There was no kitchen – we cooked on a gas ring on the floor.

"Most of the time, all we could afford to eat was pasta. We ate cauliflower for a month when it was in season. If we got an egg or a sausage, it was a feast. That sounds grim, I know, but it was so much better than what we had lived on on the streets. At least we were eating something. Compared to sleeping in an abandoned van, I was in a bed, surrounded by friends I could trust."

Most of the guys had been gang leaders on the street. Now they had something of Christ in them, and some of the light of the gospel was shining through their spiritually immature characters.

"Jambri had to be disciplined for punching a guy in the face, and Raul Casto could take a guy's head off when he wasn't careful. He once gave me *platos* for two months. He didn't even give me any reprieve over Christmas. If someone had been in Betel for six months, and had not gotten anywhere in God, Raul would back them into the corner, and tell them they had a choice: convert, or leave.

"Now there is so much more grace and patience. I can't explain the lack of mercy when there was so much love ... but those early days forged heroes.

"Our lives were so much rougher, harder on the streets. What may seem brutal now was so much softer than what we lived in the drug world.

"There was something overshadowing us, calling us forth, covering us in spite of our failings. The missionaries' supervision and their daily devotionals gave us the ongoing direction we so badly needed. We had very little Bible knowledge. But the little we knew had impact. The devotionals we did were never complicated – Raul, for instance, had only read the sports page before he came to Betel. The first book he'd ever read was the Bible.

"Among those first men in the Mejorada house were Raul, Tito, Pino, Juan Botanico, Pedro, Ramon, Jambri, Javi, Ivan, Oscar, Marcos, Alberto, Miguel Mechanico, and Manuel el Vasco. Raul founded the work in Barcelona, and later became the senior national pastor. Tito pioneered Almeria, Malaga, and New York City. Pino led the centers in southern Madrid, and now heads the work in Malaga. Juan Botanico went with Raul to found Barcelona, became its senior pastor, and then founded Tarragona, Lerida, and is presently pioneering in Bilbao in the Basque region. Pedro went to Cuenca, Tarragona, Murcia, and Albacete. Ramon became the leader of Mejorada, until his death from AIDS.

"Jambri started the work in Naples, and ran the work from a hospital bed until his death. Javi is now the senior pastor of the Madrid congregation. Ivan helped Tito in New York, and is presently on the leadership team in Madrid. Oscar has grown the work in Lisbon; Marcos leads in Porto, northern Portugal. Alberto helped open Malaga, led Albecete, and now heads up outreach and home groups in Madrid. Miguel leads the work in Galicia. Manuel led the Cuenca work – while doing time in prison! He died of AIDS in Malaga, but led the work there from hospital until the very end."

Juan Carlos led the centers in northern Madrid, and opened the work in Alcala de Henares. He heard Elliott, Raul and Jenny tell stories of their missionary trips to Equatorial New Guinea, and dreamt of starting new works in the third world. When Raul's fragile health was compromised by the tuberculosis he contracted in New Guinea, Juan Carlos resigned himself to the fact that no Betelito with AIDS could serve in the emerging countries. Their weakened immunities were just not strong enough for the more primitive conditions.

A further blow came when his second daughter was born

HIV-positive. He and his wife, Mary Luz, were full of faith, and ready to serve anywhere, but when Lydia's health continued to be so fragile, it was a very hard eighteen months. She didn't cast off Mary Luz's antibodies, and the doctors said she wouldn't.

"It felt like we embraced the very cross of Christ. I was not afraid of death, but I feared for Lydia's. Even today, there is a great weight on my heart. I watch the other children grow, and she stays so small and frail.

"Elliott and Mary lost their youngest son in 1991, and their sacrifice and faithfulness continue to be a tremendous strength to me and Mary Luz. We watched them carry on in ministry, and their testimony stifles the feelings we have of being defrauded by God.

"I used to think those in Christian ministry were chosen by God and that suffering wouldn't touch them. Our illusion of the Christian life – of blessing and healing – was fractured. Before, I was like an eagle soaring. With Lydia's AIDS, I went into a dive, and crashed into the rocks. The Teppers' faithfulness picked me up, and though my theological simplicity is gone forever, I can live with the complexities now. It has caused me to throw myself even more passionately into the battle. Instead of a life of despair, I am impelled forward."

"When Lydia was three years old, God began impressing the nation of France on our hearts. Elliott discouraged us, because France was so hard to the gospel, and we wouldn't be able to receive the same medical care we could get in Spain. It was a season when pastors and leaders were dying of AIDS every month. Everyone was wondering if they would be next.

"Every month, I kept asking for release to France. It finally came to a head. I told Elliott: 'I'm going to France, because I don't have time to waste. I'm going to die, but before I die, I want to do an apostolic work for God. France is not far away. We can come back if we have to. Let me go and work while we still have strength, and when I'm too sick, and too weak, I can come back to Madrid like Raul and Jambri did.'

"Elliott looked at me. He told me later what went through his mind: 'Who am I to quench an apostolic heart. That's the spirit of Betel.' We were sent off with God's abundant blessing."

Juan Carlos and Elliott explored the southern coast of France, and felt the port city of Marseilles was where they were to locate. Drugs, Mafia, prostitution, and high immigration meant there was great need.[4] On arrival, the Marseilles churches refused to receive them. No one helped them, and locally, no one supported them.

But God intervened. On one of the initial visits to Marseilles, in April 1996, Juan Carlos had a providential, chance meeting with a Spanish-speaking pastor of a local Reformed Church. He directed them to another Spanish-speaking leader, Señor Rene Pragnon, the retired commander of the Marseilles police force. He quickly became a friend, and over time, Betel's champion, patron and guarantor. He wrote letters of recommendation, and co-signed each of their loans and contracts for vehicles and properties.

Further, Rene was an elder in an Assemblies of God Church. He had formed a charitable association to care for the homeless, and for years they had tried to run a Christian hostel and drop-in café. They saw little success, and in March 1999 he offered the building to Betel.

Because drug addicts in France receive so much government assistance – doctors, social workers, psychologists, an apartment, and 2500 francs per month ($350), plus synthetic morphine, there is nothing like the *Ventoso* or the *Vertedero*. In Lisbon and Madrid, Betel can go directly to the addicts. In Marseilles, the addicts are not directly approachable. The S.O.S. Café gave Juan Carlos a door of entry for the work, for it gives him and his team the opportunity to meet addicts as they come for free food and coffee, the TV sports channel, and the chess tournaments.

Until the opening of the coffee shop, the early days were at best chaotic. Betel-Marseilles was only drawing the very marginalized, those whom the system didn't want to help. An alcoholic psychotic, Josef Marie, had lived at Betel for six months, and then suddenly left. A month later he phoned Juan Carlos in the middle of the night. "If you'll come get me, I'll come back."

Juan Carlos took two *chicos* with him and drove into the slum. Josef Marie was on the street, waving them into a dark alley. They followed him into his ground floor apartment. On one wall he had a picture of a nun in an old-fashioned habit, with an enraged face. In another corner there was a statue of the Buddha. The place was filthy, and Juan Carlos was glad he wasn't there alone.

Josef Marie was nervous and restless, and motioned for them to sit down in three chairs. He sat down in front of them. They began to talk, and he said that he couldn't come with them back to Betel. He started raving nonsensically. The one coherent sentence was his repeated declaration, "I have to get vengeance." He pulled out a revolver from underneath a sweater at his side, and pointed it at them.

"In his psychotic state, we knew that he was going to kill us. I knew that I was going to end my life in a dirty apartment in Marseilles, and all my dreams in God were going to end in the same kind of place I started. We tried to reason with him for half an hour, and still at gunpoint, we asked if we could pray with him. Josef Marie looked at us, gripped the pistol with both hands, grimaced, and said, 'You're right.'

"He suddenly let go of the gun. It fell out of his hands, and dropped to the floor. The bullets popped out of the chamber, and rolled about."

Juan Carlos brought him to the center. "He settled in and became very happy, but then left suddenly because his social worker convinced him that Betel was a cult. He ended up in a mental hospital."

A schizophrenic named David lived with them for a month. One day he snapped. They were at work at the *Rastro* – David had disappeared, shaved his head bald, and returned with a case-hardened motorcycle chain. He started screaming for his clothes. He whipped the chain around his head, and smashed the telephone to smithereens. He hauled off and punched a Betelito in the face, splitting his mouth open, and knocking out two teeth. The guys pulled the injured Betelito towards the back of the store, but David threw a steel stool at him. As it spun end over end, the plastic seat split the man's head open. Juan Carlos yelled, "All we've done is good to you; why are you doing this to us?" From three feet away, David spat in his face, and said, "I'm going to kill you, and send you to Paradise before your time."

With that, he turned and left. Two days later, he came back to the *Rastro* and asked for forgiveness, and re-admission to the community. Forgiveness he received.

Since those early days, Juan Carlos has established a network of healthy relationships. He took us to the Betel stall in the Arab market, where they sell used clothes. My brother Paul was filming video footage, and an Arab woman, their stall neighbor, asked aggressively, *"Qu'est-ce que vous faites?"* "What are you doing?" *"Un documentar de Betel."* A big smile broke across her face. *"Ah bon! Ils sont mes amis."* "They are my friends." The next morning, she stopped by at the men's house, with a pot of Algerian stew – for twenty-eight!

Juan Carlos and Mary Luz are quick to say that they do not begrudge the years of hardship. "When we were in Madrid, we lived under the covering of the church. So much was looked after. We felt very secure. In Marseilles it is has been an exercise of our faith, for we live with a spiritual pressure we never faced in Spain. Through it the Lord has given us a capacity to walk by faith, something we really didn't have to do before. In Madrid, we had others standing with us; here, it feels like we're very much alone.

"I've wanted to call Elliott and tell him, 'I can't do it any more; I'm finished.' There have been times when there hasn't been a new guy join the community – we've gone six months without someone new. We've had seven in the community, and four would go. Of the first six leaders I brought from Spain, all but one have left. Sometimes I've felt like a captain in the army, watching my army desert me.

"I wrestle with the fear of failure. In those dark times, the Lord faithfully gives me a word. I read about entering and taking the Promised Land, and I wonder how Caleb and Joshua felt, what were they thinking. I read the missionary biographies, C.T. Studd, and Hudson Taylor. They had difficult moments and failures. One phrase from C.T. Studd has helped. He had lost his reputation, and lost all his support. 'When a man loses his reputation, that's when Christ can do something great in his life, because he has nothing left to lose.'

"I know that a lot of my Betel friends felt I was stubborn, and had missed the call of God in going to Marseilles. Sometimes I have felt like a crazy man who dragged his family off to France, but just before I've given up, the Lord has given me encouragement. We've met the right people at just the right time. Recently, more 'normal' people – addicts – started to come, and there is a spiritual hunger in the guys that we had not previously seen.

"We pray as never before, and we are waiting on God more than ever. There is a direct correlation between the time in prayer, the wave of new people, the café, and the men's house we're presently in. That was a very significant breakthrough – such a large house, in the heart of Marseilles, with its huge garden. When we went to look at it, it was empty, but there was a tract stuck in the door. It was a quotation from Isaiah 41:10:

> *"Have no fear, for I am with you;*
> *be not afraid, for I am your God.*
> *I shall strengthen you and give you help,*
> *and uphold you with My victorious right hand.'*

We felt the Lord was saying that the house was ours, and that we were not to worry about the rent. We took that miracle moment to be His promise that He would sustain us. We needed supernatural encouragement, because the rent was beyond our means, and it took all of our reserves to get the contract and pay the first month's rent. Every month since, we've had what we needed to pay the bills, and we've grown from six guys to twenty-two. The Lord has so impressed 1 Kings 17:12 upon us. That's the story of the widow and the miraculous provision of oil. As long as we keep bringing the 'pots,' the Lord will keep supplying our need.

"I feel such a stirring of mercy for the hopeless ones – Francisco, Augustine, and José Paris – guys who have failed other Betels. I remembered a word that I'd read many times, Ezekiel 37, the story of the Spirit and the dry bones. I looked it up and meditated on it, and as I did, I felt like the Lord said that that word applied directly to the men I had picked up and rescued. The sense I have is that the Mejorada spirit of Betel's early years will be revived. These men are not just being rescued; they are being built up to be a great army once again.

"I know that there is both victory and mystery in Christ, and that at Betel, we walk very close to both life and death. We appreciate life more than most, and we penetrate more of the mystery because we know how short our lives will be. We know that one day, in heaven, we will come 'further up and further in.'[5] Once we cross the veil, we will be perfect."

I read philosophy for three years, spent four years in seminary, received denominational ordination, and went on to do doctoral studies. Juan Carlos has an understanding of ministry that I never received in any of my classes! I asked Elliott about the ways in which Betel identifies, prepares and ordains their pastors.

"The supreme and only requirement for ordination is the evident call of God in an individual's life. It is not possible to prepare, train, and to coax from an individual what God has not put in. It's futile and ultimately destructive to ordain someone who does not have God's call and blessing on their life.

"The challenge is to identify that heavenly calling in a person, and to bring it forth in God's perfect timing without distorting the process. We try to discern that calling in our people even at a very early stage of their Christian lives. At first it's just an impression in our spirits, but it is usually followed by different evidences of that calling.

"We notice certain giftings as our people live together – who's giving leadership, and who is nurturing the immature and the struggling? As our young leaders give devotionals, we listen for the budding powers of inspiration and exhortation, and the ability to explain biblical truth; we look for spiritual wisdom and discernment in their lives and ministries. There are also two very visible fruits: people get converted through their ministry, and the residences under their care grow and stay healthy relationally. The opposite is also true – if people are always leaving, it's often because of leadership problems.

"The preparation and training of someone with God's calling on their lives is simply to stand alongside them as they begin to walk out God's work of preparation in them, and offer counsel, correction, encouragement, and covering. If emerging leadership is to be fully commissioned for greater authority in ministry, they must learn to submit to us as their immediate and pastoral authority.

"As to formal training in the Word of God we give our people at least one year of Bible training in our Adullam Bible School.[6] It is an intensive half-day training school for those monitors who have been in Betel for at least a year, and desire to prepare for the ministry. The course includes basic Bible survey courses of the Old and New Testament; an in-depth study of a Gospel, Romans or Galatians, and the Book of Acts; spiritual warfare; and a book that is our leadership 'manual,' Watchman Nee's *The Normal Christian Worker*.

"We usually wait until there is no doubt as to a person's calling and character before we ordain. We want to avoid placing titles on young leaders as long as possible – we've watched it feed too many fat heads! Before there is a public laying on of hands, we like to wait until the Cross has done its preliminary work. In short, we wait until there is evident Christlikeness and grace in a person's life."

At Betel, the majority of those who are raised up to give leadership come with little or no formal training or educational background. Watchman Nee's candid and practical instruction reads almost as if it were written specifically for recovering drug addicts; it has served as *the* training manual for all of the original Betel pastors. It has been translated into Spanish and is handily in view in the church offices and lounges. If one is to understand how Betel as a community holds together and why, Nee's *Christian Worker* is foundational. The book describes a detailed character profile of Betel's leadership.

The Normal Christian Worker objectifies and determines the leadership goals and values that are to be sought, leaving an up-and-coming Betelito concluding, "So *this* is what I'm supposed to do ... So *this* is why those in leadership behave like they do ... " Nee's practical instruction also serves as a grid by which Betel leadership holds one another accountable. I wish I had discovered the book a long time ago – it would have saved me and my leadership untold grief!

The opening paragraph reads:

> "The personal life of a worker of the Lord is intimately related to his work. Therefore, we have to consider matters of character and conduct when considering the qualifications necessary to be in God's employment. This relates to the constitution of character and the formation of habits. A man must have not only a certain amount of spiritual experience, but a certain constitution in his disposition; the Lord must constitute a certain kind of disposition within him...
>
> The outward man must be molded into proper shape. It takes grace and mercy from God for this to occur; character is not built up in a day ... God will reconstruct a new character in him through resurrection." [7]

Molding character through resurrection necessarily implies crucifixion. Death and resurrection grace are working dynamics in Betel's leadership.

Oscar Matesanz is eight years younger than Juan Carlos, his eldest brother. Oscar is very close to Juan Carlos. "I idolized him when I was young, and craved the money and the reputation he had. I told myself, 'When I grow up, I want to be like him.' I hung around with his friends, and got myself into all manner of trouble."

Oscar watched as Juan Carlos' life hit bottom hard. "A dog on the street had a better life than he did." Five years of heroin took their toll on Oscar. He couldn't keep a job, and his family didn't know what to do with him.

Juan Carlos had entered Betel, and repeatedly asked Oscar to join him. Oscar felt his life would never sink as low as his brother's had. His father was also pleading with him to get help. To appease his family, Oscar thought he'd go to Betel, and stay long enough to kick his habit, then leave and live a normal life. He was amazed to see drug dealers, thieves and gang leaders, so changed. Many of these were *chicos* he'd known on the streets. Among them was the house leader, Juan Carlos.

Oscar left Betel six months later. Heroin's draw was stronger than anything he'd experienced while he was clean. "That next

year was the worst year of my life. I felt so completely alone."
He felt he'd never be free of drugs, and came recklessly close to
overdosing time after time. But there was also some sense deep
within that kept him from killing himself: he'd often go to the
place to buy his drugs singing worship songs he'd learned at
Betel months earlier.

"I overdosed once at my parents' house. I woke up in the
hospital. When I came round, I felt as if I had been given a
warning from God: 'This is your opportunity to make your life
right.'"

After Oscar was released from hospital, Juan Carlos picked
him up and brought him to Betel. He was embarrassed to see his
old housemates – they had gone to such lengths to help him,
and he'd walked out on them. But he had nowhere else to go.
Physically, he was a wreck – he'd been using dirty syringes, and
so was covered with abscesses; he'd lost sixty-five pounds. Back
at Betel, he regained the weight in three months.

"Miguel, my shadow, reached into my life, and lifted me out
of the dumpster. That's what it felt like – my life was garbage,
and his joy, his freedom, his continuous giving to me lifted
me out of the feelings of worthlessness I had always felt. It
was more the life he lived with me, than anything he ever
said."

One day, during devotions, something unusual came over
many of the *chicos*. They started weeping; most of them had
prostrated themselves on the floor, crying out to God. Oscar was
one of them. That day, he pleaded with the Lord, "Help me to
know You more."

Not long after, Oscar was out on the streets, selling the Betel
calendars door to door when he met a young man whom he had
served as a shadow. He had run away several months earlier. As
they talked, the guy held out a wrap of heroin, and offered it to
Oscar.

"A huge battle raged within, for three seconds, until the fear
of God came over me, and it felt like something broke. I felt
something I'd never felt before – *victory*. With it came a deeper
sense of joy than I'd ever experienced. It was a greater high than
the heroin would have given me!"

Oscar spent a year at Adullam, Betel's training school. "I took
the Bible classes because I wanted to learn. They were times I

really enjoyed, although we fell asleep nearly every afternoon – they shouldn't have classes during siesta time!

"I had a horrible life before I met Christ. As a junkie, my life was so unstable – drug highs, and huge lows. My life had been one long rollercoaster. Through that time at Adullam, the Lord overwhelmed me with His love. I came to know His forgiveness, and freedom from the condemnation I had carried. In many ways, I think my heart learned more than my head did.

"One of the books we studied was Watchman Nee's *The Normal Christian Worker*. It is a very important book in my life, but the truth is, I realized reading that book that there isn't anything normal about it – it's for supermen!

"I was especially touched by the chapter about Peter's instability. The Lord showed me that there was no way I could do what was ahead in my own strength. My own abilities had brought me to nothing. If I sought only Him, He would truly give me the life I always wanted. Somewhere I learned that 'To trust God is to live as God requires.'

"At a *cumbre* a few months later, I suddenly realized that things had leveled out. With that realization, it was as if the Lord then asked me, 'You are either with Me, or without Me. Which is it?'

" 'I'm with you Lord, and I'm staying in Betel.' "

Oscar was sent to the house in Almeria to help the pastor, Tito Herrera. When Tito went to New York City two months later to begin pioneering a new work, the couple who were to take over Almeria had difficulties that required discipline. Oscar was suddenly in charge. He'd been a Christian for only three years.

He called Elliott to ask, "I've never preached before – what am I supposed to do?" Elliott said, "There's no one else – I'm trusting you."

Oscar felt two things – no one had ever believed in him like that; and, he still didn't know how to preach. "I was forced to look to the Lord for day-to-day guidance and strength. When I look back on those years, I can trace miracle after miracle, even in the midst of the many mistakes."

During the five years of Oscar's leadership in Almeria, the work grew from twenty-five to eighty men. They sent teams out to start new works in Melilla, North Africa, and Granada. While managing the original *Rastro* in Almeria, he opened three new thrift stores, plus one in each of the new works. All six did very well financially, and Oscar was feeling very comfortable – until he heard of a new work that was being started in Lisbon. The stories from the *Ventoso* unsettled him.

The founding pioneer suffered sudden health problems, and at a *cumbre* shortly after, Elliott put out the Jonah challenge: "Is there a reluctant missionary who is resisting the call of God, to leave Joppa – the comfortable city – and go to Nineveh?"

Oscar and Nines, his wife, looked at each other. After the *cumbre*, Oscar felt the Lord was calling them to take a big step forward. Neither he nor Nines wanted to leave Almeria – they lived in the married residence, and the community they lived with had become family for them. The thought of leaving felt like they would be losing everything. There was a time of silence between them; Nines spoke first: "You know, we don't have a home in Almeria. If we moved to Lisbon, we could get our own house."

That marked the transition for them – their hearts warmed quickly towards the move to the new work in Lisbon.

In fifteen days, in July 1997, Oscar was in Lisbon, having spent the two weeks at home transferring the leadership responsibilities to Fernando, his senior leader in Almeria. In another two weeks, Nines had joined him. A junior leader from Almeria joined them, along with three *chicos*. A leadership couple from Madrid came to help. This leadership team of eight joined the eight from Madrid that had been gathered by the first pastor.

There were a lot of fights in the early months. It seemed that every day, the Portuguese and Spanish cultures clashed. Whether it was rooted in an historical animosity, no one was sure, but it was rough on everybody. Issues of trust, honor and servanthood were being established. Oscar and Nines slowly won the hearts of the community, but over the course of the first year, the other Spanish leaders returned to Spain. There were times when Oscar and Nines wanted to return with them.

During that same year, a number of Portuguese leaders emerged. But not without cost. There were times when Oscar wondered if he wasn't going to be crucified. "The Portuguese were causing me so much grief. I recognized that I was growing bitter towards them. One day the Lord showed me that no matter how they treated me, whether they neglected me, or disobeyed me, or used me, I had to love them, just as He loved me in my disobedience and my neglect.

"It was another of those intensive growth periods in my life, one of those hard times of character formation. I certainly didn't enjoy it, but I know more about humility, and patience, and trusting in the Lord. Through it, I know more of what it is to seek Him, and His will. There is lots of fruit produced out of the suffering – there have been many conversions, and leadership formation, and we *know* that Lisbon is the Lord's place for us. We love the Portuguese, and we know that they love us.

"I can't explain how or when the change came; all I know is that the Lord opened my eyes, and gave me His heart for the Portuguese. He reminded me that regardless of culture and tradition, the hearts have the same hurts, and the same needs.

"The Lord said that I was the one who had to change, not them. That if I was to win their confidence and respect, it would only come through love – through me showing them His love." [8]

The following reflections by Lindsay McKenzie bring some analysis to bear on Betel's leadership formation.

"Our emphasis in Betel over these last sixteen years has been on one-to-one discipleship, and our preaching has emphasized the cross of Jesus Christ, and a life of faith. When a dependence on drugs and alcohol is replaced with a dependence on Jesus, the drug abuse problem is dealt with, as are other greater problems like pride, lying, selfishness, greed, sexual aberration, and co-dependency.

"We are unashamedly out to train and produce preachers, pastors and missionaries. All our leaders are ex-addicts which means that they already have a 'life degree' in addictology. That prior experiential drug knowledge, coupled with a radical discipleship and practical on-the-job Bible training, makes these ex-addicts the best 'drug professionals' in the world!

"There's something more at work. Because of WEC's formative influences, our Betel leaders have a world vision which keeps them looking beyond their own parochial existence.

"I think what shaped a lot of what became Betel's guiding principles was a simple 'holy ignorance.' We knew nothing about rehabilitation. Elliott and Mary had experimented with drugs for a few short years while in college, but I was an average middle-class evangelical 'good boy.' Neither Myk nor I had ever smoked a cigarette! I will never forget our first meeting with the members of the newly formed International Substance Abuse and Alcohol Coalition leadership council. The meeting had become bogged down in a discussion about the merits of twelve-step programs. I had never heard of such a program, and I couldn't disguise my ignorance for too long. I finally blurted out, 'Could someone please explain to me what on earth is a twelve-step program?' Suffice it to say the room went silent for a few pregnant moments!

"Beginning the work with that kind of naiveté gave us a freedom to let God's Spirit guide us in ways that otherwise would have been cluttered up with human know-how and methodology. In our ignorance we made lots of mistakes, but we learned as we went. We simply believed that God would meet us at each step, and He did.

"Another key aspect that came in (almost by accident) right at the beginning was that of handing over responsibility and authority to the men early in their Christian experience. We have a very high trust factor working in Betel, often of necessity, as our people mature, and develop in relationships. For example, we already mentioned that Raul took direct control over the men in the house when I moved out to marry Myk. When I went back to Australia on furlough, that again required us to broaden Raul's authority to fill the gap.

"When Raul married Jenny, other single workers had to step in to take his place in the men's house. It's a continuous Betel dynamic: growth and change, and our response to that change through promotion. We often wonder if the next in the leadership line is ready for the new responsibility. It usually appears to our natural understanding that they aren't, but it nevertheless seems right. We place them in their new position by faith, and most of the time, it's worked out well. We take a lot of risks with very young men in significant leadership positions.

"When a residence grows to about twenty to twenty-five men, we break off and begin a second house, often in the next suburb or on the other side of town. This gives the next-in-line a certain autonomy and the chance to try out his leadership skills without having 'big brother' breathing down his neck.

"For instance, right now in Naples I can see a handful of men that need to be given responsibility and authority in setting up a house of their own, or else they will dry up and probably leave; not because their time is finished but rather out of frustration and boredom.

"All leaders without exception have to come up 'via the system' as products of our own discipleship. They are all homegrown leaders. Even if someone comes to us having demonstrated maturity and leadership in another sphere, they have to start from the bottom and earn their leadership stripes in the Betel context. I believe that this has helped us to avoid ugly splits and divisions.

"Our bi-monthly *cumbres*, or leadership summits, are a gathering of our leaders, junior leaders, and some hopefuls. We come together for a weekend of worship, teaching and training, and on the Sunday afternoon we hold a presbytery of our ordained pastors. Together, we make decisions, and discuss and debate issues. These leadership summits help to nurture our sense of family. As a presbytery, our pastors are answerable to each other, and typically any pastor that is showing maverick tendencies is dealt with first by his peers.

"Evangelism and reaching out to other street addicts is an integral part of Betel's ethos. The men and women in our residences are taught to see that they are to help others in the same way that they have been helped. Added to that sense of local mission is the ongoing recognition of the needs in other countries. Globalization touches even the drug world – we have Russian addicts living in Spain, Polish addicts in Italy, and Peruvian addicts living in New York.

"Betel is a self-financed ministry, and is not dependent on outside gifts and donations. Self-supporting work is an indispensable part of the overall rehabilitation process. Association Betel sends and supports new works, but there is an expectation of financial independence within the first four to six months. This isn't in any way rigid or legislated. Rather, with the new leadership, we seek the Lord and try to get a 'feel' for where He is leading. We set out when we feel He has given us a green light, whether or not the finances are in place. This keeps us free from being tied to budgets, and continuously teaches our leaders about the practicalities of walking by faith.

" 'Free entrance – free exit' is another important aspect to life in Betel. We really don't have a screening process for those who want to enter, except that they express the desire to get off drugs and quit smoking. We go to the streets and drug-dealing centers, and plead with the addicts to come in.

"We used to require that an addict had to come to four consecutive church meetings before we would consider admitting them into residence. That didn't last long, because we discovered that we could never second-guess who would go ahead and who would fail. The most promising guy would miserably disappoint us, and the one that seemed a perpetual loser would end up proving himself to be leadership material. That's still the case.

"Our centers are urban-based. Many other rehabs are cloistered away in the country. Because we need to be close to the city in order to run the businesses, our residences are never more than thirty minutes from the central business district. That means that our guys are faced with a reality check very early in their walk to freedom. Once they've detoxed, they are often in or near their old drug neighborhoods. The difference is that they now have a 'shadow' who can be their guide and strength.

"People are always asking us about Betel's growth. What are our 'secrets?' We have none. Eternal lostness is very real to Betel; our guys have been there. That knowledge puts fire into their preaching and serving. Christian character is produced more effectively and rapidly in the community 'pressure cooker' context. Those two together – a passion for souls coupled with a godly character – makes for a powerful tool in God's hands."

On the inside covers of Elliott's Bible are hand-written quotations and maxims that define Betel's leadership. Two 'Studdisms' conclude this chapter:

> "Christ's call is to feed the hungry, not the full; to save the lost, not the stiff-necked . . . to raise living churches among

the destitute, to capture men from the devil's clutches and snatch them from the very jaws of hell, to enlist and train them for Jesus, and make them into an Almighty Army of God. *But this can only be accomplished by a red-hot, unconventional, unfettered Holy Ghost religion, ... by reckless sacrifice and heroism* in the foremost trenches...

The difficulty is to believe that He can deign to use such scallywags as us, but of course He wants Faith and Fools rather than talents and culture. All God wants is a heart, any old turnip will do for a head; so long as we are empty, all is well, for then He fills us with the Holy Ghost." [9]

Notes

1. C.S. Lewis, *The Magician's Nephew* (Penguin Books, 1951), p. 130.
2. Matthew 28:19, the Great Commission.
3. Herman Hesse, *Demian*, The German Library (New York: Continuum Publishing Company, 1998), p. 166.
4. Marseilles was the location for the 1971 drug movie, *The French Connection*.
5. This is the greeting that the children and the Narnians receive as they enter heaven: "Welcome, in the Lion's name. Come further up and further in." (C.S. Lewis, *The Last Battle*, Penguin Books, 1951, p. 160.)
6. See 1 Samuel 22:1ff.
7. Anaheim: Living Stream Ministry, 1994, p. 1. The work is alternatively titled *The Character of the Lord's Worker*.
8. As of February 2000, the work has prospered markedly. In Lisbon, there are now four men's houses, with sixty men living in community. Three couples live in apartments, and the two *Rastros* are very profitable. Above the main *Rastro* is a church facility that seats 200.
9. Norman Grubb, *C.T. Studd: Cricketer and Pioneer* (Guildford: Lutterworth Press, 1970), pp. 151–2, Grubb's emphasis.

Chapter 9

Unseen Realities

"Have no fear, little flock; for your Father has chosen to give you the kingdom." (Luke 12:32)

It's not just Elliott who prizes Studd's spiritual legacy. Myk McKenzie sent me this in an unsolicited email:

> "I can't resist including this little quote from *Fool and Fanatic*, quotations from the letters of WEC's founder, and Betel's 'grandfather,' C.T. Studd.
>
>> 'God is the head of WEC, the government is on His shoulders and we have given Him our word to walk in His paths. Before I left England God made me declare on many platforms that we went trusting neither in man, nor in committee, except in that of the Committee of the Eternal Three. In His great love God has allowed us to suffer desertions, detractions, defamation and the loss of many friends, so called, but He has only bound us closer to Himself and held our heads straight for the next fence. The greatest honour God has ever given me is that He had confidence in me, the most foolish and weak of His children, that I would not turn tail, lie down, whine or sulk, but just take His bit in my teeth and forge ahead. Do you wonder why my soul jumps for joy? JESUS IS WITH US, HALLELUJAH!
>>
>> There is glory in my soul at the thought of this glorious proof of His presence.' " [1]

Betel can only be fully understood as a supernatural enterprise. The success of this work is grounded in the government of God. Through intimate fellowship with Him, there comes an ongoing attentiveness to His direction and provision. This is something Betel's leadership is continuously challenged to live.

The growth of the Association has required additional administrative staff. A WEC missionary, Jim Regan from the Liverpool area, joined the Madrid family in 1995, and met many of the tremendous organizational needs. He oversaw the head office, created job descriptions, centralized accounts, attended to daily banking functions, and computerized the financial systems. He also linked all the Betel accounts electronically, and began the governmental process of registering Betel with the Spanish social services. This set the senior directors at greater liberty to seek God and minister spiritually, without having to worry about many of the office's problems.

However, it was discovered that there was a limit to the sphere of administrative authority. Raul Reyes, the founder of Betel Germany, called from Krogaspe with an urgent need of a van for their thrift store. As an emerging work they needed help from the Association's projects fund – but, as always, needs exceeded present resources.

Elliott told Raul he would see what they could manage. He asked Jim how much money was in the fund and was told there was considerably more than what Raul needed. Jim then went on to list the month's expected expenses – which more than exceeded the balance. By Jim's estimate it would be irresponsible to use the funds in hand to help Raul.

After Elliott reported this to Raul, the pastor's discouragement stirred Elliott. Here was a young man of faith who seemed to have just hit a wall. He was being asked to sacrifice his all; shouldn't the sending church stand with their pioneer?

Elliott felt that they had just compromised something of their calling, so he spent some time in prayer. He asked the Lord what they should do. Within his spirit, he just as clearly heard the Lord ask him a question: "What is that steward doing in the chamber of the prophet?"

"I knew immediately what God was asking. He wasn't despising the judgement of our missionary administrator. Rather, He was pointing out that certain decisions must be made prophetically, in the dimensions of faith, even if those decisions seem to cut across sound natural judgement."

Elliott went to Jim, told him to send the money to Raul and noted, "When we need the money for the coming expenses, it will be there." The check was sent to Raul, and in the coming month more than double that amount was received to cover the expenses that Jim was anticipating.

Elliott concluded this anecdote with these words: "This was a defining moment for Betel – our life of faith, and the conduct of this ministry could not and would not be limited by our bookkeeper's ledger. We will always contend with that fine line between faith-risk and recklessness, but we will not surrender the growth of the work to conservative accounting prudence and efficiency." That from a man with a MBA from Harvard Business School.

A heightened expectation of the Lord's gracious provision pervades Betel, from the mundane to the miraculous. Friends of the Teppers, Bill and Melinda Fish, were visiting Betel Spain. While driving, they saw a fruit stand sign that read: *"Chirimoyas 2 Kilos por 200 pesetas."* They stopped, and Elliott bought two kilos of fruit.

"When we returned to the car I put the plastic bag on the floor of the van, and Chirimoya juice ran out. I looked at the Fishs. 'They're too ripe – that's why they're so cheap. We just got taken.' Just then my eye caught a hundred pesetas lying on the highway. I went over and picked it up and said, 'Well, never mind. God's given us back some of the money.' Melinda said, 'It isn't fair. These kinds of things are always happening to you. The next thing – who knows, another house will fall out of the air into your lap!'

"As soon as she had finished speaking, my cell phone rang. I answered it and it was Pino, our pastor in Malaga. 'Elias, a woman has just offered us a house as a gift. Should we take it?'

" 'If it's for free and if you can use it, sure.'

"Bill, Melinda and Mary had heard the conversation, but asked for further details. I told them of the circumstances of the call, and in her most theatrical Texan drawl Melinda cried, 'I don't believe it! I don't believe it! It's not fair! You are not on the same page as the rest of us mere mortals!' "

Stories of timely intervention are numerous. They sound very similar to those that George Muller told of in his work with the orphans in Bristol, England, a hundred and forty years ago.[2]

In 1996 Betel-Naples planted a work in the province of Bari in a town called Spinnazzola. The work had only been open a few months, and was not yet self-supporting. The monthly rent was due – 250,000 lire. With all of the start-up expenses the men had only 40,000 lire left. They prayed together and asked God for help. Then they prepared the evening meal.

After supper, five strangers appeared at their door. The group explained that they were from a church in a nearby town and had heard of the new Betel Center in Spinnazzola. The men invited them into the lounge room, and the introductions continued. After chatting for a few moments, one of the guests pulled out an envelope. "Our church took up an offering for the Center." When the leader opened the envelope, there was exactly 210,000 lire inside – the balance needed for the rent.

Two of the Italian leaders had been looking for a place to open a thrift shop in Bari. They found a place that seemed ideal, and felt as though the Lord would open the way to sign the lease. Back in Naples, a man walked in off the street. He had been around for a while, and everyone considered him "relationally challenged." He was an eccentric businessman, and talked incessantly when given the chance.

The Betelitos took turns spending time with him. That day, three of them quickly declined: "Not my turn; I talked to him Tuesday." "I spent an hour with him last week." It was decided it was Lello's turn. Everyone else disappeared quickly.

Later, Lello rejoined them. He had a big grin on his face. "None of you guys wanted to talk with him – boy, did you get that one wrong! You know why he came by today?" Lello held out a cheque for 5 million lire – money that they were able to use to start up the *Rastro* in Bari.

Material blessings are only one of the various ways the Lord demonstrates His favor on Betel.

Milagros – "Miracles" – was dying slowly. She had lived an extremely rough life as a bank robber and a heroin addict. She never stopped swearing. Because of her foul mouth and bitter spirit, she scared most of the Betelitas she lived with. Ironically, she died of cancer of the tongue.

A few days before her death, Milagros had an open vision in which she saw the Lord. She was very weak, but it was so vivid that she sat up in her bed and stretched out her arms. The woman caring for her, Yolanda, tried to settle her.

"Can't you see Him? It's Jesus! He's so beautiful. And He's told me that He's coming for me." She smiled, relaxed, and died in complete peace a few days later.

She had arrived at Betel three months before her death, and in ninety days had traveled from hell to heaven. At Milagro's funeral, the testimonies of her transformation were so compelling that her addict-brother joined Betel.

Open visions are rare. Most of Betel's spiritual direction comes as they wait on the Lord before His Word, and nurture providential relationships.

Raul Reyes came to Betel Madrid from Amistad Puebla Mexico, after hearing Elliott tell of the work of Betel. For five years, from January 1990 to April 1995, he served as a missionary, and lived and worked with the addicts in the Mejorada house. He befriended Lutz Damerow, a German from Neumünster, a small town outside of Hamburg. Lutz was visiting Betel for the summer, and stayed with Raul and the other men in Mejorada.

It was a spiritual turning point in Lutz's life, and when he returned to Germany, he talked four friends into visiting the work in Spain. On their return, the friends told Betel stories to whomever would listen. Two local farmers, Reimer and Helma Schulte-Steinberg, were impressed with what they heard. If Betel would start a work in their area, they had a farmhouse property that could be used as a residence.

The house was in ruins. It had received no care whatsoever for sixteen years. But it was rent-free, and the farmer offered to provide a heating system and some materials for the refurbishment of the building.

Hamburg is a strategic city in the drug world, and a gateway to the Baltic countries and the Eastern Block. Betel leadership felt that a new work in northern Germany could certainly meet the high need in the greater Hamburg area, and would serve as a launch pad for further Betel plants.

The present work certainly has an international feel about it. While visiting Betel Deutschland, we surveyed the men around the breakfast table. We asked after their homelands, their years of addiction, and their time at Betel.

Israel is the house leader. He has never done drugs but his brother was an abusive heroin addict. Betel's ministry brought radical transformation to his brother's life, and Israel was so impressed that he serves Betel as a career missionary. Vito is from Italy, and was addicted to heroin for twenty years. He has been at Betel for three years. Antonio came from Spain, and was addicted to cocaine and heroin for fifteen years. Betel has been his home for the last four years. Andreas is from Germany, and was an alcoholic for eight years. He's been in Betel for two years. Thomas is also from Germany. He had a seven-year heroin habit, and has been in Betel eighteen months. Volker, from Hamburg, was addicted to heroin for twenty years. He too has been in Betel eighteen months. Luis is a missionary from Mexico and has been at Betel eleven months. Jewgeni, a Russian, was addicted to heroin for four years. Betel has been home for nine months. Felix is newly arrived from Switzerland, and is just through his detox after ten years of heroin. Frank is a local, and has been at Betel six months, after two years of alcoholism. Rene is also a German: five years of heroin, nineteen months at Betel. Johannes, Germany, fifteen years of heroin, 135 days at Betel. Edmond, Usbekistan, five years of heroin, six days at Betel. Sebastian, Poland, six years of heroin, five weeks at Betel.

In January 1995, a team was assembled from the Madrid center – Raul, Mario, and Israel, all Spanish speakers, and commissioned to plant Betel Deutschland. When they started a thrift shop in Neumünster, their neighbors all said that they would never be able to pay the rent. Their confidence rested in a promise of restoration that the Lord had impressed upon them from Zechariah 14:9 and 14:

"The LORD *will become King over all the earth; on that day He will be the only* LORD *and His name the only name ... and the wealth of the surrounding nations will be gathered up."*

They have never missed a month's rent.

The "wealth" of the surrounding nations was not just material: Raul married one of Lutz's local German friends, Meike!

In three years, the pioneers had renovated the farmhouse. The horse stable was transformed into a kitchen, dining room, washrooms and showers. The cow stable became the workshop. The living-room was renovated, and turned into an eighteen-bed dormitory. Above the workshop in the barn is a huge furniture storage area; behind it is another six-bed dormitory. They rebuilt the garage and patio.

When Betel Deutschland first began the work, the village was not at all happy with the thought of drug addicts living in their backyard. But as they watched how industrious the men were, it dispelled their fears. The neighbors in the village have been very impressed with their work, and Betel is not only well accepted, but sought after. They regularly receive work contracts for renovations and building projects in the community, and one real estate company in Neumünster retains some of the Betel men to paint and refurbish their rental properties.

The new work also began to receive food donations from local grocers and bakers. Because the guys picking up the food were so polite and happy, their smiles continued to build rapport. Furniture donations picked up markedly, especially as Betel prayed for better quality goods!

Raul beamed as he told their story. "It seems that the more we need, the more the donations come in. As the number of men in residence increases, and our expenses go up, the more work we have. And as the work has prospered, the health of the men has improved. Volker will tell you *his* story. His doctor really is astounded."

The work has not been without its challenges of faith, and its timely moments. In December 1999, there was no money. The insurance premium was due for the community's seven vehicles. A first-time gift from a local church group covered their expenses.

Every month, they are able to pay over $9,000 in expenses for *Rastro* and office rent, vehicle operation, house expenses, and food – for a community of fifteen residents and five leaders.

In September 1998 Betel-Deutschland leadership felt stirred to pray 1 Corinthians 2:9, asking for *"things beyond our seeing, things beyond our hearing, things beyond our imagining, all prepared by God for those who love him."* The more they prayed, the more they saw an increase.

Through 1998 they looked for property in Hamburg to start a new *Rastro*. They saw a vacant store they thought would serve them, but the owners wouldn't rent it to them. For a year they prayed that the Lord would direct them to the right place. Raul saw an advertisement for a store on the street that they felt would best serve them. When they went to check out the address, it was in the very block they had hoped for.

Their bookkeeper, a Christian, told them they were crazy to even think about opening a new store with a $3,800 monthly rental; it was too far beyond their means. The community prayed and fasted – some of the men, twice a week – and they felt that this was a door the Lord was opening.

As they pursued the offer, they learned that the owners wanted a three-month security bond, which was completely beyond Betel's financial reach. However, the previous tenants offered Betel more than three months' rent if they would renovate and paint the place to meet their rental release requirements! They also wanted out of their five-year lease a year early, and gave Betel a bonus for taking it over for them.

Their bookkeeper grows ever more astonished as she watches Betel's cash flow and profit. "What you are doing is impossible, but it works!" She recently invited them to her church one Sunday to testify to God's miraculous provision – and through the course of the service, charismatic prejudices came tumbling down.

In a corporate prayer time, Betel Deutschland became especially burdened for the many prostitutes that work the red-light district. They received the impression that if they could start a coffee bar in town, they would have an opportunity to meet new people and give the women a safe and stable place to work.

Raul saw an advertisement for a property in the paper. It fitted their needs for the coffee bar, and more. It would give them a large meeting room for their infant church and for the office space they needed.

In his devotions that morning, Raul read 1 Chronicles 22:10–15, and was especially encouraged by the last verse: *"You have at your disposal a large force of workmen, masons, sculptors, carpenters, and every kind of skilled craftsman."* Without knowing it, another of the leadership team, Lina, Mario's wife, confirmed the very same word in her prayer time that night.

The day after they signed the contract for the lease on the new coffee bar, a stranger gave them ten pounds of coffee, something they'd never before received. From within their own ranks, Volker, a licensed electrician, did the electrical work, and Dimitrij from Siberia did the ceramic tiling and carpentry. The furniture shop collected and repaired tables and chairs. An unsolicited donation of $1,500 was received, just when the bills for the coffee bar were at their highest.

Before they could occupy the building, fifteen windows in the facility needed replacing. They were out of money, so they asked the Lord for provision. They went to a demolition sale and found thermopane windows the exact size they required. They even got privacy glass for the washrooms!

"As we've watched the farmhouse and coffee complex being renovated, the men are themselves being restored. They're growing stronger, and we believe the Lord is fulfilling His Isaiah 61 promises: His Spirit is graciously upon us, and He is binding up the broken-hearted, setting the captive free, and releasing those in prison. He is raising up oaks of righteousness, and restoring ruins long laid desolate." [3]

Volker Hübler is one of their walking miracles of restoration. He is forty-two years old and has been in Betel Deutschland for eighteen months, since August 1998. He used drugs for twenty years. By 1983, he was fully addicted to heroin and cocaine. [4]

"I used to sell drugs in the Hamburg train station. One day while I was dealing, someone gave me a Betel flyer. I put it in my pocket and carried it around for six months. It was a miracle that I didn't lose it, or that it wasn't destroyed. It passed through the washing machine many times. Jesus held His hand over it all that time.

"When I finally looked at it, all I could read was the phone number and the words, 'There is a way to get out.' Something inside me said, 'Yes, there must be a way.' The desire to stop using drugs had been in my heart for the last two or three years. I tried methadone, and rehabs, but I wasn't getting anywhere.

"I was injecting twenty times a day, and every time, I'd stare at the needle and ask, '*What* am I doing?' I wanted to die. I couldn't go on. I was very sick physically at that time, more dead than alive. I couldn't leave my apartment because I was living on the second floor. If I went downstairs, I never would have made it back up again.

"I was only able to get to Betel with my girlfriend's help, and a lot of drugs."

"After twenty years of addiction, the withdrawal and the first three months at Betel were like dying. I couldn't walk more than thirty steps. People here in Betel prayed for me, talked to me, and looked after me. I was never alone. The guys kept telling me about Jesus, and what Jesus had done in their lives.

"Those first months, I used to ask myself, 'What am I doing here? These guys are *crazy*. They live without women, without money – how can you live without money?!' I couldn't live without money. Money was everything to me. Money was life. You have to have money to survive.

"Here, Betel buys you everything you really need, and they *give* you the things you can't buy with all the money in the world. Now I know I don't need money if I have those things, the things that really matter.

"But back then, I kept thinking, 'I need to get out of here.' But I couldn't, because there was something at Betel which kept me. I saw something in the guys, and I thought, 'Wow, look at them – what do they have that I don't? They're always happy and at peace.' That's why I stayed."

Volker threw his head back and laughed. "Now I'm *crazy* too!

"At Betel, we live like monks. That's what I thought when I first got here. For the first few months, I didn't like it. After a while I thought, 'Maybe it's better for me to live like a monk. Maybe it's the way out.'

"I used to smoke fifty cigarettes a day. At Betel, you are not allowed to smoke. That's one of the rules. The leaders know that it's hard – nicotine is harder to kick than heroin. But they also know that unless we are willing to make a total break with our past, we will never be free from it. That seemed like a monk's decision to me – to leave the world – my old world – completely behind."

"Before I came to Betel, I had been reading the Bible regularly for the last six years of addiction. I went to Sunday school as a child and I knew about Jesus, but I lived without Him. I turned my back on Him. But as I was destroying my life I kept remembering, 'There is a God.' The Word was like a magnet. It kept drawing me. As I read my Bible, God's Word began to live in me. It started to become life in me. It just keeps getting bigger and bigger.

"It took two or three weeks at Betel before I gave my heart to Jesus. I'd been listening to Vito and Antonio tell me what Jesus had done in their lives. They would share their testimonies in the devotionals, while we were working together in the kitchen. It made me think, 'Well, maybe it's a way for me.'

"Here in Betel I was born again. I am really happy today. I can laugh – I have never laughed so much in all my life. I have no more fears, I have peace in my heart, and I can sleep at night. I have never felt so good. I know that Jesus is the only way and I have to follow Him.

"I *am* a new man, and it really is a miracle, because Jesus has changed me totally. When I came to Betel I really was almost dead. My body was totally destroyed and I had nothing. I had liver-problems, and terminal hepatitis B and C – I'd had it since 1984. A couple of weeks ago I had a bad pain in my tummy that I thought needed to be looked at. I went to the doctor, and he wanted to do blood tests. That was a big problem for him, because my veins are all collapsed. He couldn't find a useable vein anywhere in my body. It took two hours for him to draw blood. I offered to help, but he wouldn't let me.

"When the doctor saw the results of the tests, he couldn't believe it. He said, 'I know a little bit about your drug history – this is a great miracle. You are healed.' There are no signs of hepatitis B or C. They are totally healed. I was on no medication, nothing. No medicine. Only Jesus.

"That's why I say, for me there was no other way. There was no help in the world. Only God could help me, and He really did."

"I don't know how long I will be staying in Betel – I know that I don't want to leave. Especially in these last months, I have received so much I want more and more and more. I haven't enough of Jesus. There is something special here at Betel, something of His presence I know I won't find anywhere else. I want the Spirit of God to use me more, so that I can be more of a blessing to others.

"My heart is to stay here at the farm in Germany, and build a house for women addicts and their children. There is nothing here in Germany for them like there is in Spain. We need a place for everyone who wants out of drugs. A place where all you have to do is say, 'I need help.' I'd like to build it because I lost my wife and all my girlfriends to drugs. I lost my daughter – she was born as a drug addict.

"There are so many young children out on the streets. I want to do something to help them. It hurts my heart to see the red-light district crowded with addicts and prostitutes."

Betel-Birmingham has its own miracle stories to tell.

As teenagers, Kent and Mary Alice Martin each felt called to missions, and worked towards preparing their lives for work on Spanish-speaking fields. As newly-weds, they met Elliott when he was on a deputation visit at their home church in Bethlehem, Pennsylvania. His stories of the Spirit's work at Betel arrested their hearts. Elliott was doing what they were dreaming about – he was evangelizing the outcasts, discipling new converts in the context of community, and sending out equipped leaders to plant new churches.

In April 1991, the Martins left the States to join Betel. They anticipated spending a few years in Madrid learning the Betel ethos, and then hoped to be used to pioneer new works in Spain or other Spanish-speaking contexts.

In May 1995, an unexpected invitation came to visit Birmingham, England. It came from Terrance Roslyn-Smith, the president of SEED (Social Enterprise, Evangelism and Discipleship), a group of British church and drug-rehabilitation leaders. Some of the members had visited Betel Madrid months earlier. SEED's goal was to begin revolutionizing British rehab by helping to establish income-generating models like Betel. They wanted to know more about Betel's ability to be self-financing.

Elliott and Kent responded to the invitation. They were scheduled to meet with the committee for two and a half hours, and then visit Windmill House, a nearby Christian rehab work. At the meeting, Elliott and Kent were asked, "What is Betel looking for, and how can we help?" The following priorities were itemized:

1. Betel needed a property with multiple buildings. This would give the new work the flexibility to isolate residents undergoing drug or alcohol withdrawal if required by the government.

2. It was hoped that such a property could be secured from the government, a large foundation or Christian trust for little or no rent. It was recognized that bringing older buildings up to fire and access codes have cost other organizations upwards of half a million dollars.

3. Betel in Britain was to be defined as a "religious community," not a "drug rehabilitation center." As a community of faith, Betel would not have to meet the restrictions applied to licensed professional residential care programs.

4. The ideal site of a new Betel would be in the "fringe" countryside, placing it beyond the pressures of urban vices, but near to business opportunities within the city.

Alex Elsaesser sat through the meeting, and seemed almost disengaged from the discussions. He spent most of the time reading an earlier book about Betel, *Rescue Shop Within a Yard of Hell*.[5] When the meeting ended, it was Alex who took Elliott and Kent on the tour of the local rehab work.

After a twenty-five-minute drive from the city center, they arrived at Windmill House, a sprawling five-acre estate in the rolling countryside. Alex proceeded to tell Elliott and Kent that five years ago he had obtained a lease for Windmill House, with the hope of caring for drug addicts and alcoholics.

Alex showed them the first building on the site. It was equipped as a furniture restoration shop. Elliott and Kent stared at one another. They told Alex that Betel is a self-supporting enterprise, and is largely dependent on second-hand furniture sales and restoration.

Next, they toured the three-story main house, a beautifully kept forty-room mansion overlooking a huge lawn. The lounge, the games room, the well-equipped kitchen and dining hall seemed all made-to-order. Upstairs, they were surprised to find dorm rooms with multiple bunk beds. They understood that the authorities required that residents have private or semi-private rooms.

"Yes, that's true," Alex responded. "If you come under the laws for drug rehabilitation centers. But we don't. We've explained to authorities that we're simply a 'caring Christian community' which provides residence for the needy."

"That's the exact legal posture we've just been advised to explore, to see if it's even possible," Kent said. "And here you are doing it!"

Returning outdoors, they walked through the two smaller houses and a multi-room garage towards the back of the property. Five buildings in all.

As they strolled across the spacious lawn, Alex opened his heart. "We've set this whole place up to take in addicts and the needy. The only problem is that we haven't been able to make Windmill House function as we'd like. It's time to let it go." He said that he had been asking the Lord for direction as to who might take over the work.

"We invited you today to see if Betel would consider opening its program here."

Alex explained that Windmill House was leased from a secular trust founded by the Cadbury family. The Cadburys, of chocolate fame, were originally Quakers. They have a history of philanthropic benevolence. The Cadbury mansion currently met all fire and building codes. And while maintenance costs were high, monthly rent on the entire estate was just $45. Elliott and Kent were speechless. Every aspect of their ideal center seemed to be realized. In one hour's time, with no prior knowledge or planning, Betel of Britain had gone from theory to reality. Over a cup of tea, the three of them talked through details of the transition. Alex asked, "When can you take it over?" Elliott and Kent hadn't thought through a time-line; they stammered, "Eighteen months." Alex was hoping for January 1996, in six months' time.

Other pieces fell into their laps. On an unsolicited visit to the Betels in Spain, a Christian lawyer offered to donate his services to legalize Betel of Great Britain as a charity.

A few months later, Kent and Mary Alice were invited to meet David Partington, a Director of SEED. He is considered by many to be the most influential voice in Christian drug rehabilitation in Britain. But Betel works on a very different model. Kent wondered if it would be difficult to convince David of Betel's viability.

David quickly cut to the chase. "What Betel is doing in Spain is the future of rehab in Britain. Government funding is expected to be cut back, while hard drug use in Great Britain has tripled between 1989 and 1992. Glasgow, a city of only 470,000, has an estimated 12,000 injecting addicts." David's enthusiastic support for Betel, coupled with WEC's solid missionary reputation in the UK, opened doors far quicker than expected. Church groups and rehabs as far away as Glasgow and Edinburgh were soon wanting to know when they could begin referring desperate addicts to Betel.

Back in Madrid, a team was formed: Kent and Mary Alice were joined by fellow WEC missionaries Victor and Sandra Bautista, and two recovered Spanish addicts, Eduardo Almagro and Antonio Fernandez. As "Betel of Britain," they took over Windmill House in January, as Alex had hoped. Within months they had a dozen men in various stages of recovery. They were soon able to open a charity thrift shop. They were, however, vehicularly challenged. One day a gentleman came into the shop and started asking questions about Betel. He was the Director of the Aston Re-investment Trust and the local representative of the Charities Aid Foundation; within weeks he had arranged for a trust loan that enabled Betel to buy a desperately needed seven-ton truck.

Four years later, Betel of Britain operates three trucks, a double-decker outreach bus, four vans and as many cars. One furniture shop has become four. They are presently renovating an inner-city warehouse that will be used as a thrift shop, a church, and an outreach center. Currently, the community at Windmill House thrives with thirty-eight men and five women in recovery, five missionary families, their children, and several single workers – a total of sixty-five people.

Time has shown just how miraculous a provision Windmill House was. The search for a second residence to expand the work has been anything but quick or easy. Others' experience concurs. Upon learning that Windmill House was a gift that was the result of an unanticipated afternoon meeting in May 1995, an astonished visitor commented, "Our charity has been searching twenty-five years and still hasn't found a property like this one."

The supernatural government of God has a single distinctive: He is always the One initiating, and we are always the ones responding. Most churches and ministries live this dynamic the other way round – we initiate, and hope and pray that the Lord blesses our efforts to His glory. But miracles, be they of provision, or intervention, or restoration, only come according to the divine order – His initiative, and our response. The founding of Betel of Britain certainly seems to have been a motion proposed and carried unanimously by the "Committee of the Eternal Three."

Notes

1. *Fool and Fanatic?* compiled by Jean Walker (Bultstrode, Gerrards Cross: WEC Press, 1980), p. 19.
2. *The Autobiography of George Muller* (New Kensington, PA: Whitaker House, 1984).
3. Verses 1–4.
4. The interview with Volker was conducted without a translator. English is his second language.
5. Stewart and Marie Dinnen (Reading: Christian Focus Publications, 1995).

Chapter 10

Behind the Mountain, a Whisper

"Unless a grain of wheat falls into the ground and dies, it remains that and nothing more; but if it dies, it bears a rich harvest."   (John 12:24)

Since 20 January 1994, the Toronto Airport Christian Fellowship (formerly the Toronto Airport Vineyard) has been hosting renewal meetings six nights a week. Gerald Coates, the leader of Pioneer People, was one of the guest speakers at the third anniversary services. On the Saturday night, 17 January 1997, he began to prophesy in the course of his sermon. I was seated in the second row.

"Guy, I saw your next book: *Fire in the Church*. Fire in the Church, fire in the Church. You are going to write things that you've never seen before but they're in your heart and they are in your mind. It's a new sort of church, Guy...

This book is going to go around the world. Different models of church. Models for deaf people, models for elderly people, models for sick people, models for black, models for brown, models for multi-ethnic communities, models for the rich, models for the poor, models of music, models of theology...

People are going to read this book and they are going to feel they've come home. They've come to this great lake where they can drink.

Fire in the Church – what God is doing with this thing – this fire that has taken a hold of us. Some of us can't go to bed at night because of this fire. We wake up early in the morning because of this fire; we feel so shallow and limited and fraudulent, but we long for what only God can do. The revival fire of God ...

Revival is on the heart of God. It's not for us, Church. It's for the millions dying of AIDS, and the broken-hearted mothers and fathers and brothers and sisters of criminals in prison. Of blacks, browns, and yellows ostracized for the pigmentation of their skin. It's for the millions of broken lives and families ...

Fire in the Church, fire in the Church, fire in the Church ...

This lot may look informal and undisciplined, but they are going to be the most disciplined army that the world has ever seen. Not with legalism but with love. Not with rules but with grace. Not with fear but with kindness. That's the sort of discipline that God is looking for ... " [1]

Several months later, I was invited to preach at Betel. Elliott had heard of my involvement with the renewal at the Toronto Airport Christian Fellowship and had read my first book, *Catch the Fire: the Toronto Blessing*. He asked if I would come to speak at the *cumbre* which was to be held from 7 to 10 November 1997.

Though the invitation unsettled me a little, I had a very clear sense that the Lord wanted me to accept the request. As I prepared for the conference I spent considerable time praying, and asked over and over, "What do You want me to say to recovered drug addicts?" I didn't feel that I received a great deal of revelation, but there was a growing sense that I wasn't just responding to Elliott's invitation. Rather, I felt that the Lord was sending me to Madrid and to this church called Betel.

Mid-Atlantic, I was staring out the airplane window, praying. A verse of Scripture echoed in the recesses of my jet-lagging brain: *"Has not God chosen those who are poor in the eyes of the world to be rich in faith and to possess the kingdom he has promised to those who love him?"* After a bit of a concordance search, I found the reference: James 2:5. As I meditated on the text, I had a clear sense of the Spirit saying, "I am sending you to Betel, not so much for you to teach them, but for them to teach you."

⊂∽⊃

The second night of the *cumbre,* I met with some of Betel's leadership in an upstairs office. We prayed together until the congregation began worshipping. As we left the office to join them, I paused on the open balcony and looked down over the 750 passionate worshippers who had gathered. Tears filled my eyes and streamed down my face.

Here were such broken lives, *redeemed* by the grace of God. The radiant glory of God on their scarred faces was unlike anything I'd ever seen. The sense of their commitment and abandon to God and His Kingdom was almost tangible.

Through the tears, I said out loud, "They do not belong to this world. They're living on the edge of eternity." I felt that this Betel fellowship drew me closer to that edge than I'd ever been before. I wasn't just having a "warm, fuzzy charismatic moment alone with God."

A month later, Elliott sent me a report on the *cumbre.*

"Over fifty unsaved gave their lives to Jesus. We know these men and women, and we are not counting the many recommitments in this number.

Nikki, an aggressively militant, angry Muslim, and a heroin addict, has been in Betel for five months. He had been extremely antagonistic to the gospel, but is one of those who gave their lives to Jesus. He is now a gentle man, and is showing remarkable kindnesses to others. His doctors are also astounded – they expected him to be dead by now. They can find no trace of his terminal TB or AIDS.

Loli and Miguel, our pastors in Galicia, told us that Loli's unsaved brother from Madrid stopped by the church to see them. He has had no interest in the gospel and was not seeking God. But during the meeting he was overcome, weeping and trembling in the presence of God. He was one of the last to leave the meeting.

The Almeria leader, Fernando, says that most of the hardest, resistant men have been converted. He himself left the Sunday meeting and sat weeping in the van for a long time. When he tried to explain what was happening he said, 'I felt God hugging me.' Fernando never knew his father.

In the Mostoles house, a new addict just off the street was converted. His comment: 'This high is better than drugs!'

The Mejorada house leader said of his detoxing addicts: 'Every single one of them has given his life to Christ and our house has been transformed! One cried with joy for four days.'

The men from Mariblanca returned to their farm after the Sunday night meeting. Some were staggering as if drunk. A number went walking around saying over and over again, 'Here am I, Lord, send me.' They are functionally illiterate and only newly discipled.

A young Italian recently confessed his life's secret. He had been involved in a drug murder, and lived as he put it, 'a hell of guilt.' Sunday, watching everyone else drawing near God and finding God, he cried out. His testimony: 'The Spirit of love cleansed me and now I know God loves me.' The church is astounded by his brokenness and humility. His honesty has impacted the whole house community.

Eduardo testified that during the first few days of the conference, he was like the prodigal's elder brother,[2] and refused to attend the feast. He was jealous of everyone else's joy. He confessed that he was eaten up with bitterness for life's injustices. On Saturday after the leaders' meeting, he began to laugh at everything and could not stop. The knot of bitterness disappeared from his heart and he feels like a new man. His house leader commented: 'His sour expression is gone and even the fixed lines in his face have changed.'

Our Betel lawyer could not sleep for the joy and peace of God. His home has been revolutionized.

Our mid-day intercession hour after lunch has doubled, and many of the new converts are attending."

Elliott concluded the email: "It has been that kind of week – grace and love from heaven, more than we dreamed possible."

Five months later, in April 1998, I was with Mike Bickle of the Kansas City Fellowship. We were speaking at a conference in

Melbourne, Florida. Over an extended meal together, I told him about my aeroplane reflections on James 2:5, and my experiences at Betel. Mike has a huge heart for the poor, and a greater passion to know more of the glory of God than anyone I know. At the end of the afternoon, Mike looked at me and said, "It sure seems that the Lord is calling you to know so much more of His splendor, His beauty, and His glory." Mike affectionately called it "Project Glory."

Two years have passed. I have been privileged to be with the Betel Association of Churches five further times, and I have been studying, meditating, praying, and reading around the theme of "glory." This concluding chapter puts a prophetic frame around the redemptive and transformative work of the Spirit in and through Betel. While the balance of the book has been the telling of individual, personal stories of transformation, what follows is a larger, corporate story from the gospel of Jesus Christ. It is a partial fulfillment of Gerald's prophetic word regarding "Fire in the Church," and Mike's "Project Glory."

I have devoted my adult life to studying the work of the Spirit in the Church of Jesus Christ. It has been a wonderful opportunity and privilege to have preached in over 150 different churches. So far, Betel has no equals. More than any other church I've been associated with, they understand that the Church is a supernatural enterprise. Ministry cannot be reduced to a program or a structure, but must continuously attend to the call, direction and intervention of the Spirit.

Betel understands that the Church does not have a mission. Rather, the Mission has a church. Betel's *raison d'etre* is clearly defined and lived – they exist to reach substance-dependent and marginalized people with the love of Jesus Christ.

Their worship comes from a deep, sacred source that is rooted in a gratitude greater than any I've ever experienced, personally or corporately.

Betel's peer care is also most remarkable – again and again, ex-addicts explain why they're off the streets: "Love's grip was stronger than heroin's."

More than any church I know of, Betel disciples new believers more quickly, and more thoroughly.

The same can be said of their leadership development, and their ability to plant new churches.

Betel's exercise of faith and prayer is extraordinary, as is the ongoing sanctification of the believers.

Their mystical understanding of ministry is also most uncommon – there is a strong sense that what counts is not what they do for Jesus, but, rather, the life that He lives in them.

Lastly, the power of grace, mercy and forgiveness is truly life changing in Betel.

To reduce Betel to "ten transferable principles," or "five keys," however, is to miss that which sets Betel apart. What makes Betel so dynamic is relationship, not reproducible structure.

My second visit to Betel in September 1998 began in Ciudad Real Spain, at the Betania Conference Center. The Betel pastors were gathered, and I was to teach and minister for two and a half days. On the morning of our last day together, one of the senior pastors, Juan Botanico of Bilbao, spoke to Elliott during breakfast. After the morning worship Juan came forward and addressed the gathering. He shook his head. "I really don't want to do this – I haven't wanted to do this for the last twenty-four hours. I've spoken with Elliott, and he feels that I have to."

He looked around the room. "What I feel the Lord is telling me to do is to take Elliott by the hand, and then lie down at his feet. Crazy, no?" Juan stared at the floor for a moment. "I want to be obedient more than I want to be sane, so here goes!"

Elliott came forward, and Juan lay down on the floor, holding Elliott's hand. Moments later, Elliott lay on the floor beside Juan.

What followed was a stunned silence, until another of the senior pastors, Luis Pino, came over, lay down, and took Elliott's other hand. One by one the other pastors joined the three of them on the floor, hand in hand. Chairs were quietly moved, and a circle of prostrated pastors stretched around the room.

My ministry team and I prayed from a distance – this was clearly a time just for Betel. Their physical posturing seemed to be something of a prophetic pantomime: as they lay on the floor, the sense of spiritual alignment that was taking place was, again, almost tangible. None of us had ever seen anything like the radical humility of these pastors, their chosen obedience, and their loving submission to one another.

I returned to Betel the following year, again with a ministry team. My friend Alan Wiseman was one of them. He has a remarkable prophetic gifting and an uncommon ability to hear the voice of the Lord. We began the tour in Lisbon, and then drove seven hours to the Betania Conference Center to meet with the pastors, as we had done previously. At supper the first night, I felt that the Lord gave me two prophetic words for Betel. I began to pray for further revelation. At the same time Alan heard the Lord whispering, but could not yet hear what He was saying.

During the next morning's worship, Elliott answered his mobile phone, and then called a break. He announced that Betel's brand new furniture van had just been stolen. It was a private gift from the Caja De Madrid, in recognition of their work with drug addicts. Elliott called us to prayer, specifically for the safe return of this vehicle. Passionate and militant intercessions were poured forth, but Alan and I both felt very uncomfortable. We couldn't join our prayers in calling forth the rightful return of the van. Alan felt there was a quiet message being given by the Lord through this experience. We waited and listened.

Later that morning Alan began to hear in his spirit the same whispering he heard the night before. This time he could hear the words, and began writing in his journal.

We worshipped for a while, and then Nines Matesanz, Oscar's wife, began prophesying. Her word was based on Jacob's struggle with the angel of the Lord. What we gathered through the translation was that Nines felt that this was a time when they, the leadership of Betel, were also wrestling with God. It would be a breakthrough moment for them; through it they would know more of God's presence and power than ever before, but they would leave Betania limping, just like Jacob.[3]

In the evening's teaching time, I traced a cycle of rise and fall, success and failure, and applied it to the history of Christian experience. The pattern begins with brokenness before the Lord, and the recognition of our intense need for God. Because He gives grace to the humble, we experience His blessing and favor. Inevitably, we presume upon that grace, become confident in *our* achievements, and cross a threshold into presumption and sensed privilege. Our pride becomes our undoing, and the cycle begins again, as we repent and bring our brokenness before the Lord again.

The teaching hinged on the two prophetic words I had been given the evening before – "favor" and "privilege." The Lord's favor had so clearly been on Betel – but they stood at the threshold. Would they cross over into privilege?

The theft of the van seemed to be a test, a prophetic challenge. Like Jacob, were they willing to wrestle?

The evening's teaching was audiotaped.

> "The van was a gift, in recognition of your achievements. A gift, but not a possession. It is the Lord who gives, and the Lord who takes away – blessed be the name of the Lord.
>
> If it's a gift, you can never own it. As soon as you start feeling, 'That van was *ours*,' then you've crossed over from favor into privilege. This is not a call to passivity or carelessness. In the face of that theft, you must do your spiritual warfare, but your warfare is worship. It is not so much binding thieving spirits, as it is giving thanks in the knowledge that the Lord goes out to fight before you.
>
> With the van, it is yours to claim spiritual ground, but not ownership."

I returned to the cycle of rise and fall.

> "You can never outgrow brokenness, and there is no bottom to humility.
>
> If you become proud in your own strength and achievement, the Lord will lift from you His grace.
>
> The favor of the Lord is on Betel, and will continue to be so, as long as you continue to humble yourselves. The prosperity that you are enjoying is wonderful and right, but it must take you back to gratitude and humility, not to pride and privilege."

I then read from Alan's journal:

> "Last night I heard the Lord calling you from the other side
> of the mountains. He was calling you in a whisper and I
> could not hear what He was saying. This morning I heard
> the whisper again. He was calling, 'Come back.'
>
> It was His intention to call you in a whisper, and if you
> do not respond He will level the mountains to make it
> easier for you to come.
>
> The mountains are the strength of His providence which
> can easily become the place where you would settle and
> find comfort. But the Lord's providence is not your home,
> nor your comfort. His voice and His presence are your only
> home. Come over the mountains or He will remove them,
> to make it easier for you to come."

To our astonishment, the leaders were cut to the heart. One by
one they began to come forward and kneel on the floor, a signal
of their repentance. As I went round the room blessing their
obedience, many of them were weeping, or, at my touch, burst
into tears. There was, once again, an almost tangible sense of
the glory of God.

The rest of our team sat at the back of the room speechless.
Part of it was awe, and our own worship. Part of it was paradox.
How could we as affluent and privileged North Americans have
given such a call of repentance to these ex-drug addicts? Ours
was far more the sin than theirs. Yet these humble men and
women were teaching us what brokenness really meant.

I have been meditating on Alan's word to Betel as I have worked
on "Project Glory." I've reflected on the mountain image, and
its connection with glory. It has become a word that not only
explains the dynamics at work at Betel, but becomes a much
larger call "to those who have ears to hear."

In the Book of Exodus, Moses meets the Lord on Mount Sinai
three times. In chapters 19 and 24, he ventures not just to
the top of the mountain, but into the "glory of the Lord," the
smoke, the cloud, the thunder and lightning that surrounded
the mountain.[4]

Nine chapters later, in Exodus 33:18, Moses asks to know more of the Lord's power and presence, and prays, *"Show me Your glory."* The Lord answers his prayer, but not quite in the way Moses asked. It was certainly not with thicker cloud, louder thunder, and brighter lightning.

Moses asked for more glory, and the Lord answered, *"I shall make My **goodness** pass by, and I shall pronounce in your hearing the name 'Lord.'"* There is a parallelism at work here, for earlier in verse 17, the Lord said that He knew Moses *"by name."* Just as God knew Moses, so through this revelation, Moses comes to "know" more of the Lord.

Moses again climbs to the top of Mount Sinai as he was instructed, and in Exodus 34:5–7, the Lord speaks from the cloud, but this time *without* the thunder, lightning and fire.

The Lord passed in front of Moses and proclaimed:

> *"The Lord, the Lord, God – compassionate and gracious, long-suffering, abounding in love and faithfulness, remaining faithful to thousands, and forgiving wickedness, rebellion and sin . . . "*

In this theophany, "glory" and God's character are equated. Suddenly, there is some content to this elusive word "glory."

God's glory is revealed in compassion; God's glory is revealed in grace; God's glory is revealed in patience, and abounding love and faithfulness; God's glory is revealed in forgiveness.

It is the revelation of the Lord's goodness, and not the *Shekinah,* the fire and thunder, that visibly transforms Moses. Only after this third experience is his face radiant with the glory of God, so much so that he has to veil himself when he is before the people of Israel. It is as if the veil buffers the glory of God to a rebellious people. Because she is stiff-necked, Israel cannot see the glory of God.[5] The veil signals that, once again, mercy triumphs over judgement.

Before we proceed, one other observation from the text. I was puzzled by the fact that in Exodus 34:6 there is an unusual doubling, *"The Lord, the Lord . . . "* It does not occur anywhere else in the Old Testament in that form. It's only found once in

parallel accounts of the Gospels. In Luke 6:46, Jesus asks, *"Why do you call me 'Lord, Lord,' and never do what I tell you?"*
Matthew 7:21–23 expands on the question:

> *"Not everyone who says to me, 'Lord, Lord' will enter the kingdom of Heaven, but only those who do the will of my heavenly Father. When the day comes, many will say to me, 'Lord, Lord, did we not prophesy in your name, drive out demons in your name, and in your name perform many miracles?' Then I will tell them plainly, 'I never knew you.'"*

There are too many parallels to Exodus 34 for this to be coincidence. Prophecy, deliverance and miracles are what many count as the evidence of God's manifest glory. Jesus clearly says, "Not necessarily so." The religious, then and now, are scandalized. How can there be miracles that do not please the Lord?

It hinges on the "knowing" of Exodus 33:19: knowing as we are known. It is possible to be so enamoured with supernatural power that we fail to show the glory of God – His compassion, grace, long-suffering and forgiveness, His love and faithfulness.

The miracles of Jesus were always rooted in compassion. Again and again, as preface to the healings we read, "His heart went out to them."

There's more yet. In 2 Corinthians 3:18, the Apostle Paul uses the Exodus 33–34 theophany to distinguish not only his apostolic ministry, but the very distinctive character and nature of the ministry of the Spirit.

There were some in the Corinthian congregation who were less than impressed with Paul as an itinerant preacher. They felt that he had an unimpressive presence, not to mention a questionable prison record. His spiritual authority was criticized, and many found his ministry inferior to those whom Paul referred to as "super-apostles."[6] The Corinthian letters were written to confront a pervasive spiritual pride and elitism that was at work in this very charismatic church. The two letters addressed specific difficulties that had arisen from that root elitism. The platform for all of Paul's teaching and correction is declared in 1 Corinthians 1:29: *"no place is left for any human pride in the presence of God."* Paul's argument in 2 Corinthians 3 builds on that foundation; what he hoped to establish was nothing less than the transformation of the believers into the very glory of God, the image of Christ.

Throughout his letter, Paul names his apostolic sufficiency – it was only "in Christ." He pushes "glory" to the forefront of his argument in chapter 3, and uses Exodus 33–34 to contrast the old and new covenants at work. He did not compare himself with Moses, however. If that were the contrast, Paul would have logically concluded that because there was a greater glory revealed in the New Covenant, he would have had to wear a thicker veil than Moses did!

Rather, Paul contrasts Israel and the believers in Corinth. Moses had to cover his face with a veil because Israel's hearts were hardened. Not so for the Corinthian believers. Because they have turned to the Lord, the veil has been removed. Israel could not or would not perceive God's glory; Paul attempted to help the Corinthians understand more fully what had been revealed to them by the Spirit.

The Apostle uses Exodus 33–34 very freely.[7] In 2 Corinthians 3:14, Paul makes a fluid transition, from the veil that covered Moses' face, to the veil that covers a closed heart, or, as the New International Version translates it, a dulled mind. The issue for Paul is not theology, but devotion.

In verse 16, he tightens the focus: *"Whenever* [one] *turns to the Lord, the veil is removed."* The reference is to Exodus 34:34. Whenever Moses went back into the tent of Meeting, back into the Lord's Presence, he removed the veil that covered his face. Paul made that a general, inclusive principle – when *anyone* turns to the Lord, the veil is removed – not from the face, but from the heart.

The Apostle then makes a very hasty jump, asserting,

> *"Now the Lord of whom this passage speaks is the Spirit, and where the Spirit of the Lord is, there is liberty."*
> (2 Corinthians 3:17)

The question is mute: liberty for what? To do what?

The most suggestive interpretation is to turn to the Lord, to keep returning to the Lord. Under the Old Covenant, Moses, alone, was infrequently on the mountain before the glory of the Lord. But under the New Covenant, every believer in Christ lives by His Spirit, continuously.

Verse 18 poses the greatest interpretative challenge. Literally translated it reads,

> *"But we all, with unveiled faces, behold as in a mirror the glory of the Lord, and are being transformed into the same image from glory to glory, just as from the Lord, the Spirit."*

There are two controlling verbs: the New International Version translates the first verb as "reflect," though the majority of historic and current translations and interpretations favor "behold;" the second verb is "being transformed," literally, "metamorphosized." Grammatically, the "beholding" serves as explanation to the stronger verb that indicates transformation. Just as Moses was changed in the presence of the Lord on Mount Sinai, so the Corinthians are being changed in the presence of the Lord, as He is at work in their hearts. However, they behold Him, not alone, atop a holy mountain, but as they live life with one another! One suddenly understands Betel's "holy jealousy" in a new light, and the question that resounds: "What is it that you have that I don't?"

As the Corinthians humbly looked at one another, and at Paul as their apostle, they beheld the transforming grace of the Spirit at work in their midst. This grace was making them all more and more like Christ, "with ever-increasing glory." Paul makes this explicit in 2 Corinthians 4:6:

> *"God ... has caused his light to shine in our hearts, the light which is the knowledge of the glory of God in the face of Jesus Christ."*

This glory, however, is "para-doxical" in that it is glory, *doxa*, that is made manifest in the laying down of life, as Christ did. Paul uses a most homely image to make his point:

> *"We have only earthenware jars to hold this treasure, and this proves that such transcendent power does not come from us; it is*

God's alone. We are hard pressed, but never cornered; bewildered, but never at our wits' end; hunted, but never abandoned to our fate; struck down, but never killed. Wherever we go we carry with us in our body the death that Jesus died, so that in this body also the life that Jesus lives may be revealed."

(2 Corinthians 4:7–10)

The glory that Paul would have the Corinthians see is one that was revealed in the very midst of suffering and sacrifice. Calling their spiritual pride and elitism into check again, he would have them understand that the "glory life" is not devoid of or beyond suffering; rather, the glory of God in the face of Jesus Christ is and continues to be revealed in the very midst of seeming weakness and the laying down of life. Suffering and persecution do not pose question marks against his claims to apostolicity. On the contrary, his conduct in the midst demonstrates the very work of the Spirit, revealing ever more of the power of Christ to redeem. The rebuke and challenge comes full circle in 2 Corinthians 13:3–5:

"You will have the proof you seek of the Christ . . . who, far from being weak with you, makes his power felt among you. True, he died on the cross in weakness, but he lives by the power of God; so you will find that we who share his weakness shall live with him by the power of God. Examine yourselves: are you living the life of faith? Put yourselves to the test. Surely you recognize that Jesus Christ is among you?"

True glory is not so much seen with the naked eye, but is revealed in and to the heart. It is a further revelation of the goodness of God, the Exodus 34:6 revelation, and the love that is poured out, for others. The life, death and resurrection of Jesus is the ultimate revelation of that love.

"For the love of Christ controls us once we have reached the conclusion that one man died for all and therefore all mankind has died. He died for all so that those who live should cease to live for themselves, and should live for Him who for their sake died and was raised to life. With us therefore worldly standards have ceased to count in our estimate of anyone; even if

once they counted in our understanding of Christ, they do so no longer."   (2 Corinthians 5:14–16)

Shortly after my return from the February 2000 Betel tour, I was worshipping with our house group, and the phrase "cheap grace" floated into my consciousness. Dietrich Bonhoeffer wrote *The Cost of Discipleship* in 1937, eight years before he was martyred by the Nazis. The opening line of the book reads: "Cheap grace is the deadly enemy of our church." [8]

As the house group continued to sing and pray, my mind and heart were back in Spain. It seemed that "cheap grace" was not so much the issue for our day, but *"cheap glory."*

In many church circles around the world, there is a growing cry to know more of the glory of God, the *Shekinah*, the shining, manifest presence of God. A favorite text is 2 Chronicles 5:13–14, the account of the dedication of Solomon's Temple:

> *"The house was filled with the cloud of the glory of the* Lord. *The priests could not continue to minister because of the cloud, for the glory of the* Lord *filled the house of God."*

As exciting and awe inspiring as such an experience would be, Betel has shown me that there is so much more.

Again, it comes by way of another mountain-top revelation of glory. Luke 9:28–36 is the theophany on the Mount of Transfiguration. Jesus is clothed in radiant light, and Moses and Elijah appear and speak of His departure and the fulfillment of His destiny. Rabbinic tradition maintained that Moses, like Elijah, was translated into heaven and did not see death. But Jesus' departure was to be *very* different. Nine verses earlier, Jesus had declared to His disciples what that destiny was:

> *"The Son of Man has to endure great sufferings, and to be rejected by the elders, chief priests, and scribes, to be put to death, and to be raised again on the third day."*   (Luke 9:22)

From the midst of the glory cloud, a Voice declares, *"This is my Son, my Chosen; listen to him."* That implies the question, "What was Jesus saying?" The last recorded words in all three Synoptics were addressed generally to the crowds:

> *"Anyone who wants to be a follower of mine must renounce self;*
> *day after day he must take up his cross and follow me. Whoever*
> *wants to save his life will lose it, but whoever loses his life for my*
> *sake will save it."*   (Luke 9:23–24; *see also*
>   Matthew 16:24–25; Mark 8:34–35)

The glory of Jesus is inseparably tied to His suffering and death, and by implication, the believer's glory is similarly made manifest.

Though subtle, this is made explicit in John's Gospel. There is no account of the Transfiguration in the Fourth Gospel. John was with Peter and James on the mountain – why wouldn't he record such a momentous event? Perhaps because the experience was so profoundly imprinted on the Apostle's spirit and understanding. The Transfiguration is certainly implied in the sudden inbreaking of the first-person in the prologue: *"We saw his glory..."*[9] The phrase directly parallels Luke's account in 9:32: *"they saw his glory..."* John 1:14 has another direct parallel: *"we saw his glory, such glory as befits the Father's only Son;"* isn't this the echo of the Voice, *"This is my Son, my Chosen..."*

In John's Gospel especially, glory and suffering are continuously juxtaposed. In His High Priestly prayer, Jesus declares, *"Father, the hour has come. Glorify Your Son, that the Son may glorify You."*[10] The "hour" in John is the hour of crucifixion.[11] The fullness of Christ's glory is revealed, not in His shining presence, but in the laying down of His life.

This revelation stands as commentary on John 1:14:

> *"The Word became flesh, he made his home among us, and we*
> *saw his glory, such glory as befits the Father's only Son, full of*
> *grace and truth."*

In Jesus, the compassion, the grace, the patience, and abounding love and faithfulness, the forgiveness of God, are all incarnated. God's character is made flesh and blood, for all to see. The whole of John's Gospel is then framed by what it means to listen to Jesus as He calls His followers to take up their cross. Though I've known all this for years, I'm starting to see things very differently.

Earlier in John's Gospel, the Apostle quoted the prophet Isaiah:

> " 'Lord, who has believed what we reported,
>   and to whom has the power of the Lord been revealed?' "
>
> (John 12:38)

There is another saying of Isaiah which explains why they could not believe:

> " 'He has blinded their eyes
>   and dulled their minds,
> lest they should see with their eyes,
>   and perceive with their minds,
>   and turn to me to heal them.'
>
> **Isaiah said this because he saw his glory and spoke about him."** (John 12:40–41)

I have wondered at that last line – why was a revelation of the Lord's glory blinding?

My studies convince me that it's not because the glory of God is so brilliant in its intensity, but rather because it doesn't look like what we thought it would. Because we expect glory to look a certain way, we can't see it for what it really is.

We're not alone. On the Mount of Transfiguration, when the disciple Peter was overwhelmed at the glory he witnessed, all he could do was blather about building booths to commemorate the moment. Luke adds this comment: *"he spoke without knowing what he was saying"* (Luke 9:33). The natural mind cannot and will not perceive or understand the glory of God. The greatest event in all of human history took place in front of a rag-tag crowd in the middle of a garbage dump outside the city.

Some would argue that the suffering of Jesus is swallowed up in death, and His glory is now revealed in and through the

triumphs of His resurrection. So thought one of the twenty-four
heavenly elders in Revelation 5:5:

> *"the Lion from the tribe of Judah, the shoot growing from
> David's stock, has won the right to open the scroll and its seven
> seals."*

However, it was not the mighty, victorious Lion that the
Apostle John saw in his vision.

> *"Then I saw a Lamb with the marks of sacrifice on him,
> standing with the four living creatures between the throne and
> the elders ... The Lamb came and received the scroll from the
> right hand of the One who sat on the throne ... and they* [the
> elders] *were singing a new song, 'You are worthy...'"*

(Revelation 5:6–9)

I am in complete awe that for all eternity, the Lamb carries on
Him the marks of His sacrifice.

Any visitor to Betel is profoundly struck at the glory of God
manifest in their midst. With some of the studies from "Project
Glory" in hand, there is some sense as to why it is so striking,
and so uncommon.

It is a glory that costs. It is a glory revealed in and through
suffering. It is the glory that is only revealed in the laying down
of life. It is a glory that is lived in the face of death, continuously. *This* is the manifest glory of God in Betel.

One last Scripture passage. Philippians 2:6–11 stands as one
of the great hymns of praise to Christ.

> *"He was in the form of God;*
> *yet he laid no claim to equality with God,*
> *but made himself nothing,*
> *assuming the form of a slave...*
> *and was obedient even to the point of death,*
> *death on a cross.*
> *Therefore God raised him to the heights..."*

Commentators agree that the phrase the *"form of God"* is a euphemism for His majesty and glory. Many Bible notes suggest a parallel reference to Hebrews 1:3: *"He is the radiance of God's glory, the stamp of God's very being."* Jesus revealed the fullness of that glory in laying down His life. His "emptying" of all was His "obedience."

In Philippians 2:12, the Apostle Paul calls that same obedience forth from those who would follow Christ. *"You too must be obedient..."* The laying down of life is something which he had modeled himself. He states in Philippians 2:17:

> *"if my life-blood is to be poured out to complete the sacrifice and offering up of your faith, I rejoice and share my joy with you all."*

Few of us have this verse underlined in our Bibles.

In Betel, this kind of obedience is modeled. Jonathan Tepper, Elliott's son, told me the following story.

"Back in 1985, there was a man, Lucio, who had severe mental problems. He didn't have drug problems, but gravitated towards the guys because they were a loving community. He was talking to Lindsay and my father and Raul in Lindsay's living-room. Lucio said he was going to the bathroom, but went to the kitchen instead and came back holding a *big* knife. He was very agitated, and they were trying to calm him down. He lunged at my father, but Raul went straight towards Lucio and wrestled the knife out of his hand. He did it without hesitating. I believe he saved my father's life, and maybe Lindsay's as well."

Jonathan also provided some detail to a story that Juan Carlos told of the early days in Marseilles. "I worked with Betel-Marseilles during August 1998. Remember the story about the schizophrenic named David? He wasn't just schizophrenic. He was psychotic and very vicious. He was a huge guy, 6ft 10in. When he flipped out and came back to the *Rastro* with a motorcycle chain, we thought he was going to smash someone's skull with it.

"I was one of the ones that helped the guy that got punched in the face. When David threw the stool, and it split the Betelito's head open, I got splattered with his blood.

"David was standing at the entrance to the *Rastro,* and we were all towards the back of the store. Juan Carlos immediately put himself in front of everyone and pushed David out the door. He was protecting all of us, but especially wanted to keep one particular Betelito out of the fight. He had been convicted of murder in Spain. Juan Carlos didn't want him to get hurt, and he didn't want him to get in any further trouble with the law. Juan Carlos didn't think about his own security. He just jumped in between the guys."

There's more. Most of the men and women of Betel have spent their lives on heroin. Now, whatever life they have left is spent on Jesus, and the work of the Kingdom.

Just as heroin was "unto death," now, their lives in Christ, are also "unto death." Their AIDS-infected blood is unto death, but in Christ it is, like His blood, poured out so that others may live. The words of the Apostle Paul suddenly have a greater meaning than ever before:

> *"we carry with us in our body the death that Jesus died, so that in this body also the life that Jesus lives may be revealed. For Jesus' sake we are all our life being handed over to death, so that the life of Jesus may be revealed in this mortal body of ours. Thus death is at work in us, but life in you."*
>
> (2 Corinthians 4:10–12)

We are all going to die. That's an inescapable fact. Because of the gospel of Jesus Christ, we get to choose *how* we die.

Two Betelitos have found their way into a very special and sacred place in my heart. Their lives have not only taught me about the glory of God made manifest, but have shown my spirit how to "dance until I can fly." Their stories conclude this chapter, and the book.

Javi Gonzalez was addicted to heroin for nine years. He lost his job, his car, his house – everything but his wife Pacqui. They ended up living on the streets. The two of them would sleep in abandoned cars, the Metro stations, or in city parks. One night, it was so cold, there was frost an inch thick inside the car in which they were sleeping. It was a turning point for Javi.

"I asked, 'God, please, let us die. I don't want to live like this any more.'"

Javi knew Raul and Tito from San Blas, and he knew that they were living with missionaries. He wanted to join them, but only because he had been in an accident – while on the streets, a car had hit him and smashed his leg. He needed a place to heal. Javi asked Raul if he thought he could join them, and Raul made it quite clear that the house wasn't a convalescent home. Javi was only welcome if he wanted to change his life.

Javi was fed up with drugs, but didn't want to give up smoking. As it was one of Betel's requirements, he stayed away. Two years passed. "That whole time, I felt two things – one, that I was a coward, and two, I hoped that I could be free of drugs, that our family could be restored, and that I could get a job."

The sense of desperation kept growing within him, until a friend called Tito on Javi's behalf, pleading for help. Tito said, "If he's ready, tell him to come."

I asked Javi if he remembered when that was. His eyes sparkled. "I know the *exact* date – 8 March 1989, between 6 and 7 p.m.!"

"I had totally abandoned myself. I hadn't taken any care of myself for three years. I weighed a hundred and twenty-five pounds. My face was covered with cuts; my head had an oozing sore from the lice. My hair was shoulder-length, and filthy. My toes were sticking through the holes in my shoes. As soon as I arrived at Betel they took me to the showers, and when I got out my clothes were gone. They had thrown them away!

"They gave me new clothes, and looking at them, I had two feelings. I was grateful that I didn't have to wear rags any more, but I was also so ashamed that I couldn't look after myself. I couldn't even wear the new shoes – there were so many sores on my feet, they hurt too much.

"After they cut my hair, and I shaved my beard, I stared into the mirror for a long time. I realized that my life had hit a deeper bottom than I was ever aware of.

"The guys' kindnesses really shook me – I remember one breakfast. There wasn't much food, and they gave me their cookies. I looked at them and they smiled. Somebody said, 'We've been eating for a while.'

"Manuel was my shadow much of the time. He was my mentor, my friend. I really love him. There are so many stories to tell ... I remember once we were in a van and the brakes failed. Every time we had to slow down, Manuel steered, and I had to let myself out the back of the van, and try to stop it by dragging my feet on the pavement! It was a very long drive home.

"Manuel's life, the way he managed things, the way he reacted – he lived Jesus. He, and all the guys, they became like older brothers that I wanted to be like. When I came to Betel, my heart was completely empty, so there was lots of room for love.

"But for those first two months, I was like a dog who gets a bath. They poured all their love over me, and cleaned me up, but then, a moment later, I'd shake it all off, and roll around in the dirt again. I'd sneak off and smoke, and my attitude wasn't really changing.

"One day, I was at work digging a hole for the septic tank in Mejorada, and the Lord showed me the condition of my heart. I suddenly saw the way I was rejecting every opportunity I was being given to change. My pride and my rebellion were having a hard time digging that stupid hole, but at the same time there was something my heart was saying: 'You can't have just a bit of Jesus – you can't just have the benefit of Jesus without commitment. It's all or nothing.'

"I felt incredibly sad. I asked for a break, and I went to my bed. I started to cry. I wept and wept and wept, for an hour and a half. I fell asleep, and when I awoke, I realized that something had changed inside. It was a fight that ended – I gave Jesus everything; He won, I lost, and losing, I won! The rebellion was over.

"I stopped smoking, I stopped acting out and breaking the rules. I quit sneaking off, and lying. I stopped hanging around the new guys in the house, talking about football, and girls, and drugs. Instead, I became friends with the guys that were serious about Jesus. I started reading my Bible, and two days later a visiting group gave me a prophecy that the Lord had called me to be a leader in Betel. I couldn't see it. There was no way I'd ever stand up in front of a crowd. Two months later, I received other prophecies that spoke of leadership."

A year later, Javi started classes at Adullam, the Bible school. "At first, it was very hard. As a child, I didn't really go to school. Our teacher, Armando, a Mexican missionary, tells that some of us were such poor students, we didn't even know how to hold a pencil. He might have been thinking about me! I wasn't a good reader. As he'd fill the blackboards, there were many days when sweat would break out on our faces, and the cry would go out, '*Mas despacio!*' 'Slowly please!'

"To discipline our lives as students was a great challenge. Armando taught us how to read the Bible systematically, how to pray and wait on the Lord, how to think structurally and orderly. As I took notes and struggled with my reading, it got easier, and it became such a special time. It was like my mind was so open – I was so hungry to learn. I still have my notes from school, and I continue to use them as I prepare my sermons. Elliott's class on the life of Jesus was so important for me. It laid a foundation under my life.

"It wasn't just classroom work. Whenever I saw a drug addict on the streets, something rose up inside me, a conviction – I was one who had found the solution. Christ had set me free from drugs, and they could be free too. Deep within I knew the Lord was saying, 'I have called you, I have set you apart, I have called you to tell them what I have done in your life.'"

In June 1993, Javi was sent to Cuenca to join the leadership team, and in March of the next year, he was ordained as the work's pastor. The three years there were preparation for his move back to Madrid. Elliott is the International Director and Senior Pastor of Association Betel; Javi is the Senior National Pastor over the Madrid congregation. He oversees four men's houses, two women's houses, the couples' house, several apartments, three *Rastros*, the mechanics' shop, and one of the chicken farms.

In February 1998, Javi was with Juan Carlos, Elliott, and Keith Bergmeir, another staff missionary, in the business district of downtown Madrid. They were on their way to negotiate the purchase of an old factory that would serve Betel as a larger church facility, administrative offices, and several business opportunities on site. They had parked in a car park and, as they walked through a pedestrian tunnel, they were discussing the size of the loan they needed $3.3 million.

"When we turned a corner, I cried out, 'Wait – stop!' I suddenly had a flashback – there, against the wall, Pacqui and I used to sleep on a cardboard carton, covered only by the one coat that we had. And here I was, in a suit, a tie, polished shoes, nice aftershave. I couldn't help saying out loud, 'This is where I used to live, like an animal, and here I am, going to negotiate a 3.3 million dollar deal – times sure have changed!'

"It seemed to all of us that this was a picture of Betel. From the very bottom, the Lord changes someone who is completely useless, into someone who has a destiny. I very rarely wear a suit, but that day I felt like I should never take it off. The Lord had taken my filthy rags, and clothed me in royal robes, and put the image of Christ in me. Even the aftershave – His fragrance, His beauty – surrounds me wherever I go. I have such gratitude – it is such a privilege to be someone who is used by God to work for His Kingdom."

I had the honor of preaching at the *cumbre* which took place in Madrid from 24 to 26 September 1999. During the congress we prayed for healing. I asked those who were sick or in pain to put their hand on the part of their body that hurt most. If they needed healing for their whole body, they were to put their hand on the top of their head. Once that instruction was translated, most hands went topside. After praying corporately, the ministry team began praying for individuals. I prayed for Javi. AIDS is taking a serious toll on his health.

He was lying flat out on the floor, and I was struck by how funny his nose looked, pressed as it was against the tile.

As he rested in the Lord, I prayed for him for about twenty minutes. He stirred, and slowly sat up. We were eyeball to eyeball. I was overwhelmed with love for him, and overwhelmed with his love for me. It was an incredibly deep heart connection, a moment in which *compassion* took on new meaning...

What made it so strange was that Javi and I have almost nothing in common – language, culture, background. But none of it mattered. It was all heart.

Through a translator, Javi broke the silence: "I have asked the Lord many times why He doesn't heal me. I'm living in the midst of the glory of God ... we see so many miracles, but why not my healing?

"As you prayed, I felt so much love, God's love, covering me, filling me, from the top of my head to my very toes. I felt like He completely enfolded me in His love. With that love, I don't need anything else.

"There is so much love, my healing doesn't matter; my death doesn't matter – I'm so full of God's love ... only He matters. That moment of love is a moment that leaves me longing – only for Him."

Five months later, I asked Javi to reflect on that time. He grinned. "I have now a new way to rest in the Lord. I have a deeper peace than ever before. I have made a complete surrender; I have let Him have complete control of my life. I trust Him as never before."

Javi looked off into the distance. When he spoke, passion overflowed. "Heroin had my life. It drew me to the very bottom. It took me to the limit. I faced death; the end. In Jesus, there are no limits. There is only more. More and more, ever more of His love. More and more of His life. I don't ever want it to stop. I want to know all that He has promised.

"Heroin took everything from me. Drugs lied to me – they promised, but they didn't fulfill. God has given me everything, and He is completely faithful in all of His promises."

As we began this book with worship – *'La victoria esta en Jesus!'* – so we finish.

The victory that can be ours in Jesus is, at one level, exuberant and liberating. At another level, it is so very much deeper, and life sustaining. Javi Gonzalez and Nines Matesanz have the place in my heart that they do because they have shown me these depths.

Their lives, their "living sacrifices" [12] unsettle my well-ordered life. Being with them challenges my habitual need to be in control. Their humility points the way – to trust, to freedom, to love.

Nines was a rebellious teenager. She was pregnant at sixteen, and when the baby died at two months, she went into deep depression and despair, and lost herself in drugs. For six years, she was addicted to heroin and cocaine. When she couldn't get what she needed, she'd abuse alcohol – simply "anything and everything." Nines stole so much from her parents that they kicked her out of their home. Life was then "sex for drugs." However, it wasn't long before the heroin ravished her body. She was consuming so much, and she'd lost so much weight, no one wanted her. "I did anything I could to score."

One night, Nines was shooting up, and two Betelitos came by, handing out flyers. She told them to get lost. They stayed, and tried to keep her from injecting. She was trying to concentrate, as she was having difficulty finding an uncollapsed vein. With the needle in her arm, Nines looked up at the two men. " 'Leave me alone, go away. You're talking to the wrong person. I don't have a drug problem.'

"It was a ridiculous scene. I was covered with abscesses, and I'd completely lost myself. Those last six months of addiction, I lived in an abandoned van, near the gypsy camp where I got the heroin."

Later that night, alone in the van, she started to cry. "I don't want to keep living like this any more. Either I die, or something changes."

To get the two guys to leave her alone, Nines had taken the Betel flyer. She pulled it out of her pants' pocket. She went to a pay phone, and called Betel. Elliott answered. Nines asked, "Is this a rehabilitation center? It's free?"

"Yes, it's free, and God is going to give you a lot of love."

That last line scared her. "Elliott's Spanish had a strong foreign accent, and no one talked that way about love on the streets. I really wondered if this 'Betel' wasn't a weird American cult that would send me off somewhere as a sex slave."

Nines was desperate enough to risk it, however. The next day, 11 February 1989, she followed the directions to Betel. It has been her home and family ever since. Within six months she was made a *responsable* and, two years later, a house leader. On 3 October 1992, she married Oscar Matesanz and four months later they were sent to Almeria to assist the leadership team. In July 1997, they moved to Lisbon to take over the work there.

❧

Both Oscar and Nines are HIV-positive. Chronic hepatitis has compromised Nines' liver. For twenty days in November 1999, she had to be in hospital for the sclerosis. She needs a liver transplant, but as she is HIV-positive, she is at the bottom of the waiting list.

"For years, I have asked God to heal me. Many, many of my friends have prayed for me. My health seems to be degenerating. I have struggled for answers, for understanding. I don't understand, but I have peace. I am learning to rest. If I didn't have God, I'd be completely miserable. But in Him, I have hope. I continue to pray for my healing. Every day. I receive ministry for healing every chance I get. And as I wait on Him, I am learning, as the Apostle Paul said, to be content in *all* my circumstances, the good times, and the hard times.[13] I know that I can either worry, and get really depressed, or I can be grateful as I wait in hope.

"When you are living a situation like mine, sometimes you wonder, 'Why me, and not somebody else?' There's no answer to that question. You have to accept it as it is. I've discovered that I'm not alone. God is there for me, and He will never leave me. There are people – wonderful people, who surround me with their love.[14]

"If I give up, if I stop hoping, then I don't bring God any glory. It is very heavy. But there's no other way. Those around me won't see the miracles He's already done in me. He's delivered me from drugs, He's healed my heart, and my soul – there's love in my heart now. I wait for Him to heal my body."

"I've learned that God doesn't need our work for Him. He can use anyone. He decides whom He's going to use. It is not we who produce for God, but He who gives us the opportunity to participate with Him. He is the one who lets us share with Him the work of His Kingdom. We are not able to feel all of how He feels in this life. But we share a part, not so much with our minds, but more with our spirits. My illness, and the suffering, has drawn me more to Him than to the work. Because of my illness, I can't work with the *chicas* like I used to. Now, rather than producing, my work is waiting in His presence.

"I can still lead worship, but that has changed too. I am more sensitive, and more able to listen to God. I am learning to rest in

Him more, and learning to hear His voice. I am more peaceful now, and I'm more able to listen to what He is saying.

"This is the best part of my illness. The doctor tells me I have to rest. I can't work, but I can worship. In worship, He takes all my worries; He carries the burden. It's like a swimming pool – it's so wonderfully refreshing to dive in, and so restful just to float; to float in the love and the presence of God. I know that in His presence, anything can happen.

"A year and a half ago, the Lord put a particular song on my heart. I sing it all the time, especially when I'm discouraged. It is called '*Espero en ti*', 'I wait in You.' We've translated it into Portuguese for the church."

Nines laughed. "After eleven years, I'm learning to wait. As I wait, I've learned that God is still using me to His glory. I can't work like I used to, but my worship, my time with Him, the love that I can give to Oscar and our son Ruben, and the *chicos* and *chicas* when I can, it is a great privilege to be used by God, and to understand, to know more of His heart, and to share that revelation with others. All is His glory. All."

LA VICTORIA ESTA EN JESUS!

Notes

1. Transcribed from the evening's audio cassette tape.
2. Luke 15:11–32, especially verses 25–29.
3. Genesis 32:22–32.
4. Exodus 19:6–19; 20:18–21; 24:15–18.
5. Exodus 32:9, 22; 33:3, 5 and 34:30.
6. 2 Corinthians 11:5–6 and 12:11.
7. N.T. Wright, "Reflected Glory: 2 Corinthians 3:18," *The Glory of Christ in the New Testament*, ed. L.D. Hurst (Oxford: Clarendon Press, 1987), pp. 139–150; Scott Hafemann, "The Glory and Veil of Moses in 2 Corinthians 3:7–14," *Horizons in Biblical Theology* (1992), 14 (1), pp. 31–49; Martin Scharlemann, "Of Surpassing Splendour: An Exegetical Study of 2 Corinthians 3:4–18," *Concordia Journal* (May 1978), pp. 108–117. Joseph Fitzmeyer, "Glory Reflected on the Face of Christ: 2 Corinthians 3:7–4:6," *Theological Studies*, 42 (1981), pp. 630–644.
8. Norwich: SCM Press, 1959, p. 35.
9. John 1:14b.
10. John 17:1.

11. John 19:28.
12. Romans 12:1.
13. Philippians 4:11–13.
14. The back cover photo is of Nines in Mary Tepper's arms.

Appendix 1
Drugs and Drug Taking

The most common illegal drug used worldwide is cannabis, or marijuana. It goes by many street names: weed, grass, marijuana, dope. It is usually smoked in a rolled cigarette, a "joint." Sometimes it is baked in food; chocolate brownies are a favorite.

The effects of cannabis are almost instantaneous, and last 1 to 4 hours. The user becomes relaxed, and often talkative. Relational tensions ease; everything "mellows." For many, sound and color become intensified, and creativity is stimulated, as self-awareness increases. Once the effects have worn off, there is no hangover as with an alcoholic binge. What one is left with is a "woolly head."

"Grass" is considered the threshold drug. For instance, research worldwide has demonstrated conclusively that children who use cannabis are 85 per cent more likely to use cocaine than those who've never tried it.

How does one move up the drug ladder? One step towards addiction is prior contact with dealers. Those who sell cannabis typically deal in harder drugs too. Often there's a freebie: "Here, give this a try. This will wreck you way worse than grass." Amphetamines are typically the next rung. "Speed" is the most common street name; "crank, crystal," or simply "uppers" are all declarative, as amphetamines are stimulants. They are ingested orally as pills, or ground into powder and sniffed, or dissolved and injected. Amphetamines give a very intense rush, lasting 4 to 6 hours. Users become hyper-alert, hence the name, "speed."

But what gets sped up has to wind down. When the drugs wear off, physical exhaustion sets in. The mind still races, however. Sleep is painfully elusive.

For this reason, amphetamines are often used cyclically with "downers" – barbiturates or other depressants. Diazepam and temazepam, Valium and mogadon are some common barbiturates. In low, medically prescribed dosage, they are used as sleeping pills or tranquilizers, and are taken to depress the nervous system for 3 to 8 hours, and induce sleep. A speed addict may take 8 to10 tablets at a time, attempting to come quickly down off of his high. The goal on this rollercoaster is to achieve "good days, good nights." Over prolonged use, amphetamines characteristically generate a paranoia that can become extreme. This, in turn, often calls forth extreme violence.

One of the newer drugs on the streets is ecstasy. Its chemical name is abbreviated MDMA, short for methylene-dioxymeth-amphetamine. On the drug spectrum, it is considered halfway between speed and LSD. Users experience a loss of inhibitions, a sense of euphoria, a rush of energy, and a sense of empathy for others. The high peaks in 2 hours, and usually lasts 3 to 4. Long-term use brings frequent panic attacks, confusion, anxiety, depression, paranoia, and serious liver damage.

Ecstasy is known as "the dance drug," and is big in the rave and club scene. Because it is such a strong stimulant, heat stroke, hyperactivity, exhaustion and dehydration have been the cause of thousands of deaths.

LSD, lysergic acid diethylamide, or "acid," is a hallucinogenic. Bits of paper the size of a postage stamp are soaked in a solution of LSD before being swallowed by the user. It is about an hour before the drug takes effect; the trip lasts 8–12 hours. Perceptions of color, taste, sound, sight and sense of time become distorted. While tripping, users "see" sound, and "taste" colors. Some claim mystical, or ecstatic experiences. Reality and illusion blur. For instance, Brian would often drive while tripping on LSD. When asked how he managed, he said it was quite simple. "I just follow the yellow line. If it goes up a tree or over a building, I follow the hallucination; I just stay on my side of the line, wherever it goes."

LSD exaggerates whatever the person is feeling – hence the down side, the "bummer." Feelings of insecurity, depression, loneliness become magnified. With LSD, there's no way of exiting a bad trip.

Cocaine, or "coke," is a white powder that is usually ingested or "snorted" nasally. It is also smoked (free-basing), or injected. It too is a powerful stimulant, speeding up the body in a manner similar to amphetamines. Its effect is shorter and more intense. A crack addict gets his rush in under 8 seconds: "Smoking crack, with the first exhale, I'd see a thousand flashing lights." The high lasts less than an hour for coke, only minutes for crack. Users experience an intense release of energy, mental intensity, confidence, and feelings of invincibility.

But the laws of physics are inexorable: the greater the high, the steeper the fall.

"Chasing the high" can cost an addict several hundred pounds in an evening.

It is money squandered, for the euphoria of the first hit eludes heavy users. Instead, there grows a sickening mix of restlessness, nausea, agitation, anxiety and paranoia.

Heroin, "smack," or "horse," is derived from the opium poppy, and is 50 per cent stronger than morphine, its chemical cousin. Heroin is smoked, swallowed, sniffed, and is the most commonly injected illegal substance. It used to be the end-stage drug, but when cheap heroin floods a local market, it can become very cheap and accessible, sometimes costing as little as the price of a beer.

Heroin depresses the nervous system; it mimics the body's natural endorphins, our built-in pain killer and pleasure source. Endorphins are released both in injury and in orgasm.

Using heroin brings relaxation and contentment, like one is "wrapped up in a heroin blanket." It slows reactions and brings a sense of detachment. The high lasts 4–5 hours.

Non-sterile injections cause abscesses and permanently damage veins. Imagine a garden hose that is continuously being punctured; before long there is so much leakage that there's no more flow.

But addicts need to increase their use just to maintain "normality." Withdrawal is especially painful. Cold sweats, nausea, aches, chills and muscle spasms characterize an addict's "cold turkey." Because of the heroin, the body shuts down the natural production of endorphin, as it perceives too much within the system. When the heroin is missing, the body is endorphin deficient, and is without its natural painkiller. Hence the anguish of withdrawal.

Heroin kills one and a half per cent of its addicts annually. This does not include AIDS deaths, contracted because of the use of dirty and or shared needles.

The authors of *Buzzed* conclude their study of drug taking with this provocative declaration: "The bottom line on addiction is that *anyone with a brain can get addicted to drugs.*"

Further reading

Cynthia Kuhn, Scott Swartzwelder, Wilkie Wilson (All PhDs), *Buzzed* (Duke University Medical Center, New York: W.W. Norton and Co., 1998).

Fernandez Humberto, *Heroin* (Centre City, Minnesota: Hazeldon, 1998).

Patrick Dixon, *The Truth About Drugs* (London: Hodder and Stoughton, 1998).

Appendix 2

Community Rules

Those wishing to enter the Betel community may do so free of charge, on the condition that they voluntarily stop using illegal drugs and alcohol, and comply with the following rules:

- Residents are to participate in the full schedule and activities of the community, keeping a structured day from 7 a.m. to 11 p.m.
- Smoking or the use of any tobacco product is not permitted.
- Personal money is to be deposited with the staff upon entry. Money not spent on personal needs will be returned upon departing the community.
- Betel is free to enter – no one will be denied entrance due to lack of finances. However, in countries where residents are entitled to government welfare benefits, special entrance conditions may apply.
- "Betelitos" travel in pairs. All residents are to be accompanied by another resident or staff member during their first few months.
- Upon entrance, individuals are to inform Betel of their present state of health, particularly of any contagious diseases, and of all pending legal judgements. (Individuals with organic or psychological illnesses may be denied entrance if: the disease is actively contagious, it requires specialized medical attention, or impedes the normal functioning of the community.)

- The use or consumption of drug, alcohol or tobacco substitutes is not permitted.
- Family visits require prior notification.
- New residents generally do not leave the premises for the first 15 days. (While everyone maintains the right to depart Betel for any reason at any moment.)
- It is recommended that married couples who enter together be separated temporarily, into the single men's and women's communities, until the directors consider them prepared to reunite.
- The possession of illegal drugs or alcohol by a resident may be motive for expulsion from the community.
- Each resident retains the right to access appropriate provisions of the local Health Authorities and Social Services.

Appendix 3

Betel's International Address and Telephone List

Betel International Headquarters

C/o Antonia Rodríguez Sacristán
8 CP 28044
Madrid
Spain
Tel: 91 525 2222
Fax: 91 525 8907
E-mail: betelmadrid@retemail.es

Betel International

USA

New York
78–05 Roosevelt Ave
Jackson Heights
NY 11372
Tel & Fax: (1-718) 533 9861

Germany

Krogaspe
Hof Rabenhorst
24644 Krogaspe
Tel: (49-4321) 53692
Fax: (49-4321) 962780

Hamburg
Hamburger Str. 180
Tel & Fax: (49-40) 20972385

Italy

Naples
Via Roma, 509
80017 Melino
Tel: (39-081) 711 5215
Fax: (39-081) 711 5409

Genoa
Viale Bernabó Brea No. 47 Int. 23
16131 Genoa

Bari
Via Flemin, 31–33
70031 Andria (Bari)
Tel & Fax: (39-0883) 54 4815

Portugal

Lisbon
Rua do Cruzeiro, Lote 121
Almada Charneca da Caparica
2825
Tel & Fax: (35-11) 225 7691

Oporto
Rua Antero de Quental, 370
CP 4050 Porto
Tel & Fax: (35-12) 5502832

UK
Birmingham
Windmill House
UK Weatheroak Hill
Alvechurch
Birmingham B48 7EA
Tel: (44-1564) 822356
Fax: (44-1564) 824929

France
Marseilles
198 – Rue de Lyon 13015
Marseille
Tel: (33-4) 91587182
Fax: (33-4) 91025415

Mexico
Puebla
Prolongación Reforma, 6908
Col. La Libertad
Puebla
Pue. C.P. 72130
Tel & Fax: (52-22) 302445

Betel Spain

Madrid
C/o Antonia Rodríguez
Sacristán 8 28022
Tel: 91 5252222
Fax: 91 5258907

Albacete
C/ Capitán Cortes, 57
02004
Tel: 967501419
Fax: 967510410

Algeciras
Avd. Virgen del Carmen, 53
11202
Tel & Fax: 956587008

Almeria
C/ Doctor Carracido, 19–21
04005
Tel: 950234127
Fax: 950276362

Barcelona
Crta. Molins del Rey a Sabadell
Km.13 Poligono Industrial Can
Roses nave 91 (Rubí) 08191
Tel: 93 5886324
Fax: 93 6973205

Bilbao
Ctra. de Bilbao a Galdakano, 1
48004
Tel & Fax: 94 4128223

Castellón
C/ Navarra, 119
12002
Tel: 964203122

Ceuta
C/ Canalejas, 23 Bj.
51001
Tel: 956517529
Fax: 956510744

Ciudad Real
C/ Caballeros, 14
13002
Tel: 926212226
Fax: 926215581

Cuenca
Ctra. Alcazar, Km.1.700
16001
Tel: 969233754
Fax: 969233371

Granada
Avda. de América, 53
B. Elzaidin 18008
Tel & Fax: 958131410

Guadalajara
C/ Wenceslao Argumosa
Tel: 949229769

Malaga
Avda. de José Ortega y Gaset, 286
29006 Polígono Viso
Tel: 95 2334926
Fax: 95 2355509

Mallorca
C/ Francisco Fiol y Juan, 7
07010
Tel & Fax: 971753882

Melilla
C/ Jacinto Ruíz Mendoza, 13
Bj.izq
29805
Tel & Fax: 95 2673614

Orense
Ntra. Señora de la Sainza, 8-bj.
32005
Tel: 988253751
Fax: 988254304

Sevilla
C/ Asensio y Toledo, 6
41014
Tel: 95 4680845
Fax: 95 4689059

Tarragona
C/ Riera de Miró, 27–29
43204
Tel & Fax: 977756618

Valencia
C/ San Vicente Martir, 153
46007
Tel: 96 3410433
Fax: 96 3809223

Vigo
C/ Balaidos, 13-Bj.
Tel & Fax: 986244541

If you have enjoyed
this book and would like
to help us send a copy of
it and many other titles to
needy pastors in developing nations,

please write for further information,
or send your gift to:

Sovereign World Trust
PO Box 777
Tonbridge
Kent TN11 OZS
United Kingdom

www.sovereignworldtrust.com